Bleeding Orange

Bleeding Orange

Trouble and Triumph Deep in
the Heart of Texas Football

John Maher
and
Kirk Bohls

St. Martin's Press

New York

Design by Susan Hood

Library of Congress Cataloging-in-Publication Data

Maher, John, 1950–
    Bleeding orange : trouble and triumph deep in the heart of Texas
football / John Maher, Kirk Bohls.
        p.   cm.
    ISBN 0-312-06305-9
    1. Texas Longhorns (Football team)—History.   2. University of
Texas at Austin—Football—History.   I. Bohls, Kirk.   II. Title.
GV958.T45M34   1991
796.332′63′097631—dc20   91-19079
                                                                    CIP

10 9 8 7 6 5 4 3

To our parents, Kay and Leon Bohls and
Anne and Howard Maher.

Contents

Contents

Acknowledgments

This book would not have been possible without the help of the many people who consented to sit down and talk with us at length. To all of them we owe thanks for their time and cooperation.

Working on this book made us appreciate even more the effort expended by former *Austin American-Statesman* sports editor Lou Maysel, whose book *Here Come the Texas Longhorns* served as an invaluable reference for the history of Texas football.

We'd also like to thank our friends and colleagues at the *Austin American-Statesman* for their support and help in this project.

We're grateful to John Millard for his insightful feedback and to Basil Kane for his aid and enthusiasm in this project.

Mostly, however, we'd like to thank our wives, Vicki and Sally, for their patience, love, and understanding.

Bleeding Orange

1

Happiness in the Valley

"Marvin! Have you found the game?"

"Have they started yet?"

"Is there any score?"

Marvin Moos is stranded in a broken-down bus in the middle of Pennsylvania with a lot of very important people from the University of Texas huddled around him and a pocket transistor radio wired to his ear. The coaches' wives, university vice presidents—they all want the damn radio to stop crackling and buzzing so Moos can start relaying the play-by-play of the 1990 season-opening game they're supposed to be attending in style, Texas vs. Penn State.

The ill-fated road trip began shortly after dawn, when Cindy McWilliams, the blonde ex-cheerleader wife of Texas football coach David McWilliams, and a private jetload of other dignitaries were whisked to Williamsport by Texas's biggest booster, Jim Bob Moffett. The mining and real estate magnate was only too happy to spend a little of the $13 million he makes a year on the friends of his very favorite football team.

Moffett's corporate jet had no trouble negotiating the 1,385-mile trip from Austin, but the bus chartered from the airport soon overheats and hisses to a stop halfway down the sixty-five-mile route to State College. The driver calls for a new bus, but he can't raise the game on the radio.

Now it's up to Moos, whose wife, Joyce, is an executive assistant to Texas president Bill Cunningham, to try to tune in the biggest opening game in the ninety-eight-year history of Texas's proud football program.

Let the tailgating Penn State fans—who'd started pulling up in their Winnebagos, Airstreams, and assorted vans at Beaver Stadium on Thursday night—burn their inch-thick steaks, pop their ice-chilled Buds, drink in the 70-degree sunshine, and think the game was just another good excuse to stage the world's largest tailgate party in Happy Valley.

Joe Paterno would be prowling the sidelines for Penn State. Joe Pa, as he's known in the secluded land of blue blazers and club ties, is getting ready to tee it up with yet another solid, no-frills team. That's why he's won 13 of 14 home openers in two dozen seasons as head coach in a fiefdom so friendly that he's still listed in the notebook-sized State College phone book.

As for Texas, well, the opinionated fans of the largest and richest university in the biggest state south of Alaska normally tolerate only two kinds of seasons, 10–1 and 11–0.

McWilliams, meanwhile, is coming off two straight losing campaigns, the first time Texas's pride had been stung like that in fifty-one years. The 5–6 team of 1989 not only stumbled through the worst game in Texas history—a 50–7 home loss to Baylor—but it was also rocked by published allegations of betting and steroid use.

The homegrown McWilliams had been heartily welcomed back from Lubbock after a one-year head coaching stint at Texas Tech. Some of those same fans, the ones that say they bleed orange for their school, are now grumbling and wondering how Texas could ever have hired a coach with so short a head coaching resume. Was the likable, easygoing McWilliams just ex–Notre Dame coach Gerry Faust in ostrich-skin boots?

"Faust was more overly headstrong," Phil Ransopher, a Texas public address announcer, reasoned earlier in the fall at Scholz Garten, a traditional pregame gathering spot in Austin. "It takes David's computer a little longer to belch out the answer. David's a mathematician. He's become an elliptical orator. He'll talk in a funky circle and come back where he started and you'll say, 'What did he say?' It drives the kids nuts, it drives the coaches nuts, and it probably drives Cindy nuts."

Ever since last year's season ended with a sixth straight loss to hated rival Texas A&M, the hottest topic in Austin has been just how many wins McWilliams needed to keep from getting the last year of his five-year contract bought out. You couldn't win an argument by predicting anything less than 7–4, even though Texas athletic director DeLoss Dodds kept protesting that McWilliams's job was safe. The speculation only increased when McWilliams blurted on a radio talk show that he might be willing to go back to being an assistant for Texas if he couldn't get the head coaching job done at his beloved alma mater.

Rumors of a badly split staff had some of the staunchest of Texas supporters fearing the worst.

"There's not the camaraderie on the staff," says one Texas ex who's been following the camp since the glory days of Darrell Royal in the 1960s. "Not even an us-against-the-world mentality. It's a rudderless ship that lacks leadership."

"I think we're looking at three and eight—and the scary part is, I can't find the three," Ransopher adds. "The football program will get worse before it gets better. Even with the banner recruiting years, we were getting kids we wouldn't normally get because they felt they could play here. That's the kind of kid you *don't* want. We're still kind of in a black hole down here. The rest of the country doesn't know how bad we are."

McWilliams's forte is recruiting, and he feels very confident about the seniors he's about to send out against Penn State. But, in the turmoil of last year, even recruiting slipped. Allen Wallace, publisher of *SuperPrep*, has listed Texas's 1990 class of freshmen as one of the most disappointing in the country, along with those of Boston College and Louisiana State—two schools that will end up firing their coaches. Robert Heard, the rogue journalist and former AP correspondent whom infamous sniper Charles Whitman couldn't quite kill from the Texas tower two decades ago, wrote in his December 1989 newsletter that Texas was losing the recruiting battle to conference rivals Texas A&M, Houston, and Baylor.

In his small, but consistently prickly, newsletter printed in black, white, and burnt orange and aimed at 1,500 of the most diehard orangebloods, Heard summed up the situation this way: "Right now we are face down in our own vomit, and R. C. Slocum, Jack Pardee and Grant Teaff are stepping on our head. Rival recruiters are staggering under the weight of the bullets, axes, bombs, swords, and kitchen sinks that Texas has gift-wrapped and handed to them."

In the off-season, when McWilliams drew his line in the sand by retaining his entire staff—including several members he was advised to fire—Heard wrote, "There are three groups who applaud McWilliams's announcement: The assistants who would have been fired; those academicians who deplore big-time football; and supporters who want to fire everyone in the football program from DeLoss

Dodds on down and who are convinced the program will crash and burn."

A longtime UT official added sadly, "Somewhere Texas has lost that 'We're Texas and we're going to win because we're Texas' attitude. Texas football teams once expected to win. Lately, Texas has been hoping to win. They've gone into some games expecting to lose. We're two and seven in our last nine home games. That does something to the psyche. Texas is looking for that knight in shining armor to ride downfield to make it right."

Now, as kickoff at State College nears, Texas's knight errant is wearing a pair of freshly unpacked gray coaching pants. Someone made the pants too long. They unfurl on his feet as an equipment manager scrambles around on his knees, hastily pinning them up while McWilliams mutters a line right out of a Laurel and Hardy movie. "This is a fine way to start the season."

Over in the other locker room, Paterno just rolls up his suit pants in his ready-for-another-Johnstown-flood style that has become a trademark.

Tucked away in the back pocket of McWilliams's pants, however, there's a victory speech. It's nothing to make anyone run through a wall, but it's one he scrawled on the back of an itinerary the night before the game in his room at the Holiday Inn when he became convinced his team would win. He desperately wants to pull it out after the game to show the team just how certain he was they'd pull it off, even though Texas's school record four straight opening-day losses has included a couple of season-shattering defeats.

McWilliams, a former player and assistant coach for Texas legend Darrell Royal, and his team rumbled into State College Friday afternoon in a cavalcade of mammoth Trailway buses. They had all the sweatsuits, travel bags, and other trappings of a traditional football power as they hastily checked into a wing of the Holiday Inn while the buses idled and waited for them to pile back on and head to a brief workout. But the last time Texas had been ranked number one and really felt like Texas was six years ago, when they'd just lined up and flat whipped Paterno's team in the New Jersey Meadowlands, 28–3, as if Penn State were Harvard or some other Ivy League school.

The Texas team that pulled into State College Friday was still looking for a way to recapture that past magic and to forget about games like last season's contest with Penn State. In 1989, Texas beat Penn State everywhere except on the scoreboard, where the Nittany Lions came out ahead 16–12 when a punt blocked by linebacker Andre Collins was turned into the winning, fourth-quarter touchdown.

To acquire some old-time toughness, like that of the 1963 national champion team when a 188-pound McWilliams played defensive tackle and center, Texas players had been waking at 5:30 so they could make predawn practices. They'd forsaken their world-class, climate-controlled weight room for a hole in their stadium where the heat was always cranked up around the 100-degree mark and the air was so thick with humidity and acrid sweat that it would just about rain during a workout.

"There were spiders, crickets—I had to dodge a bat one day," says Stan Thomas, the huge Texas offensive tackle. "There was rust all over the barbells. That first week you've got guys throwing up in there. You could hardly breathe."

The players, led by the seniors, endured it because they were sick of losing and not going to the Cotton Bowl and always having to answer questions about what in the hell was wrong with Texas.

"We sat back and watched every senior class go out as losers," says Stephen Clark, the senior tight end who had gone in to talk with McWilliams shortly after the 1989 season closed on yet another sour note. "The coaches can only do so much. We were victims of all the negativism. It was like a disease. All the seniors before us were bitching and bitching and bitching, about the dining hall, about weight lifting, about practices, about everything. We had to change ourselves. We had to practice like champions and quit making it like a chore and start having fun again."

The Texas players wanted to win, but after so many years of losing, they weren't quite sure how to do it. They'd been losing for so long that some were beginning to say that the football team wasn't an aberration. Instead, it was a product of a university that had once been run with passion, fierce pride, and hardball politics that had now grown tired and top-heavy.

Now, as kickoff approaches, DeLoss Dodds makes his way to a glass-enclosed room on the press box level. He takes a roster card, folds it into a neat pyramid, and places it on top of his wooden briefcase. Close by is his ever-present pipe and his whiskey-flavored Borkum Riff tobacco. Dodds is CEO-slick, with a national reputation for being a shrewd negotiator. But the one part of his job he really hates is firing people, so much so that he usually "reassigns" or "backfills" them. He's had to do that to one football and two basketball coaches during his nine-year stay at Texas. He doesn't want to do it again. Dodds has voiced his support of McWilliams; yet it was Dodds who orchestrated an extensive review of the entire football program after the disastrous 1989 season.

On the sidelines, McWilliams is in his typical stance, with his legs crossed. He's confident in his talent, but he's also coaching a team that yielded two huge plays early in the last two opening losses to Brigham Young and Colorado.

Up in a booth, ready to start screaming into his headphones, is boisterous, Louisiana-born Lynn Amedee, Texas's hired-gun offensive coordinator who sports the three Cotton Bowl rings he helped arch-rival Texas A&M win. Defensive coordinator Leon Fuller, who rarely raises his voice, is down on the field ready to go with his man-to-man defense that critics are saying has been outdated by college football's increasingly sophisticated passing attacks.

And now Texas's kickoff team trots out. It's one of the special teams that McWilliams began working with personally after those units failed in game after game in 1989.

That's why first-teamers like Stanley Richard, a converted corner-back and a potential star at safety, are on this kickoff team. So is Van Malone, "Showtime" as the back of his letter jacket reads. Malone made the David Letterman show when he was in high school for game clips that showed him flying and flipping through the air on offense and defense. Now, he's the "gunner," or wedge-buster, for Texas. That means he's thinking about nothing except splattering as many Penn State bodies as possible.

Seven yards behind the ball, kicker Michael Pollak is trying to remain calm. A fifth-year senior, but still a walk-on, he's never kicked an extra point or a field goal in college. His longest field goal in competition is a 38-yarder he hit in high school. Instead of trying to win the starting job in spring football, Pollak had jumped at the opportunity to spend that semester studying in Vienna and traveling around Europe, where he was on hand to pick up a piece of the Berlin Wall after it came down.

On the bus to the stadium, Pollak quietly practiced mental imaging. As the bus moved past the acres of tailgaters with their gas grills and the clusters of coeds walking to the game, Pollak imagined himself warming up on the sidelines. He envisioned himself coping with the roar of the crowd and the nervousness that would try to short-circuit his body. In his mind's eye he saw himself making field goals, and driving the ball deep on kickoffs.

As he runs up on the real ball, though, Pollak's left foot slips slightly on the slick natural grass that Penn State players consider a big part of their home-field advantage. The ball tumbles down to Penn State tailback Gary Brown at the 2. As Brown makes his way up the field, Malone vaults into the air, jackknifes like an eighteen-wheeler on an

6

icy road and makes like a human bowling ball on Penn State's three-man wedge. But, he takes out only one player, leaving a split.

Texas linebacker Anthony Curl misses an arm tackle on Brown, and Pollak now sees three blockers in front of Brown, who keeps coming and coming and coming. Pollak dives for Brown near midfield but he only nicks him in the ankle and . . .

"They've run the kickoff back," Moos says forlornly to the captive audience on the bus.

Cindy McWilliams, who'd been on the edge of her seat right behind Moos, slumps back. Silence overwhelms the bus.

Brown doesn't make it all the way to the end zone because linebacker Winfred Tubbs, a converted fullback, keeps on sprinting until he hauls Brown down on the Texas 3. Once again, McWilliams and Texas are starting the season in the worst possible way, in a goal-line defense. The defense holds on two plunges by 224-pound fullback Sam Gash. On third-and-goal from the 2, tailback Leroy Thompson runs right up the gut for a Penn State touchdown.

Suddenly Texas is down 7–0 and everyone from the players to the silent riders on the bus are filled with the same premonition of dread. Oh, no. It's happening again. The first cracks in the newly laid foundation of confidence are starting to appear as the offense, quarterbacked by boyish-looking sophomore Peter Gardere, starts first-and-ten from the 21.

From the booth, Texas offensive coordinator Lynn Amedee opens with a couple of runs by Adrian Walker. Then he mixes in a pass to senior back Chris Samuels, good for 10 yards and a first down at the Texas 35. After another run by Walker and two incomplete passes, Gardere finds Texas's answer to Bo Jackson, receiver Johnny Walker. Walker, whose $172,000 baseball bonus from the Atlanta Braves organization allows him to tool around to class in a new champagne-colored Mercedes-Benz 190E, makes an 18-yard grab to the Penn State 29.

After an incompletion, Gardere changes his snap count from one to two. Surprise. The cerebral, mistake-fearing Penn State defenders jump offside like some kind of high school team. The drive, however, bogs down, leaving Pollak to attempt his first-ever field goal under real game conditions in college. The 30-yarder is good and Texas has steadied.

When Moffett, Cindy McWilliams, Joyce and Marvin Moos, and the rest of the stranded party pull in on a new bus with the first quarter ending, Texas is still down 7–3, but very much in the game.

The team and the traveling Texas fans get a big emotional lift on the first series of the second quarter, when on fourth-and-one from the Texas 27, Paterno passes up a field-goal attempt only to see Gary Brown stuffed on a run by middle linebacker Brian Jones. Jones is the first black at Texas to be given the sacred number 60 previously worn by Tommy Nobis and other white Texas linebacking greats.

Later in the quarter Texas defensive end Oscar Giles sacks Penn State quarterback Tony Sacca, whose fumble sets up another field goal by Pollak, a 29-yarder. A little more than a minute later the half ends, 7–6.

Texas players are upbeat in the locker room, and they get downright rowdy when Adrian Walker starts the second half with an in-your-face, 88-yard kickoff return. Amedee calls Samuels's number for the first and only time on a running play. Samuels is having trouble getting his cleats to bite into Penn State's hard turf, but he's able to sweep right six yards for the score. A scrambling Gardere completes a pass to Keith Cash for the 2-point conversion and Texas is up 14–7.

Now the Longhorns are in control. Compared with the sophisticated run-and-shoot offense that Texas has faced against Southwest Conference foe Houston for the last few years, Penn State's routes and Sacca's arm look easy to handle. Gardere's cadence still has the Penn State defenders on a yo-yo. When the Texas offense does sputter, the Penn State returners have fits with the erratic, driving kicks of left-footed punter Alex Waits.

When Texas redshirt freshman Phil Brown breaks a 42-yard run behind Duane Miller's block, he's well on his way to a game-high 95 yards rushing. Dodds is puffing contentedly on his pipe. Then, when Pollak hits his third field goal, a 20-yarder, the resigned Penn State crowd starts thinking about what they're going to grill and drink after the game.

But, as the fourth quarter opens, Sacca finds Terry Smith for a 48-yard gain to the Texas 29. Four plays later the Nittany Lions have scored on Brown's 5-yard run. But the 2-point try fails and they remain 4 points down 17–13.

On the Longhorns' next drive, Pollak gets a chance to get the margin back up to 7, but his 30-yarder pulls to the left. The Lions miss a 31-yarder, and after another short Texas drive and a Waits punt, Paterno's team gets the ball again.

The Lions have had to use all their time-outs on defense. There's only 1:06 left on the clock and Paterno's normally conservative team is 76 yards away from the Texas end zone. Not even the losing Longhorns of the past two seasons could find a way to give this one back.

Hold on. Sacca hits a couple of completions, and a 15-yard pass interference penalty that stops the clock moves the ball all the way to the Texas 27. A 7-yarder to Smith gets the ball to the 20, but the clock is just about to expire. Penn State rushes to the ball. Texas doesn't have time to call a defense. McWilliams is—Where is he? He's all the way down at the other end of the field, as if he can't stand to watch the final moments.

It's sandlot time, helter-skelter stuff. Penn State receivers streak long and the Longhorn defenders scramble to pick them up. Brian Jones sees a back drift over the middle, picks him up, and just hopes that everyone has found a man.

Oh, no. Not again. Brown, the very player who ran back the opening kickoff, is open in the right flat and if Sacca sees him, all the hope and hard work, the camaraderie, and the confidence could vanish in what could be one of Texas's most crushing defeats ever.

Sacca throws. But it's over the middle, where Stanley Richard slaps it to the ground. Texas wins!

The field spills over with Texas players who have never, ever won an opening game. In the corner of the end zone they create a thirty-player pileup as they jump on one another in ecstasy.

In the center of the end zone, safety Lance Gunn is prancing around like he's in a trance. *"We shocked the world. We shocked the world!"* he yells to no one in particular.

"Merry Christmas, Texas. Merry Fuckin' Christmas," a bearded Penn State fan screams from the end zone at receiver Johnny Walker, who raises a triumphant we're-number-one finger in response. Other Penn State fans, however, shout congratulations.

In the locker room, McWilliams pulls out his prepared victory speech and reads, "This should be a springboard for us," to whoops of joy

"This is like a movie script," Brian Jones says. "But the best is yet to come."

"We won the game before we hit the field," Van Malone boasts. "We had the attitude that we were going to win."

"We wanted to show everybody on the East Coast how Texas plays football," says offensive guard Duane Miller.

On the other side, Paterno is subdued after seeing his team hit with nine penalties for offsides and illegal motion, have a field goal attempt blocked, and a punt snuffed by Malone.

"We didn't play with a lot of poise or precision," he sighs. "We played sloppy. We didn't play with any consistency, and you have to give Texas credit for that.

"With all of the people around the football, it was pretty tough to get outside. They play man-to-man on the wide-outs and everybody else around the football . . . Texas is a better football team. They're better organized offensively."

On the way back to Williamsport, the Moffett party has no problems with their bus. And, as the Longhorns leave Happy Valley and wend their way back on a three-hour trip to the larger airport at Harrisburg, punter Alex Waits tunes in a sports talk show on his radio. He is stunned to hear Penn State fans talking about how good Texas played instead of bitching about why the Nittany Lions lost.

The Texas cheerleaders and some of the team's fans have to wait until the next day to leave State College and its tiny two-gate airport. As a small group is waiting to board their propeller-driven commuter plane, Gordon Appleman, a member of the Texas Athletics Council, arches an eyebrow when asked if he thought the team looked good.

"Not really," he says. "We were kind of lucky."

2

The Way They Were

Elvis is talking Texas football.

It's 1970 and he's backstage at the Las Vegas Hilton, safe from the flashbulbs that start popping as soon as he so much as peeks out of the stage door. The King's entourage is still keeping guard and there are five ladies hanging around, but Elvis isn't putting on a show by wearing a cape or one of those jewel-encrusted belt buckles big enough to eat off of.

He's being just folks from Tupelo, Mississippi, talking with a country boy from Longview, Texas.

"The funny thing about it is, it was like he was tickled to meet me," recalls former Texas quarterback James Street, today an insurance agent in Austin. "We were talking about the Big Shootout . . . we must have talked for more than an hour. Elvis was saying that Texas deserved to win and Bill Medley, you know, of the Righteous Brothers, he was arguing that Arkansas should have won."

That's how big Texas football was when Street led the Longhorns to 20 straight wins capped by a national title following the 1969 season. President Richard Nixon braved the protests of hillside antiwar demonstrators in Fayetteville to watch Street complete a miraculous fourth-down pass to lone receiver Randy Peschel in a come-from-behind 15–14 win over Arkansas.

Evangelist Billy Graham was shaking hands in the Texas locker room while Nixon was declaring, "This was one of the greatest games of all time. . . . The wire services will name Texas the number one team."

Street and his teammates didn't let Nixon down. They went on to the Cotton Bowl and beat Joe Theismann and a Notre Dame team that broke its 44-year ban on post-season bowls to get a shot at number one ranked Texas.

In the heady aftermath of that championship season, Street appeared at the spring showing at Neiman Marcus in Dallas. He hobnobbed with John Wayne for a day and a half in Dallas while he wasn't busy posing for pictures with Miss Texas Phyllis George. "Slick," as he was nicknamed back then, didn't do impressions of the Duke. But he did a pretty fair Elvis.

At least Farrah used to think so when he performed over at her apartment.

How big was Texas football? Texas coed Farrah Fawcett didn't even date Street, the starting quarterback; she was just the girlfriend of one of Street's buddies, former Texas player Greg Lott.

"It was like being the Beatles," says Street, who that year was even too busy to take up Lyndon Baines Johnson's offer to visit him out at his ranch.

National championships. Mob scenes at the airport and the Drag, as the main artery by the Texas campus, Guadalupe Street, is called. A win streak that eventually stretched all the way to 30 games.

In the 1960s Texas coach Darrell Royal even had a hotline to the White House and the good old boy network headed by LBJ. In 1963, six days after President John F. Kennedy was assassinated, wounded Texas Governor John Connally called from his hospital bed to congratulate Royal on a victory over arch-rival Texas A&M.

On Saturday nights, writers used to stop by 2001, the hospitality room at the Villa Capri motel, not only to talk about football as long as the bourbon flowed, but to sit at Royal's knee and find out what was really going on in the world and in Austin.

When Royal said Matt's El Rancho had the best Mexican food in town, writers flocked to the unpretentious eatery and ordered just what Royal would get, even though it wasn't on the standard menu. They'd get some chicken enchiladas that, as often as not, wouldn't be accompanied by a bill.

Royal introduced them to a redheaded stranger named Willie Nelson when he was just an unshaven, unknown guitar picker. The folksy Royal was country before country was cool. Will Rogers with a game face. An Oklahoma native and University of Oklahoma star quarterback who became, in his words, a dipped and vaccinated Longhorn. A child of the Depression who would be entrusted with the football fortunes of the brassiest, most boastful university in America, one that has won more football games than every school except Michigan and Notre Dame. Texas, with typical immodesty, calls itself The University. And at Texas a Dust Bowl kid who had climbed through eight coaching jobs in as many years settled down to become The Coach.

The youngest of seven children of Burley and Katy Royal who survived the Dust Bowl days of the mid-1930s—and that's all you did, survive it—Royal didn't initially aspire to much more than a regular paycheck and a breath now and then that didn't bring the sour taste of red grit.

"We did have some clear days," says Royal, who slept with a wet washrag over his mouth as a child to try to keep the dirt out of his mouth and lungs. "But it seemed like it was in the air all the time. I lived four miles from Texas, and you could look back in that direction and you could just see it boiling. When it would come in, it would choke you. It would literally cover the house. Inside, furniture would be dirty and dusty. It would get in the sheets. A few days later the storm would be going back the other direction to Texas. We just swapped dirt back and forth.

"I remember it being tough, but I never did feel like I was singled out. Everybody up and down the street had the same problem.

"Papa, he worked anything he could find. I remember he drove a truck that delivered fuel to the farmers for a while. And I remember him talking at breakfast that he was going to go down and try to 'get on.' That meant seeing if he could get a job that day working for the WPA. There was a place right down there at the courthouse, and all the men would go down there and line up and they'd hire so many."

The baby of the Royal family saw coaching as his ticket up and out. "I studied that like a subject," says Royal, whose mother died when he was four months old. From the time he was taking his first junior high gym class in Hollis, all he wanted to be was a high school coach in Oklahoma.

"That's as far as I could dream," Royal says as he sinks back into a plush, rose-colored couch in the lounge at the opulent Barton Creek Country Club, which commands a hillside in southwest Austin. "I can't say what I do now is work, but you could stack up a pile of money a show dog couldn't jump over and that wouldn't get me to change what I'm doing."

Royal is still on the Texas payroll as a special assistant to university president Bill Cunningham. When he isn't busy helping out with fund-raising or benefits, the sixty-six-year-old Royal can often be found on the golf course, where he's a seven handicapper and a golf cart hot rodder. He and buddy Frank Broyles, athletic director of the University of Arkansas, once shot ninety holes of "golf polo," as friends have dubbed their fast-moving game, in a single day during a break in the Southwest Conference meetings in 1963.

Coaching football at the University of Texas was kind to Royal, but then he did everything a coach was supposed to do at a school that aspires to be the Harvard of the South while being, well, Texas in football.

Royal never had a losing season in twenty years as head coach at Texas. He won two AP and three UPI national championships from 1963 to 1970. DKR, as he was sometimes called, took Texas to ten Cotton Bowls, including an incredible run of six straight from 1968–1973. He finished in the Top 10 ten times in twenty years.

Royal even looked like a winning coach. "He could walk into a room, and the conversation would stop," says Jones Ramsey, who used to stir drinks with his finger instead of a swizzle stick for writers at 2001. "Darrell was ruggedly handsome and had sex appeal and charisma. Charisma, that's a disease you can't get rid of."

"Darrell was a sweet Bear Bryant," adds Ramsey, who served as a sports information director for both coaches during stints at Texas A&M and Texas.

Maybe so, but Royal's players were half scared that he'd notice them from his coaching tower or when they snuck out on the town.

"I've been in a billion dressing rooms, but I've never seen anyone like Coach Royal," Street says. "He could walk out there and just stand there and it'd get quiet. If you were jackin' around and you had your back to him and you didn't know he was there, you could hear that he was in the room. It was kind of like the silence would just come around. He would never whistle. He didn't do anything. He'd just walk out there and it would get quiet.

"In all the time we played there, he had an open-door policy. But nobody dared to go into his open door. If you heard Coach Royal's side of the story he'd say, 'God dang, guys, I was here to listen to your problems or anything else.' He's a good guy, but he's a hard guy to get close to. It's hard to know Coach Royal."

Royal, however, made a point of knowing everyone else, especially if they could have an impact on the football coach at Texas, a position that couldn't escape the politics that swirled throughout the state capital.

When he interviewed for the job, bigger names like Michigan State's Duffy Daugherty and Bobby Dodd of Georgia Tech had already backed off. However, they recommended a rising star by the name of Royal. The thirty-two-year-old Royal didn't just know the names of the five-person Athletics Council; he knew whom to call Doctor and whom to call Sir. Some of his assistants at Washington, the latest stop on his whirlwind coaching tour that stretched all the way to the professional league in Canada, were so sure that he'd get the job that their wives stopped buying groceries.

And Royal, upon replacing Ed Price, who resigned after six years with a 33–27–1 record, didn't stop there at making impressions.

"What you do is you keep your fences mended when you're winning," he explains. "Don't make a lot of demands, don't ask for a lot of different things. Try to be the same way that you were when you were building. If you get your base behind you at that time, and if you don't do anything to antagonize people, then they're the ones who come to your aid when you have those 6–4 seasons. You don't have to speak to defend yourself. It never gets off the ground."

Yes, 6–4 could be a losing season at Texas, where coach Berry Whitaker once felt forced to refute the widespread story that he had been fired by a powerful, meddlesome booster. "I'm too thin-skinned and conscientious," he countered. "Defeats killed me. I was coming down with ulcers and that kind of thing."

He maintained that it was entirely his decision to resign. That was in 1922, after Whitaker had just compiled a three-year record of 22–3–1.

Well, hell. In Royal's three best years, 1963, 1969, and 1970, he only lost one game in all. That's why ABC named him the coach of the decade for the 1960s. At Texas, the 1960s were Camelot with cleats.

Pat Culpepper, a linebacking star for Texas in the early 1960s, once wrote that unnecessary roughness penalties, holding, and even using varied snap counts to draw opponents offside would not be tolerated at Texas, even in practice.

Royal's practices—like the Turd Bowl that was held on Mondays for the third teamers—were better than some games in the Southwest Conference, the two-state league that Texas all but owned. With no scholarship limits to speak of, the Longhorns routinely corralled most of the best high school talent in football-crazed Texas. More importantly, they kept half of it or more on their bench and off other SWC teams that kept on futilely struggling to beat them.

Even Royal's best athletes played on the fear rush of adrenaline. "You were scared to death to come out of a game, because you were afraid you'd never get back in," says Bob McKay, an All-America offensive tackle in 1969.

"There was a list on the wall as you walked into the dressing room," recalls Jim Bob Moffett, who turned out to be the richest member of his seventy-seven-man freshman football class of 1958. "I don't remember one time you'd walk in that room that you didn't sneak a glance at the list. Every day, if you wanted to stay on the first team, you had to compete."

Compete: That's what a quiet, long-lashed, thick-legged high school player from a small railroading town near Fort Worth did best. David McWilliams was good enough to attract attention from outside the state Royal owned.

"That Oklahoma plane came down to Cleburne," says Culpepper, now a head coach at Lufkin High School in East Texas. "And Bud Wilkinson didn't come unless you were a top, top player."

McWilliams, however, was committed to go with Royal's program. When the Longhorns later lounged around in motel rooms the night before games in their shorts, swilling Dr Peppers, it was usually McWilliams who could be found running the projector and reminding everyone of his assignment.

In 1962, McWilliams's junior year, the Longhorns finished the regular season 9–0–1 They then lost 13–0 in the Cotton Bowl to a Louisiana State team quarterbacked by Lynn Amedee, who also hit a record 37-yard field goal in that game.

The 1963 team starred larger-than-life tackle Scott Appleton and middle linebacker Tommy Nobis, but it was the studious McWilliams who was a co-captain with Appleton and halfback Tommy Ford. The team finished the regular season 10–0 when it slid by Texas A&M 15–13 on muddy turf that was dyed green for television and was so bad that Royal jabbed at it with a rake in disgust. Six days after President Kennedy was gunned down in Dallas, Texas Board of Regents member Frank Erwin was so upset about the field that he tried to commandeer the public address system at A&M. When that failed, he issued a halftime announcement that proclaimed, "The condition of the playing field is a disgrace and a reflection on Texas A&M. No university which makes any pretense of having an athletic program would permit any such condition to exist."

From there it was on to the Cotton Bowl, where the number two ranked Midshipmen of Navy were waiting with a quarterback named

Roger Staubach. To keep up with Staubach's scrambling style, Royal's trusted and crusty defensive coordinator, Mike Campbell, had his linemen chasing sophomore backup quarterback Marvin Kristynik back and forth across the field to get ready to play a special eight-man front defense called the Staubach Chase. By studying game films, the Texas coaching staff had cracked some of the code that Navy's coaches hand signaled in to their players.

Right before the game, Navy coach Wayne Hardin announced on television—which was also piped into the stadium's public-address system—that if the Midshipmen were to beat Texas, they should be national champs. "We're ready," was all a seething Royal said during his introduction.

"Darrell was so mad," Ramsey says, "he wouldn't have to say a thing to his team. He told me later, 'You could have coached the team that day.' "

The Texas defense held Navy to a minus 14 yards in rushing, a Cotton Bowl record, and Texas strutted off the field with a convincing 28–6 win and the school's first national championship.

A three-year stretch of four-loss seasons from 1965 to 1967 had powerful Board of Regents member Erwin ready to dump Royal, but, for once, Erwin didn't get his way. "I had some of those six and four seasons and Erwin wanted to get me fired," Royal says. "I didn't know about it at the time, but I heard he brought it up at a Regents meeting and was laughed at. That ended it."

By the start of the 1968 season, Royal was also ready to make a switch. He'd had offensive backfield coach Emory Bellard working on an offense that would allow him to use his deep backfield talent and be more dangerous than the I formation that had sputtered at Texas since 1966.

That summer of '68, Bellard was sketching diagrams and having his son and some of his friends walk through plays from a funky-looking full-house formation. By fall, Royal and Bellard had Texas starting quarterback "Super" Bill Bradley and Street, his little-known backup, giving it a try.

"I told them it was impossible, you can't do it," says Street, who'd been a 155-pounder thinking about a pro baseball career even before he realized that Texas had fifteen quarterbacks in his freshman class alone. "I really think I was right. If you left that fullback up there where he had that fullback, you don't have enough time to react. You don't have enough time to read that tackle or even that area. They moved him back about a yard."

The wishbone was born, although it was a stillbirth for the first few games of the 1968 season. It just didn't fit the talents of Bradley, who was later moved to defensive back. When Texas was losing the second game of the season to Texas Tech, Royal grabbed Street by the jersey and said, "Hell, you can't do any worse."

Hell, he couldn't have done any better. Texas lost that game, 31–22 but never looked back. The Longhorns won the next 18 in a row before facing a delayed showdown with Frank Broyles's undefeated Arkansas squad at the end of the 1969 season.

Beano Cook came up with the idea to move the mid-October game to December. Roone Arledge had asked Cook, the ABC-NCAA press director, to examine the 1969 season and make some suggestions. Cook predicted Arkansas and Penn State would battle for the national championship in the 1970 Cotton Bowl, and that Joe Paterno's team would win. Preseason favorite Ohio State, Cook figured, would fall to Minnesota.

"Darrell thought we were nuts," Cook recalls. "Broyles was for it because they didn't get the exposure."

Cook nailed his prediction except for the fact that the top-ranked and heavily favored Buckeyes lost to Michigan, not Minnesota, to enhance the Texas-Arkansas matchup.

"The stage was set," Street says. "Here's the hundredth year of college football. Here's the president at the ballgame. You've got the number one team and the number two team. National TV. Most of the other games are over with. Most of the people in America who are football nuts are watching the number one and number two teams play each other. In addition to that, it's the way it unfolds. The underdog gets up fourteen to nothing, and then we start to come back."

Texas is down 14–8 and looking at fourth-and-three at its 43 and a likely loss when Royal sends in the crucial play.

"I couldn't believe the call," Street says. "I came back not to question the call, because I didn't question his calls. I questioned the formation he used. Lots of times he'd send in a play, and he'd get excited and he'd send in a formation that you couldn't even run it from. I think he just felt like I would adjust to whatever it was. I just wanted to make sure that we were doing exactly what he wanted.

"I said, 'Right fifty-three veer pass, Coach, *means* we're setting the formation to the wide side of the field. Cotton is going to the wide side of the field. The *only* receiver we got going out is our tight end, and he's going deep. Are you sure that's what we want to do?' I thought maybe he meant run left fifty-three veer pass."

Upstairs at the press box level, defensive backfield coach Fred Akers and other Texas assistants are clamoring for Royal to change the call. They'd rather try to throw to star Cotton Speyrer than tight end Randy Peschel.

Royal sticks by his decision, and Street relays the play to his teammates.

"In the huddle, the first thing I said was, 'Y'all aren't going to believe this call. But it will work. It will work,' " Street says.

"The Arkansas linebackers would always stand there and look in your huddle. So, what I did, Cotton Speyrer was straight ahead from me and I kept doing like I was talking to Cotton, and using my hands. I wouldn't even look at Randy, but I said, 'I'm talking to you, Randy. The play calls for you to go deep. I don't care what you do. Just take two stops, turn around, and I'll dump it to you. Or get three yards deep, get open, and catch the ball. If you see you can't get behind them, just turn around and come back to me. Anything. Just get open and catch the ball.' Then I said, 'Line, give me time to throw. Right fifty-three veer pass.'

"I've told Coach Royal about the fear I've awakened with. How would I have explained it to him, if, just about the time I let go of the ball, Randy stops and starts running back toward me? I know good and well that Coach would have killed me.

"I'm not sure we'd ever run that play in a game. We didn't work on it on practice that week. But, it's like Coach Campbell said, I could have thrown that damn pass fifteen times or fifty times or a hundred times in practice with no defenders out there and I couldn't have thrown it any better or he couldn't have caught it any better. It's one of those things where it's meant to work. That's part of Coach Royal's luck and that's part of my luck. We think we're going to get lucky so we get lucky."

Peschel caught The Pass that set up The Touchdown that enabled The University to win The Game by a point, 15–14. When the Longhorns came back to Austin, they were greeted by a boisterous crowd that literally wanted to rip their clothes off. Street, who was starting to suffer pangs of claustrophobia from being trapped on the plane, tried to calm the crowd that had broken through the airport barriers. Then, he bundled up in an overcoat so people couldn't tear his clothes, calmly walked down the ramp . . . and bolted for his life.

Next fall, not too long after the Longhorns had beaten Notre Dame

21–17 in the Cotton Bowl, a little, unpretentious campus restaurant named Bert's Bar-B-Q opened and posted a little "Laugh In"–era bumper sticker behind the cash register. It still reads, TEXAS IS #1 (YOU BET YOUR SWEET BIPPY).

Little did anyone realize that twenty years later the Texas football team would still be searching for a national championship and a chance to sock it to 'em again. Maybe, just maybe, 1990 will be the year.

3

Rocky Mountain Highs
and Lows

Texas is playing Colorado on ESPN in two days, and Craig Helwig can't wait.

"Big-time football," the former IBM executive bellows to no one in particular in a second-floor office at Bellmont Hall as he clenches his fist and double pumps his arm.

Yeah, baby. TV money and exposure. Pumped-up, ticket-buying fans and boasting, check-writing boosters. Just what Helwig, an assistant athletic director and Texas's head fund-raiser, wants to see.

Big-time football.

"I don't know what it is, but Colorado, Texas A&M—blood-and-guts football. Make-you-sick football," Chuck Johnson, offensive left tackle for Texas, says as he leans back in a chair, lets out a soft whistle, and winces. "I mean, when the game is over you have a headache. Stuff hurts. Most games, when they're done with, you're exhausted. But after ones like Colorado and A&M, you don't feel like eating. Your head hurts. And that's on top of the bumps and bruises and being tired. You just want to go to your room and swallow some Advil."

Although Johnson is 6-foot-5 and 275 pounds, he runs life under a caution flag. He wants to be ready for everybody, everything, every situation.

For his pre-law studies he's got a computer, that was assembled by his parents. He stays away from the popular bars on Sixth Street, Austin's rockin' and rollin' answer to Bourbon Street, because he doesn't want to run into any smaller guy who might be armed and looking for trouble. At night, when he walks around campus, he's aware of what's going on and who might be lurking in the shadows.

"I don't just take off and blow straight ahead, walking with my Walkman on, not listening to what's going on, just being glassy-eyed, walkin' where I'm goin' and jammin' to the beat," he says. "Yeah, I look both ways twice before I cross the street, I'd guess you'd say. I don't like to leave things up to chance, because that's a good way to get screwed."

Johnson, the only child of two high school valedictorians, never wants to be in the wrong place at the wrong time. But two weeks after the giddy Penn State win, he is. He's just getting over the flu, and he has to get ready for a Colorado team that hits hot, humid Austin with the kind of super squad Texas used to field in its glory days.

The Buffaloes were a preseason favorite to win the national championship that barely escaped them in 1989. They sport a frisky option offense that's an offshoot of Texas's old wishbone attack, and they have some top Texas schoolboy talent. Like the H-Boys. That's what they call Alfred Williams and Kanavis McGhee in Boulder, because they both hail from Houston. They're both headed for the NFL, where they'll have outstanding size and speed even for that league. They are the biggest, baddest bookend set of linebackers in America, a potential pass-rushing nightmare for Johnson, trash-talking right tackle Stan Thomas and tight end Kerry Cash.

On the right side of the Colorado defense is McGhee, a 6-foot-5, 250-pound returning All-American and one of the favorites for the Butkus Award given to the outstanding collegiate linebacker. Also in the early running for the same award is Williams, 6-foot-6, who has bulked up to 250 pounds for this season while keeping every bit of the 4.8-second 40-yard-dash speed that's allowed him to record twenty-two and one-half sacks in his first three years at Colorado.

Colorado, which has been recruiting heavily in Texas and California in recent years, doesn't just have athletes on defense. In Darian Hagan, from Los Angeles, coach Bill McCartney has a quarterback who can run the option slicker than James Street's hair was when he was a ducktailed greaser in Longview waiting for the wishbone to be born.

Last year against Texas, Colorado was forced to start Hagan because of a cancer that eventually claimed Sal Aunese's life. Hagan, however, showed that he was a big-time quarterback when he kept for a 75-

yarder on the second play of the game. That set the tone for what would turn into a convincing 27–6 loss for Texas.

As he watched film of that game to get ready for this year's clash, Texas middle linebacker Brian Jones was squirming in his seat. "I played terrible; it was like a horror film. I covered my eyes."

B.J., as he's called, had become one of the most controversial Longhorns of all time soon after he transferred from UCLA, where he felt his individuality was being suppressed by Terry Donahue's image-conscious regime.

"I didn't feel free," he explains. "You were always looking over your shoulder. The coaches try to mold you. They want everyone to be clean-shaven. They try to control everyone, tell you what to say to the press. They want everyone to act a certain way and they keep saying that no one is bigger than the program. They tell you when you talk to the press, dwell on the team and not yourself. Donahue is a businessman. He had a great relationship with Troy Aikman, but I don't think he gives a damn about the players out there. That's why they lose with all that talent."

Although he spent his transfer year of ineligibility paying his dues at Texas, even playing fullback on the scout team to help get the varsity defense ready, Jones made some waves big enough to surf on in the middle of Texas. He dubbed some of his lazier teammates "eaters and riders," guys who were more interested in hitting the training table, traveling to games, and impressing girls than in doing whatever it took to win football games.

On a computer printout Jones looks like a match for Williams and McGhee. He's a chiseled 6-foot-3 and 238 pounds. In a straight-ahead footrace, Jones could smoke either of the Colorado stars. His running back-like 4.55 speed in the 40 yard dash has him near the top of some pro scouting sheets. Jones even announced that he wants to be the top pick in the draft, and the best damn number 60 ever to play at Texas.

Some of Texas's old guard, who remember Tommy Nobis meeting ball carriers head-on with his twenty-inch neck, sneer at that. They prefer Jones's immediate predecessor at number 60, Britt Hager, a backup linebacker for the Philadelphia Eagles. Or even Mical Padgett, Jones's junior backup.

Jones can't read plays or change direction quickly, his critics complain. They say he's top-heavy with bulging biceps and pecs. He's an athlete, but not a football player with great instincts. The Herschel Walker of middle linebackers. On his bad days he always seems to be plugging the wrong hole. Give him a shifty cutback runner to stop and he would be lost, they say.

Coming at Jones out of the Colorado I-Bone is tailback Eric Bieniemy, a low-slung Heisman Trophy candidate with 195 pounds of muscle packed on his 5-foot-7 frame. Fullback George Hemingway is five inches taller, thirty-five pounds heavier, and more than enough of a load to keep Jones and the Texas defense honest up the middle.

Williams, McGhee, Hagan, Hemingway, and Bieniemy are just some of the reasons why most preseason observers thought Texas's only chance for victory would be a moral one after a reasonably close loss.

The Longhorns, however, are now sky-high after the win against Penn State. They believe they're back. The Buffaloes, with a disappointing 1–1–1 record in their first three games, must win to keep alive the national championship hopes they still nurture.

For Texas it's an acid test, particularly for the offensive line, which was one of the team's weaknesses in the 1989 season. They were called slow, clumsy, and weak. And fat. After the 50–7 embarrassment against Baylor, the apocryphal story circulated that Texas had to waste a time-out because one of its offensive linemen was too fat to roll over and get to his feet after he was knocked on his back.

Offensive coordinator Lynn Amedee, tired of having his quarterbacks beaten up, demanded a leaner line, one with less than 20 percent body fat lapping over its belts. Left tackle Johnson, a backup in the 5–6 season in 1989, is one of the new starters. Duane Miller is at left guard, former walk-on Todd Smith is at center, Jeff Boyd starts at right guard, and over at right tackle Stan Thomas looks like a new man.

Big Stan, as his teammates call the 6-foot-6 300-pounder, used to epitomize what was wrong with the Longhorns, who often paid only lip service to the word *team*. Thomas, the son of Stan Thomas, Sr., a former baseball player in the Pittsburgh Pirate organization, started out in baseball until he outgrew that sport. He didn't concentrate on football until his junior year in high school. The best he could do was earn all-district honors at El Centro High School in California. Both USC and UCLA talked to him, but they didn't formally offer scholarships.

Texas did. Texas was desperate.

As raw as Thomas was as a freshman, however, some teammates noticed that his quick feet made him a natural at pass blocking, a skill a lot of top offensive linemen don't master until after a few years of pro seasoning.

Big Stan was starting by his sophomore season and attracting attention by his junior year. For all the wrong reasons. If someone was holding in the line or hitting late after the play, the odds were it would be Thomas. That's because he was doing it on purpose.

"I felt unwanted," says Thomas, who wears designer wristbands and thinks of himself as a stylish wide receiver in an offensive lineman's body. "I'd do anything to get noticed. Hold, punch, whatever. I didn't care if they threw a flag. I'd damn near throw my hand up and say, 'Yeah, it's on me.' We were all playing like that. We were playing for ourselves. That's probably why we were losing."

Thomas's teammates and friends, like current Houston Oilers safety John Hagy, would get on him that he could be playing in the NFL if he was a little more serious. "I'd tell him, you've got talent, you've got to get an attitude," says Hagy, who used to live across the hall from Thomas. "He was lackadaisical. He had that hey, dude, California attitude. I think he got a little more Texan in him. Against Texas A&M last year he abused Aaron Wallace. He had a helluva game. And from that point on he's kept it up."

Thomas never really believed Hagy and the others until he started hearing the same things from agents and scouting services after his junior year. Now, in his senior year, Thomas has come back with a bench press that's up 50 pounds to 400 pounds. The scouts have his 40-yard-dash speed listed at anywhere from the 5.3 seconds he clocked in high school to 5.1. That's why Thomas expects to have his pro stock go through the roof when he gets to the scouting combines after the season.

"I'm running a four point nine now," he says proudly. He's got a new scheme for getting noticed: sustaining his block, shoving the guy across from him down the field until the whistle blows. That, and saying anything and everything to the press.

"I think the offensive line this year, people need to be afraid to play us," Johnson says. " 'Cause I mean, go over there and get down in front of Stan and you're fixing to get hit by a freight train. Come on down the line through the two guards and the center, and there's no telling what might happen to you. You're going to wind up on the ground if you have to go against Jeff, Todd, or Duane. People talk about defensive linemen, oh, they've got these great swim moves and spin moves and all this. But people don't talk too much about the head jam, the shoulder grab, the leg whip—those are some of the uniquely nasty little things offensive linemen do."

The lines aren't the only places where there's fixing to be a war. There will be a battle for the minds taking place on the sidelines, where Texas is bringing in 147 recruits to watch the game—some of the very same players that wide-ranging Colorado is hoping will follow Williams and McGhee back to Boulder.

They turn out to be a small part of the crowd of 75,882 jammed into Memorial Stadium for an occasion that starts out festive. Behind the massive scoreboard at the south end of the stadium, Craig Helwig has figured out a big-time use for the huge AstroTurfed white elephant of a playing field on the roof of the multimillion-dollar Neuhaus-Royal weight and locker room facility. Normally the roof is used only by an occasional punter or some scout teamers, but now it's packed with tents and picnic tables and contributing members of the Longhorn Foundation. For them, the 79-degree temperature is enjoyable, not the energy-sapping force it will be for the players.

The crowd erupts as Texas prances onto the field for its first home game of the year. Colorado, meanwhile, is playing this one like a heavyweight championship fight. The Buffaloes enter the ring last, even though they're the visiting team. They're proud and sassy in their black shoes, the kind the Texas players covet. They've been told they can switch to black shoes if they go all the way to the Cotton Bowl.

Michael Pollak, who's finally been awarded a scholarship after kicking three field goals against Penn State, kicks off for Texas. With the aid of a fifteen-mile-an-hour wind, he puts it five yards deep in the end zone. Colorado's Mike Pritchard kneels to down the ball, but on the non-runback both pumped-up teams get hit with personal fouls.

Early in the opening quarter Texas safety Stanley Richard strips Hagan of the ball. Jones falls on it and Texas takes over on Colorado's 17. Texas chips away for four plays and then Gardere goes with Texas's money play, the one that worked even when the Longhorns weren't winning—an alley-oop pass to one of the 6-foot-4 Cash brothers. This time it's tight end Kerry, not his twin, Keith, who gets the jump ball over a defender. When Pollak hits the kick, Texas jumps out to a 7–0 lead.

Colorado's answering march down the field seems to stall finally as Hagan is hit by linebacker Anthony Curl just as he's pitching. Bieniemy recovers, but the Buffaloes are looking at a third-and-eighteen from the Texas 38, and they're not known as a passing team. Hagan drops back and has to scramble quickly to the right, where linebacker Jason Burleson is in the flat.

Burleson is Texas's square peg that the coaches keep trying to jam into round holes. He's a former junior decathlon champ and one of the bluest chips that Texas recruited for quarterback. His stats and his sheer size and arm strength had Peter Gardere wondering why he'd even bothered to pick Texas.

But that was back when Burleson was listed as 6-foot-7. Now, after being tried at quarterback, fullback, tight end, and finally strong-side linebacker, he's been officially shrunk to 6-foot-5. As Hagan rolls right, Burleson hesitates. Should he come up or float back with Hemingway? He picks Hagan.

Later that night, while he's nursing a beer in a hospitality suite at the Doubletree Hotel in the north end of Austin, an upbeat McWilliams will say that Hemingway wasn't Burleson's responsibility, that a safety or somebody was supposed to roll over into that deep zone.

But no one does, and when Hemingway catches a ridiculously easy touchdown pass, there's not a Longhorn within taunting distance. The teams are tied and the game's still young, but Burleson's season is effectively over.

On the first play from scrimmage after the Colorado kickoff, Texas has the ball first-and-ten from its own 22. Amedee calls a play for freshman Butch Hadnot, the bruiser he thinks just might be his very own Earl Campbell. Williams, however, snuffs Hadnot's college debut for no gain. On fourth-and-eight from the Texas 24, punter Alex Waits, coming back from a torn hamstring, nails a punt that doesn't stop rolling until it's in the Colorado end zone, a 76-yard monster.

Hemingway gets 33 yards up the middle for the Buffaloes, but on the next play Hagan loses another fumble. Cornerback Mark Berry pounces on it, and Texas ends up with a 47-yard Michael Pollak field goal that makes it Texas 10, Colorado 7 just as the first quarter is slipping into the sticky night.

Colorado tries to answer with a wind-aided 53-yarder, but it's deflected by the right upright. Then on their next possession the Buffaloes, led by Bieniemy, march for a touchdown. When Pollak hits another field goal, the teams leave the field at the half with Colorado up 14–13.

The third quarter is all Texas. After the two teams both punt on their opening possessions, Thomas, Johnson, and the rest of the Texas offensive line begin to dominate the Colorado defense. Phil Brown and Adrian Walker run for most of the yardage on an 80-yard, 14-play drive that ends with Brown surging in from the 2. The following 2-point conversion fails when Texas quarterback Peter Gardere leads Johnny Walker by too much, but Texas is still up 19–14. Reserve

27

lineman Alan Luther is in front of the ESPN cameras holding up the number one sign that Texas players haven't been able to flash for years. ESPN is having trouble getting shots of Texas coach David McWilliams, who keeps weaving in and out of his players. But McWilliams looks as though he'll be the coach to end Colorado's national title hopes.

Later in the quarter, Texas adds a short field goal by Pollak to go up 22–14, but Colorado, and Bieniemy, are up to the challenge. The Buffaloes march 60 yards for a score. They miss the 2-point try to leave them behind 22–20 with ten minutes left to play.

After the kickoff, Texas offensive tackle Chuck Johnson finds himself at the wrong place, at the wrong time. Johnson has been playing even though the flu had him throwing up on the sidelines. He's there now as Texas prepares to move the ball from its own 19. Stan Thomas is there, too. So are Jeff Boyd, Todd Smith, and Duane Miller, the rest of the first-team line. And there's Phil Brown, who's shredded Colorado for 92 yards on 16 carries. And the first-team receivers. Even the second-team receivers.

Gardere is looking at a huddle that could use some introductions. The sophomore quarterback is the only starter out on the field. The rest are wondering what the hell is going on. Johnny Walker is talking hurriedly to receivers coach Clarence James. "Are you sure this is what you want to do?" Walker asks.

Walker is worried. The makeshift unit, which isn't even the standard second team, didn't take a snap against Penn State. They're only out there because Amedee is worried about the heat and humidity and keeping his starters fresh. They spent a whopping twelve minutes of the third quarter shoving Colorado's star-studded defense all over the field. McWilliams, who has given Amedee pretty much of a free hand in running the offense, is just watching the series unfold.

"We had talked about putting them in, but it was a little later than anticipated," McWilliams said. "Lynn and I talked about it before the game and at half. It wasn't a spur-of-the-moment thing."

But they couldn't have picked a more crucial moment.

The freshman Hadnot runs for four. Gardere throws an incomplete pass to running back Jimmy Saxton, who's actually the understudy quarterback in more normal situations. Then, Gardere overthows third-team receiver Kenny Neal. Fourth down, and still six yards to go. Waits gets off a 43-yard punt, but it's returned 31 yards by cornerback Dave McCloughan. The momentum has swung to Colorado.

From Texas's 35, Colorado uses seven plays to score when Bieniemy blasts up the middle from the 2. Jones isn't there to stop him. He hasn't been for most of the night in which he records only four tackles. Colorado takes a 27–22 lead with less than six minutes to play.

Texas can't answer on the next series. Then, a Colorado punt pins Texas on its own 3 with just thirty-four seconds left. Johnson doesn't get it yet. He's out on the field wondering not if, but how Texas is going to pull this game out. He's shocked when Williams sacks Gardere for a safety and the game ends two plays later with Colorado storming off the field with a 29–22 win.

The Texas players are stunned. They held McGhee to one solo tackle and had Colorado flat whipped. A distraught Jones tells a post-game radio audience that he's the reason Texas lost. McWilliams, who's walking by, pulls Jones aside and tries to reassure him that it's the team that wins or loses.

After all, the Texas coaches and administrators don't feel that bad. McWilliams, who never had the sudden feeling that his team would win the way he did at Penn State, was scared his special teams would play worse.

Now, he's getting a thumbs-up signal in the dressing room from Texas president Bill Cunningham. Neither realizes that radio talk show callers are already seizing on the wholesale substitution in the fourth quarter as yet another example of why Texas will never be back under McWilliams.

But the callers don't know that the Texas players, led by senior tight end Stephen Clark, are already working on the damage control.

"I want to talk," Clark says when McWilliams is through addressing the team. "We're too good of a team to let this stop us. Go home, think about it. Think about this game. Think about two-a-days. This is the last time we're going to lose."

"We're not going to lose another time!" Richard shouts in agreement.

Losing. The players know all too well how painful losing can be at Texas.

4

The House Divided

It's November 29, 1986, and Fred Akers is cruising toward Austin in his brand-new, white 1986 Lincoln. He's just two days removed from a 16–3 Thanksgiving Day loss to arch-rival Texas A&M that was the final blow in a tumultuous 5–6 season. It was the first losing campaign for a Texas football coach in thirty years. But Akers is in a positive frame of mind. He's always in a positive frame of mind.

And why not? He's just left his gentleman's ranch in Manor, east of town. In his dapper gray suit he looks like something straight out of a Neiman Marcus catalog. And he doesn't just look good, he gets results. He's won 86 games, lost 31, and tied 2 in his ten-year stint at Texas, which began when he succeeded Darrell Royal after the 1976 season. Twice he has been just one Cotton Bowl victory away from winning a national championship.

Now it's Saturday morning and Akers has a coach's show to tape, recruits to visit, and an athletic director to meet with.

Shortly after 8 A.M. Akers, accompanied by close friend Lou Marks of Houston, wheels into the lot of River City Productions in north Austin to tape his weekly show. It recaps a season in which twenty-one starters missed one or more games.

He pops out an hour later, just about ready to head for San Antonio and a playoff game featuring four top high school recruits.

He never makes that game. Instead, he goes to Rooster Andrews Sporting Goods on Guadalupe Street and waits.

Meanwhile, on campus, athletic director DeLoss Dodds has been meeting with members of the Athletics Council on the second floor of Bellmont Hall to determine Akers's fate. Just before 11 A.M., the poker-faced Dodds emerges and heads for president Bill Cunningham's office.

Dodds tells Cunningham of the council's recommendation and then leaves for a prearranged meeting at the new offices of Andrews, which are next to the sporting goods store owned by the former Texas team manager and placekicker.

"Rooster," as Billy Andrews is known, has been selling socks and jocks to the Texas athletic department since 1946. The former roommate of Bobby Layne, Texas's star quarterback in the 1940s, Andrews is about 5 feet and 120 pounds of unbridled Longhorn passion. His place seems the perfect neutral site for a meeting. Or a showdown.

Dodds arrives just before noon. Akers has been waiting for almost forty-five minutes. They huddle in Rooster's private office for less than ten minutes.

"Fred," Dodds sums up, "they've decided to let you go."

"Who are *they*, DeLoss?" Akers asks pointedly.

"Well, the Athletics Council, the president, and me," Dodds says.

Akers stares at him with those piercing blue I'm-the-coach eyes and replies, "DeLoss, I just hope that before you leave here, you grow a set of balls."

Two hours later, Dodds is in the Neuhaus-Royal complex at Texas announcing Akers's firing. Make that a "reassignment," as they say at Texas.

Akers and wife Diane are pulling into the underground parking lot at Channel 7 and getting ready to appear at halftime on CBS's national game of the week. Akers smiles grimly. Diane takes one glance at two somber-faced reporters and says, "Hey, nobody died."

And that's what thousands of Texas supporters thought that day. Hey, nobody died. Texas would just get a new coach, which turned out to be David McWilliams, and get back to the business of being number one.

But three years later, on November 25, 1989, orangebloods saw their once-proud football team lying in state at Memorial Stadium. Those of the 49,081 fans who stuck around for the finish—and there weren't many—saw McWilliams's team sleepwalk through a 50–7 loss to Baylor, a school that hadn't beaten Texas in Austin in thirty-eight years. The game was far worse than anything in the ten-year Akers era.

"I was dejected, just like our coaching staff was," Darrell Royal recalls. "They had to be embarrassed. I know on one of those passes

31

[current Houston Oiler receiver] Tony Jones was coming over the middle and he got real short arms all of a sudden. That was the one that was intercepted for a touchdown right before half."

Texas's effort was so bad that the subsequent 21–10 defeat by Texas A&M, Texas's sixth consecutive loss to the Aggies, almost looked like a win in comparison. The loss to A&M dropped McWilliams's team to 5–6 for 1989, the third losing season in four years for Texas.

With or without Akers, Texas just wasn't Texas anymore. The Cotton Bowl had become a long-range goal, not a given. Fans that used to bank on wins now prayed for them. Or cursed the losses.

"I just don't want to sit through another game like the eighty-nine Baylor game. Ever," says James Street, the quarterback who guided Texas to 20 straight wins in the school's glory days. "Or some of the Houston games we've played. If that's the way we're going to play on a continuing basis, I'll just quit going.

"We were in the stands for the Oklahoma game in 1989 and we're ahead pretty good. And people are sitting in the stands saying 'Run, clock, run.' Well, that's a loser's approach. Hell, you're ahead. Let's beat the hell out of them now. This is our year. But that attitude is the same attitude that I always felt when we played a TCU. 'We're going to beat Texas this year,' they'd say. They stay close the first quarter. Then you'd slowly start edging away and they start thinking, 'Here they come.' "

Not, there they go. Texas got hit with the same forces of change that blindsided Alabama, Nebraska, Ohio State, Southern Cal, UCLA, and the other traditional powers that now haven't won a national championship in at least a decade. On any given Saturday, there is no more given. Scholarship limits leveled out the playing field so that the college football giants were bringing in twenty-five freshmen just like everyone else, not the fifty that Texas once did or the seventy-five that the Longhorns once were able to quickly sift through before total scholarship limits were reached.

More and more schools found that they could play rock 'em, sock 'em, blood-'n'-guts, hi-mom football with the big boys. Colorado discovered it could beat the big red squads of Oklahoma and Nebraska. In 1990 Georgia Tech would find out it could compete for a national championship. And Southern Mississippi would surpass its wildest dreams by beating both Alabama and Auburn in the same season.

Alabama-Auburn, Oklahoma-Nebraska, and Southern Cal-UCLA —not one of those traditional season-cappers was played with the conference championship at stake in 1990.

But at Texas, more than the routine forces were at work. Its decline had help: Racism, academic elitism, and the illegal recruiting that became all the rage at many Southwest Conference schools in the 1980s. That's not to mention the nasty politics that split the state's largest university for more than a decade when Royal and his folksy ways were shoved aside for the perma-pressed Akers Era.

"It takes a long time to build a program up, but they go downhill in a hurry," says Texas Tech coach Spike Dykes, a former Darrell Royal assistant. "You can lose it if you don't recruit every year. You win with players. You don't win with buildings or stadiums or jerseys or helmets."

When Darrell Royal was winning his national championships, all of the Texas players were white. Although Julius Whittier, now a Dallas lawyer, was on the 1970 team that was awarded a United Press International championship before a Cotton Bowl loss to Notre Dame, no black football player has ever been on a Texas team that won an Associated Press national championship. The 1969 team quarter-backed by Street is known as the last all-white team to win that title.

"Yeah, it's become a stigma," Darrell Royal says.

"It [the racism] was here before I got here. I'd been told that they'd just as soon we didn't integrate, but not by the administration. We started trying to integrate pretty soon after everybody else did. It took too long, but that happened to be the schedule for this part of the country."

That's why top black players simply left the state in the 1960s. Gene Washington of Baytown, Bubba Smith and Mel Farr of Beaumont, Johnny Roland of Corpus Christi, and Charley Taylor of Grand Prairie headed north and west to major college football programs in the 1960s. With them and scores of players like them, Texas lost an early opportunity to gain a foothold in the black community—a failure that still haunts the school today.

But when Southwest Conference schools finally decided to recruit blacks, they went all out. Former Oklahoma coach Barry Switzer, who had to recruit against Texas and other SWC schools, wrote in his autobiography that he humanely helped poor recruits, although one rival coach says he doesn't ever remember Switzer helping "any but the fast ones."

In the 1980s, when Fred Akers was trying desperately to prove he was a worthy successor to Royal, six of the nine conference schools were slapped with NCAA probations. The hit list included Texas, which was guilty of handing out small payouts of eighty dollars or less, selling complimentary tickets, and letting players use coaches' cars for short campus trips. The NCAA's investigation of Texas, which other SWC schools had long claimed was an "untouchable," resulted in a two-year probation handed down in 1987. It was reduced to one year for good behavior.

Hell, robbing a bank would have constituted good behavior in those wild, wild West days. Southern Methodist's program was so corrupt that the taint touched even the governor of Texas, Bill Clements, who as a member of the SMU board of governors, decided to "phase out" rather than stop illicit payments to Mustang players.

SMU, a church school, was hit with the NCAA's first-ever death penalty. It effectively wiped out football at the Dallas school for two years.

Texas Christian was stung almost as badly.

Even though TCU coach Jim Wacker kicked off seven players, including star running back Kenneth Davis, in midseason 1985 for receiving illegal payments, TCU still was hit with one of the stiffest punishments ever dealt out by the NCAA.

Texas A&M was later slapped with a two-year probation for twenty-five rules violations, including nine major ones. And Houston got a two-year penalty that some thought would effectively kill football at the university. Even isolated Texas Tech got the back of the NCAA's hand.

SWC schools were punished, but not before they had siphoned off much of the talent that normally would have been funneled to Texas. SMU eventually piled up so many blue-chippers that Eric Dickerson alternated at tailback with future New England Patriot Craig James.

Illegal recruiting reached its height in the 1980s, but it was gnawing at Royal long before. Royal grew so weary of fighting unethical coaches who offered recruits "rags and rides" that the cheating helped drive him from the game in 1976 at age fifty-two.

"I think he got a bellyful of it," says Mike Campbell, Royal's long-time defensive coordinator. He remembers riding in Royal's car from Waco after Baylor's 1974 upset of Texas and says Royal actually considered retiring then. "I think he was tired of the cheating that was going on in college football. He knew damn well he wasn't going to cheat. I think it just got to him, and he said, 'To hell with it.' They [NCAA] weren't making them stop it. It wasn't his interest that waned. What waned was the damn personnel. We ran out of Earl Campbells."

According to several Royal associates, at least one prominent Longhorn suggested that if Royal couldn't beat 'em, he ought to join 'em.

Some say it was Frank Erwin, others that it was former Texas Governor Allan Shivers, the chairman of the Board of Regents, who handled Royal's resignation. Erwin and Shivers are dead, and Royal isn't talking on the matter. But the suggestion was made, and in fairly strong terms. Royal rebuffed it in even stronger terms.

Recruiting, however, wasn't the only reason Royal left football. The game itself had changed for him. "Losing a ball game, it just was too miserable," he says. "If we won a ball game, it was just relief. Relief that we didn't lose. When I was younger, I could slough off a loss and, boy, I enjoyed the winning. I was just exhilarated and all pumped up, really fired up."

By 1976, however, he was having dry heaves in the Cotton Bowl tunnel at the Oklahoma game in which he desperately wanted to beat Barry Switzer, only to have to settle for a 6–6 tie.

"When you start getting so that losing is that miserable and winning wasn't really that much satisfaction," Royal says, "I think any rational person analyzing it would think, 'If I stay with this, someday it will be a bitter experience.' And I certainly didn't want to do that. There's something that happens to a man about age fifty. Doctors tell me it's kind of a common thing for people to change professions around fifty, fifty-five. That's the reason you don't find many coaches in this game over fifty-five. Paterno's a throwback. You go check the rest of them. You won't find many."

Royal also had other shocks, including the death of his daughter Marian in a 1973 car accident. Although Royal says he was still into the game as deeply in his later years, one former assistant coach disagrees. "I saw the change," he says. "It bothered me. It was taking the edge off of everybody. For three or four years I saw it sort of happening. The spark was gone—it was a shock for me. And his staff was no longer as good."

Willie Zapalac, one of the best assistants ever to coach at Texas and a Royal aide since 1964, left for the pros after 1975 when Royal brought in Don Breaux, now with the Washington Redskins, to be co-offensive coordinator with Zapalac—but at a higher salary. Some Texas administrators were also concerned about whom Royal had on the sidelines, and they weren't talking about the assistant coaches. In the 1970s Royal's pickers, his musician friends, were more and more in evidence, which didn't sit well with administrators trying to give Texas a more button-down presence in academic circles.

"They said he had gotten to the point he was above everybody and couldn't be touched," another former assistant says. "It irritated them that he was so casual in everything he did. He was doing things that were not acceptable for the head football coach of the University of Texas. They told him he needed to resign."

Some of the same traits that angered administrators were the very ones that endeared Royal to his supporters. Indeed, if you could capture the multichambered heart of the strange mix that's Austin, Texas, it would look a lot like Royal, who loves country music, Mexican food, politics, casual clothes, football, golf, dizzying success, and the University of Texas.

Mess with Darrell and you're messing with Texas.

But as the university grew to national prominence in the 1970s, the powers were too blind to see that simple truth. When Royal stepped down after a 5–5–1 season in 1976, they gave him no part in choosing his successor. They even let a student representative vote on the matter, but not Royal, who was technically Texas's athletic director.

Royal made his decision to quit coaching midway through the season, after a 31–28 loss to Texas Tech. "I told [Chancellor Mickey] LeMaistre coming back on the plane from the Tech game," Royal says. "He thought I ought to talk to Shivers, which I did." Royal drove to the old-monied district of Tarrytown in West Austin a few days later to meet with Shivers, chairman of the Board of Regents, at his home.

Royal now says he considered Shivers, "a loyal friend, a good supporter, and a strong ally for nineteen years and ten months." He somehow can't—or won't—find the words to describe their relationship those final two months before Royal's retirement was officially announced.

"Shivers was chairman of the Board of Regents, and he didn't want to announce it until after the season was over," Royal says. "That was a university decision; that's what he thought would be best for the university."

Rumors of Royal's retirement were incubating after that bitter 6–6 tie against Oklahoma, the Barry Switzer team he'd been pointing to beat for a year. Royal later discussed the move with Arkansas coach Frank Broyles and found that Broyles also was ready to get out of coaching.

"Darrell said something about the game not being fun anymore," Broyles recalls. "I said, 'I've already made up my mind.' Darrell said, 'Well, you're not going to believe this, I have too.' I told Darrell, 'You're not going to do it,' and he said, 'Neither will you.'"

The story of Broyles's retirement from coaching surfaced on Friday, while a United Press International reporter who later became a boxing analyst broke the story of Royal's coming resignation.

"Larry Merchant? You mean Larry Kauffman," Royal says. "Do you know he was on the football squad at Oklahoma when I was there? He was a walk-on. I remember he was a little guy with real hairy legs. He wasn't worth a shit, but he had a marvelous attitude. He was tough; he stayed out there."

When Texas assistant sports information director Bill Little was tipped off about Merchant's story, he went to Royal's office.

Little says, "Darrell looked up and said, 'Where'd he get that story?' I knew right then there was something to it."

In spite of the storyline that two great coaches would probably be going at it for the final time, only 49,341 fans showed up for the night game in Austin that was moved to December for national television. But they did give Royal a standing ovation after Texas's 29–12 win, his 14th victory in 19 games against Broyles.

Mike Campbell, Royal's trusted defensive assistant, had known of Royal's decision. And, with about three minutes to go in the Arkansas game, the other assistants were told that Royal wanted to meet with them in the coaches' dressing room after the game. A press release was issued after that. At the time, it seemed like the end of a great career, not the start of a university-splitting feud.

"Most of us thought that it would be just a changing of the guard," says Ken Dabbs, an assistant athletic director at Texas and a former Royal assistant. "We thought he would remain as athletic director and Coach Campbell would become the head man."

"Everyone says I recommended Mike for the job," Royal says. "I would have, but I never got the chance. I wasn't asked to be in on the selection. That's okay. There wasn't any tug of war until I quit coaching, and that was for a very brief time. That's the way the people who were in control wanted it to be. I didn't buck it, and I didn't try to. I think it would have been a real mess, and it would have been the wrong thing to do. And the reason I don't think that would have worked is that I'd have been out of order. I believed in the chain of command."

Shivers, who was unquestionably at the top of the chain of command, hinted strongly at Royal's diminished status by saying, "We hope Coach Royal will assist us in the selection of the coach, and that the committee will listen to his recommendations, although not necessarily be guided by them."

The seven-person search committee was chaired by Dr. Lorene Rogers, the first woman president of the university. Rogers and Shivers flew to Maryland to huddle with Jerry Claiborne, coach of a then-undefeated Maryland. He was just lukewarm about the job and finally became adamant in his withdrawal from consideration, telling a reporter, "Do you want me to sign it in blood?"

Jim Wacker, current TCU coach, was also given a quick look. He had taken Texas Lutheran College to back-to-back NAIA national titles and was coming off a 9–3 season in his first year at North Dakota State.

Then, six days after the Royal resignation, the fifty-four-year-old Campbell was summoned for an interview. After twenty years at Texas, those on the committee should have known Campbell's brand of toothpaste—but events took a different course.

Ken Dabbs remembers, "It was raining, and he got an umbrella. I drove him over there by the Tower. He gets out of the car, he takes that umbrella, he pushes it—and that sonofagun turns inside out. He looks over at me. He's in a suit, and he can't get that umbrella down. He says, 'I can just see them now, lookin' out the window. They're saying, look at those two old boys trying to fix that umbrella. And just think, the one in the suit wants to be the head football coach.'"

An afternoon newspaper, the now-defunct *Austin Citizen*, was so certain that Campbell would be named the twenty-fifth coach in Texas football history that it ran a story with the headline IT'S MIKE on the day Royal's successor was hired. It wasn't Mike.

On the same day Campbell had been wrestling with his umbrella, thirty-eight-year-old Wyoming coach Fred Akers returned a call from Lorene Rogers. He quickly agreed to a secret meeting at a motel near the Dallas airport.

In two years Akers had turned a pathetic 2–9 Wyoming squad into a Fiesta Bowl team. He'd been a Royal assistant at Texas for nine years. Arkansas, his alma mater, was interested in him, even though Lou Holtz appeared to be Frank Broyles's first choice. Akers's name had been mentioned for coaching vacancies at Illinois, TCU, and Miami.

Akers had the record. He had the family—wife Diane was a national Miss Correct Posture beauty contest winner. And he had the manicured look, always neat, always managed—the image a university of the first order should have.

Akers chain-smoked a pack and a half of Winstons a day, but stubbed them out before talking with players. "I didn't know he smoked until about two years after I was there," says former Texas quarterback Bret Stafford. "You could smell his suit every time you saw him. You'd think, 'Where's that smoke coming from?' "

If a photographer was about to snap a shot, Akers would put on his sport coat and straighten his tie. At that first meeting in Dallas in 1976, the impeccably dressed, fresh-scrubbed Akers made an immediate impression on Rogers and Shivers, who had skirmished with Royal over his long-haired, outlaw-lookin', guitar-pickin' friends.

"There sat Fred, who looked like he had come out of a Neiman Marcus bandbox," Dabbs says. "Lorene turned to Shivers and said, 'That's the image I want.' "

On December 15, 1976, Rogers had an afternoon press conference to name the new coach at Texas. She called Campbell just minutes before to tell him it wasn't him. Royal, too, didn't learn the news until shortly before the press conference.

Instead, it's Fred. Akers is only 5-foot-9—his players called him "Little Napoleon"—but no one tries harder to have a head coaching presence. His back is ramrod straight. His voice rumbles. His eyes burn. And he's so damn positive he makes Dale Carnegie look like a whiner.

One of the first moves Akers made as the new head football coach at Texas was to offer Campbell a job on his staff. After all, it was Campbell who first spotted Akers as an up-and-comer who was coaching Lubbock High School. Campbell recommended that Royal hire Akers for his staff. But Campbell declined Akers's offer to stay on.

Dabbs, the recruiting coordinator who landed Earl Campbell, and linebacker coach David McWilliams became the only Royal holdovers on Akers's staff. They soon encountered a new management style.

Royal, who hated meetings, delegated authority. Akers wrapped himself in it. "Darrell's management style was classic," says Texas insider Phil Ransopher. "Find the best guy you can get for the job, give him the authority and the responsibility, pat him on the back if he does well, and kick him in the ass if he doesn't. If he really does badly, get rid of him.

"Darrell hired the best possible guys as assistants, and a lot of them became head coaches. He'd plan, get on the tower, and watch it happen, whereas Fred would try to do it all himself. Fred would coach the second-team kid on the kamikaze kickoff team with a hundred and fifty guys standing around."

It's a new era. The cover of the 1977 Texas media guide features Akers and star running back Campbell, and both are wearing suits.

The wishbone that Royal made synonymous with Texas football is scrapped as Akers features a slimmed-down Campbell in an I-formation attack.

"I detected one thing about Coach Akers," Campbell says. "He didn't mess around. It was strictly business with him. When he got the job, he asked me how much I weighed. I said two forty. 'Okay,' he said, 'get down to two twenty-five because you'll be running the ball twenty-five to thirty times a game.' "

By September, 5-A.M. workouts and punching-bag sessions have turned Campbell into 223 pounds of mean. He had read a newspaper story of Tony Dorsett as a Heisman winner that spring and told trainer Frank Medina he was going to win it the next fall.

Akers's first Texas team opens the 1977 season by beating up Boston College, 44–0. His Longhorns clobber Virginia, 68–0, and beat Rice the way Texas is supposed to, 72–15. Then Akers does something even Royal couldn't do—he defeats Barry Switzer. The regular season ends with Texas atop both polls as number one. In early December, Campbell picks up the Heisman Trophy and gets a soul shake from Akers in New York.

The Cotton Bowl and Notre Dame are coming up. Things are going great. Too good. Following a legend is risky business.

"I think Fred was doomed before he ever got there," says Lou Marks, one of Akers's closest friends. "From the first day in."

The chasm between Akers and Royal was too large. Its origins remain mysterious because they coexisted just fine for nine years when Royal was coaching.

At least two former Texas athletic department officials say Shivers, not wanting Royal to look over his successor's shoulder, actually tried to fire Royal when he declined to step down as athletic director. Royal denounces such reports.

"That's bullshit," Royal says. "Up until the time I announced to the president, I had zero doubt I could have stayed on. The decision was one hundred percent mine."

That wasn't the perception Akers had.

A Texas athletic department official says, "Shivers told Fred, 'Do not pay any attention to Darrell Royal.' Allan Shivers convinced Fred that he had fired Darrell, but there's no way on God's green earth he could have fired Darrell. Fred misjudged his power base. As long as Shivers was around, there was no more powerful man. Allan Shivers ran the state with an iron hand. He was the ultimate governor of Texas." Trouble was, Akers was never as popular with the Texas fans as he was with Shivers. The rift between Akers and Royal widened.

Although Royal was the athletic director, Akers never reported to him about the football program. Akers was told to answer only to Lorene Rogers. Royal and Akers went their separate ways. The two rarely spoke. Akers's assistants got the message that they weren't to hang around swapping football talk or tall tales with Royal.

Former Texas school officials say Shivers told Akers that Royal had tried to damage Akers's reputation and his chance at the Texas job. Royal denies it. Akers only says "someone" told Shivers that when he had left for Wyoming, he owed huge debts around Austin from his Running R day camp, a charge he denied then and now. Akers even requested that Shivers check out the accusation, and Shivers assigned the task to Chancellor Mickey LeMaistre. Shivers was satisfied even before he heard LeMaistre's favorable report. Asked if that "someone" was Royal, Akers now says, "God, I hope not."

New Year's Day, 1977. Akers's Longhorns are six-point favorites over fifth-ranked Notre Dame and quarterback Joe Montana. Six turnovers later, they're run out of Dallas, 38–10. "We just had a bad day, man," a testy Akers sums up. "You ever had a bad day, man? You saw ours."

Akers's teams always saved their worst days for bowl day. Of his 86 wins, only 2 came in bowls. A 2–7 bowl record wasn't acceptable at Texas.

"It was either the Cotton Bowl or it was a losing season," says Donnie Little, Texas's first black quarterback. "Nothing less than that is considered good."

"From 1977 to 1983, we should have had at least one national championship for sure, maybe two," says former Texas tight end Lawrence Sampleton. "Those teams were loaded."

"Fred can't win the big one," became the first—and most deadly—bullet for the anti-Akers faction, which grew yearly.

"The thing that Fred never understood was that Darrell never cut up Fred," Texas sports information director Bill Little says. "Darrell's friends did, but not Darrell."

Once, briefly, Royal and Akers tried to mend fences in the early 1980s, when Royal had retired after three years as athletic director. Akers set up the huevos rancheros brunch at Cisco's Bakery on East Sixth Street.

"I did call and tell him I'd like to meet with him," Akers recalls. "There'd been a lot of things said. Whether they're right or whether they're wrong, I wanted to clear the air. I said, 'If you have a problem with me, I'd like to know it.' He said, 'No, I don't have a problem.' "

Royal's verson is slightly different.

"You came to Texas thinking I was a chickenshit," Royal remembers telling Akers. "Well, I might have been. But you'll never know. You never gave me the chance to be a chickenshit. The first day you came, you should have said, 'Let's come and sit in a room and sort things out.' "

That never happened. Royal and Akers may, in fact, have been too much alike. Both came from impoverished backgrounds—Akers was one of nine children and the only one in his family to go to college —and used football to climb out of poverty. When Akers's father found a dilapidated football while cleaning out an Air Force barracks, Fred even slept with it. Both Royal and Akers were kickers and defensive backs, in addition to playing offense, for two of Texas's biggest rivals, Oklahoma and Arkansas. Both were aggressive and highly ambitious, stubborn and strong-willed.

But there the resemblances end. Royal could let his hair down; Akers never let one out of place. Texas fans worshipped Royal; Akers wondered why they didn't worship him.

In 1983, Akers has another chance. Another shot at a national championship. His team struggles on offense all year, but goes undefeated and is number two in the nation, behind Nebraska.

Late New Year's Day, the mighty Cornhuskers will be stunned in the Orange Bowl by an upstart Miami team quarterbacked by Bernie Kosar. But that game loses all meaning for Texas while the Longhorns are still up 9–3 against a lightly regarded Georgia team in the Cotton Bowl.

Texas will have seventeen players drafted off this team—five in the first three rounds—and send an unheard-of twenty-one players to NFL training camps. However, that doesn't count for anything on New Year's Day, 1984. There's 4:32 to play. Georgia has done nothing on offense all day, but Akers is convinced the Bulldogs will fake a punt on fourth-and-seventeen from the Georgia 34.

The Texas defense stays in, the punt return unit remains on the sideline. Craig Curry, a starting defensive back, drops back deep and then drops Chip Andrews's punt. Georgia's Gary Moss recovers at the Texas 23. "They might as well have dropped a nuclear warhead," Texas linebacker Jeff Leiding says.

Three plays later, Georgia quarterback John Lastinger circles right end and scores the game-winning 17-yard touchdown.

"It's like somebody dying," says Rick McIvor, the surprise starter at quarterback for a team Rob Moerschell guided to an 11–0 regular season. "That person's gone and not coming back."

Maybe, but Texas starts the 1984 season as the number one team in the country. The national title hopes fade with a tie against Oklahoma and a loss to Houston, but Texas is still 7–1–1. It has the inside track to the Cotton Bowl. Until about 2:30 A.M. the Wednesday before the Baylor game. That's when Akers gets a call from the Austin police, and Ken Dabbs gets a call from Akers to help out Tony Edwards, Texas's 6-foot-2, 255-pound middle linebacker who'd scuffled with police at an east-side Austin bar.

Dabbs says, "Fred said I'd better check on him, but Tony was too drunk to even talk to. They called for backup, and he had knots all over his head. It took two or three to hold him. All we had to do was win one of the two games to go to the Cotton Bowl. That's when it all started. I can always remember this. When Fred and I went to lunch, we went over to the dining hall, and he asked me what I thought and I said, 'Fred, you got a real hard decision to make here on what you're going to do with him.' And Fred told me—I'll never forget this as long as I live—he said, 'He's innocent until proven guilty.' And I knew then he wasn't going to do anything with him. It seemed like we lost the kids after that."

Publicly, Akers announces, "This is still America right here in Austin, Texas. And the last I heard is that a guy is innocent until proven guilty. Tony is part of our family . . ."

Part of that family had been with Edwards at the bar violating the team's midnight curfew, including freshman safety John Hagy, now with the Houston Oilers, and—more significantly—Edwards's backup at linebacker, talented freshman Britt Hager.

Akers chooses not to suspend Edwards, or anyone else. That might have worked, if Texas had won. But the Longhorns lose to Baylor 24–10 that week, and suddenly the town's football fans turn moralists. The clamor increases when Texas is then pummeled by Texas A&M 37–12. The players want to end the season right there. But Texas has agreed to back up Houston at the Freedom Bowl, and Houston turns out to be the surprise Cotton Bowl team, the only SWC champion ever to show up in Dallas with two league losses.

It takes three team votes, but reluctantly the Texas players finally decide to go to Anaheim. Sort of, anyway. They lose by an embarrassing 55–17 margin to Hayden Fry's Iowa team, the worst bowl loss in school history.

An equally frustrating 1985 season ends with a 24–16 loss to Air Force in the Bluebonnet Bowl and a massive staff shake-up. One assistant, linebacker coach Scott Conley, who is on the road recruiting, is awakened before eight at his Dallas hotel to be told by Akers he is fired. Good morning, this is your pink slip!

"It got to the point where he couldn't recruit," Dabbs says. "The alumni were against him. There was nothing positive. Animosity was running rampant among the alumni."

Late in Akers's tenure, blue-chip recruits snub the Longhorns. In Akers's last two seasons at Texas, his staff is able to coax just one blue-chipper into becoming a Longhorn.

"We had [Texas] alumni calling kids and telling them not to come to Texas. I know that for a fact," Longhorn recruiting coordinator James Blackwood says. "They thought they were hurting Fred Akers, but mostly they were hurting the University of Texas."

The administration grew increasingly concerned with how Akers's players did in the classroom. A study of black football players who enrolled at Texas between 1975 and 1981—Akers began in 1977—showed that only 27.7 percent of those graduated, while 47.9 percent of the white players did. Overall, only 44 percent of the players in that span graduated, compared with 55 percent or more of the student body.

But not until the very end does it sink in on Akers that he is in real trouble. When he is walking through the halls of the $6.5 million Neuhaus-Royal complex dedicated in 1986, he looks at some of the donor names on the rooms and confides to an associate, "These are the same people who are trying to get me fired."

Akers had lobbied for just such a locker room and training facility in his very first meeting before the Athletics Council in 1977. He even brought sketches. But he didn't see it built until 1986. When it is dedicated just days before Akers's final home game, he isn't included in the ceremony. "I wasn't even invited," he says. "I just stood in the back of the room."

The loss to A&M left him at 5–6, his first losing season. It would be one too many for Akers. In ten years he'd twice taken Texas to the brink of a national championship. Six of his ten teams won nine games or more. Eleven of his thirty-one losses were by a touchdown or less. His 86–31–2 record (73.1 percent) was the fourth-best winning percentage in Southwest Conference history at the time and still ranks sixth. Royal ranks first.

Larry Lacewell, the former Oklahoma assistant, once said of Akers's teams, "Texas has the thousand best plays in football. But none of them are connected."

While Akers's offenses were often spotty, frequently boring, and always conservative, he won with defense and kicking. And with talent. Akers sent Johnnie Johnson, Steve McMichael, Kenneth Sims, Jerry Gray, Eric Metcalf, and others to the NFL.

Twice he beat Auburn with Bo Jackson. He handled Miami and Jim Kelly. He beat Arkansas seven out of ten. He bested Bear Bryant and Alabama in the 1982 Cotton Bowl. He gave Barry Switzer fits, going 5–4–1 against Oklahoma.

But Akers could never be Darrell Royal. And he wasn't Mike Campbell, Royal's logical successor.

"In the minds of Darrell's good friends and big-money people, I was the culprit," says Akers, who in December 1990 was fired by Purdue after four seasons. "What's ironic is I think Darrell should have been allowed to hire Mike, too."

Akers was fired to reunite the Texas family. Big donor B. M. Rankin didn't bother to see a Longhorn game in Akers's final season. Howard Terry, then director of the Longhorn Education Foundation, saw one game at Palo Alto, California, because he was already there on business. Asked why he hadn't seen more, he said, "I'd lost interest."

"It wasn't his coaching," says DeLoss Dodds. "It wasn't his recruiting. It was the division of people. We were so split, so unhappy. People were just not satisfied. People didn't like Fred."

Would even winning the national title have saved Akers?

"I would hope so," Akers says. "I think it'd be too much for them to object to."

"It wouldn't have changed things much," Dodds counters. "It might have delayed things."

When Dodds officially announced Akers's "reassignment" on November 29, 1986, in the building named after Royal, Dodds read a statement that lasted all of two minutes, fifty-three seconds. Ten years flicked away in less than three minutes.

Texas had died.

At the very least, it would take four years before the Longhorns would get off their deathbed.

5

Of Quarterbacks
and Controversies

"It seems like Peter overhears us or something," says Texas coach David McWilliams as he's unwinding in the hospitality room of Austin's Doubletree Hotel after a 29–22 Saturday night loss to Colorado. "Every time we start talking about pulling him, he seems to put together a good drive."

The third game of the 1990 season is coming up, and Texas sophomore quarterback Peter Gardere, former schoolboy star at Houston Lee, is headed home to play Rice with a 1–1 record and a still uncertain future.

It was against Rice a year earlier that Gardere got the first start of his college career for a struggling 1–2 team. He immediately looked like Texas's boy-wonder quarterback.

He led Texas back from a 30–17 fourth-quarter deficit. His diving, fourth-down, four-yard touchdown allowed Texas to squeak by Rice 31–30. In the next game, against Oklahoma, he threw the winning touchdown pass to receiver Johnny Walker with 1:33 left. Walker threw high fives to Texas fans while stunned Oklahoma fans stared silently at the first loss in six years to hated Texas.

For an encore, Gardere hit on 16 of 20 passes for 247 yards to upset then-unbeaten Arkansas 24–20 in Fayetteville. After three games as a freshman starter he was Peter the Great, the savior of the troubled Texas football program, the tousle-headed toast of Austin.

After the Texas defense lapsed in a 24–17 loss to Texas Tech, he went home to Houston, leading a 4–3 team. There he ran into Houston defensive back Alton Montgomery while he was scrambling.

"Montgomery just speared him," says his dad, Peter Gardere Sr., a Houston businessman. "God, it was flagrant. If I had seen at the game what I saw in the replay, I'd have died. He hit him on his shoulder and then went to his head, and his head just shifts over about three or four inches. It just scared me to death. Oh, he just got the hell knocked out of him."

Houston did the same to Texas, whipping the Longhorns every way they could in a 47–9 slaughter at the Astrodome. Heisman Trophy winner Andre Ware not only threw for 411 yards and 4 touchdowns, he also caught a 37-yard pass from backup David Klingler on a trick play.

Gardere was pulled when his shoulder stiffened in the following win against Texas Christian, but started the next game against Baylor. "He tried to come back and he just wasn't ready," his dad says. "I know the Friday before the Baylor game I accidentally touched him on the shoulder, and I made him jump about fifteen feet. He was put in about the ten-yard line throwing against the wind. He didn't have any zip on the ball and had two interceptions in a row. Frankly, he never should have started. Then Donovan Forbes comes in and, unfortunately, Forbes gets hurt. Rather than put Mark Murdock in, which I would have done, they put Peter back in. He did nothing but just aggravate the injury. That was the worst game I ever saw in my life. Worst game I ever saw Texas play, or anybody else for that matter. It was horrible. Whew. I was glad when it was over."

Montgomery's hit in the Houston game, which weakened Gardere's already-suspect arm, and the debacle with Baylor marked the end of the short reign of Peter the Great.

"It got kind of heavy that year," his father says of the attention. "It was too much, in my book. If I could have stopped some of that, I would have. It was an unnatural high. Peter the Great. All that stuff. It sounds great, but that's heavy pressure. The trouble is you're going to fall, sooner or later. It's abnormal if you continue on that course. When the drop came off after he got injured, it really dropped."

Gardere's offensive coordinator, Lynn Amedee, says, "I often wonder about the shoulder injury he had last year. Did that take something out of his arm? I watch him throw and I watch these other guys throw, and he doesn't have the arm strength that I thought he had a year ago. When he came back from the injury, his ball started fluttering.

"On those sideline routes, he doesn't have that rope that takes the ball that far. That's why he leads his receivers all the way to the boundary and sometimes takes them out of bounds. That sideline route, he throws it out of bounds."

As the 1990 season begins, Gardere is merely an incumbent, the way backup Murdock was the previous year when Gardere came in to send Murdock, the smartest—but slowest—of Texas's quarterbacks, to the bench. The bench, however, is precisely where many Texas fans look for a quarterbacking hero.

Gardere Sr. says, "I think it was Murdock who coined the phrase, 'The happiest person in Austin is the second-string quarterback.' That's true. And it's always going to be a problem at Texas."

Murdock, a junior, still hopes to get another shot directing the team he led as a freshman. But the fans are more intrigued by another local product, redshirt freshman Jimmy Saxton.

Gardere is the son of a player whose career at Texas lasted all of eight seconds before he was almost killed by a broken neck while trying to make his first varsity tackle. Saxton is the son of Austin businessman James Saxton, who was one of the most exciting runners ever to wear the burnt orange.

James Saxton was a scrawny little quarterback who was just about ready to go to Rice when Darrell Royal landed him. Later, in what he termed an "alumni move"—one to satisfy all the armchair quarterbacks—Royal shifted Saxton from quarterback to right halfback.

"He runs faster than small-town gossip," Royal once said of James Saxton, who made All-American in 1961. "He's like a balloon full of air. When you turn him loose, there's no telling where he's going. And when the play is over, he's spent."

Saxton was so fast, so elusive, legend had it that he could run down rabbits. Now his son, a cocky, 6-foot-3 natural athlete who ran for more than a thousand yards and passed for even more in his senior year at Austin Westlake, is poised to run down Gardere if he stumbles in Houston.

"Saxton has about three or four more things he can add to the game," former Texas quarterback James Street says. "That speed that he's got, Gardere and some of them don't have. He's exciting. Even if he doesn't get the job done, he's exciting."

Gardere, meanwhile, remains a walking contradiction. He's an average-size guy on a team studded with sculpted weight-room monsters. He's a shy, reserved kid on a team of animated talkers, a baby-faced sophomore entrusted with the most important position on a team run by win-hungry seniors. He's a white fraternity brother on a team whose stars are predominantly blacks. Many of those black players took a very active part in protesting the racist actions of some Texas fraternities in the spring.

Gardere is a former soccer and baseball star and a damn good backup punter. Yet no one—least of all his receivers or offensive coordinator—ever calls him one of the team's best athletes.

As a high school senior, Gardere was wooed by Penn State, Michigan, and Texas A&M. Notre Dame brought him up to South Bend only to have him sum up, "Dad, the buildings are old and the girls are ugly."

Now, with Rice and much tougher teams on the horizon, all anyone hopes is that he can become a good "Texas" quarterback.

"Years ago, I was visiting Texas Tech," says Mike Campbell, Darrell Royal's former defensive coordinator and chief lieutenant. "They had six pictures of their All-Americans. I got to thinking that Texas had an insurmountable number of pictures. I don't mean to put down Tech, but that was the only school I'd been to. I'm sure Arkansas is the same, and Rice is worse."

Texas, the linchpin and kingpin of the Southwest Conference, has produced fifty-two All-America players, enough to easily line the long hall at the Neuhaus-Royal weight complex with portraits. It is the only SWC school that has had Heisman, Lombardi, and Outland trophy winners. It has two Lombardi and three Outland winners to go with lone Heisman Trophy winner Earl Campbell.

Texas, however, turns out a big-time quarterback about, well, every time a Bobby Layne enrolls at the school. That was once, back in the 1940s.

Although passer/runner Marty Akins made some All-America teams in 1975, Layne was the last Texas quarterback to have an impact on the pro game.

Texas's career passing leader, Bret Stafford, is currently trying to make it as a pro—in bass fishing. Although Stafford, who played from 1984 to 1987, has his name all over the Texas record book, he spent much of his career being threatened with a move to defensive back. He also spent so much time learning new offenses in the spring that he was never able to play baseball, a sport in which some scouts thought he had pro potential.

James Street, however, remains the just-win Texas prototype with whom Gardere is compared after a good game.

"I was lucky," Street says. "We never lost. You never got booed. The people that would write bad about me, they'd end up on a positive because all they'd say is he's not that fast, and he doesn't have a great arm, but he wins. Even though Darrell Royal's not coaching here and we're opening it up more, Texas is still considered the running team that grinds it out."

If there was anyone who could have started a passing tradition at Texas, it should have been Layne, who chucked the fat ball they played with back in 1946 for 1,122 yards. Yeah, Layne had an arm. If there was a football game to be won or a baseball game to be pitched, he was your guy, even if he wasn't 100 percent.

Before a 1946 Texas baseball game with Texas A&M, Layne and roommate Rooster Andrews got to horsing around, and Layne ended up sticking his foot through a plate glass window. "We go into the emergency room, and he says, 'Doc, you got to sew me up,' " Andrews recalls. "And then we go to A&M, and Bobby said, 'Rooster, you got to get me some help. You got to get me some beer.' There was a guy on the football team who was a good friend of mine. We made arrangements for him to get me eighteen bottles of beer, Falstaff. Fifteen cents apiece. I iced 'em down, put 'em down at the end of the bench, and covered them up with a couple of duffle bags. At the end of every inning, I'd have Bobby a beer ready to kill the pain. He drank ten of them. And that was the day he threw the no-hitter."

Talk about tradition. But it never grabbed hold at Texas. Darrell Royal was a quarterback at Oklahoma, but he made All-American by doubling as a defensive back in the one-platoon system. He also excelled at punting. He'd work on that skill for two hours after practice while his teammates were eating. Royal ate solitary, warmed-up dinners at his rooming house.

To Royal, only three things could happen when you passed, and two of them, interceptions and incompletions, were bad. While Royal's ground-bound wishbone was broken at Texas after he left coaching in 1976, it lasted a lot longer in Texas high school football, where the university recruited almost all of its players.

"Texas high school football is not set up for the big passing attack," says Randy McEachern, a Gardere look-alike who led Texas to within a game of a national championship in 1977, largely by handing off to Earl Campbell.

"On a good day we usually passed fifteen times," he says of his high school days running the wishbone. "The magic was in dealing the ball off. Nobody knew how to stop it. Texas has been a running team from the word go, and they passed when they needed to. If you look back at some of Coach Royal's teams, the smaller quarterbacks had the heart. Texas quarterbacks have been leaders. They've not had strong arms, but a lot of them had quickness and could throw a little."

That's all Fred Akers really wanted his quarterbacks to do. He wanted to win with kicking and defense and a runner he vainly hoped would be the next Earl Campbell. Akers put in a run-and-shoot offense one spring at Texas, and told *Austin American-Statesman* sportswriter Mark Wangrin he might use the formation 50 percent on passing downs. He never used it in the fall, when games mattered.

"His belief was defense, kicking game, and then score enough points to win," former Texas quarterback Robert Brewer says. "If quarterbacks checked off and threw in the middle of the field, he'd pucker up.

"It's taking longer than it should have, but I think recruits are going to realize we're throwing the ball more. When we get back on top, it's going to be real attractive. I think the next Earl Campbell at Texas could be a quarterback. Since Bobby Layne, we haven't had an all-everything pro quarterback. I think the people here, if we had one of those, would just fall in love with him."

Through the years, Texas has landed blue-chip quarterbacks, even glamorous ones, but they never managed to become pro-style stars.

Walter Fondren was an heir to the Humble Oil fortune, but Texas let him throw only 49 passes in 1957.

Bill Bradley entered Texas as "Super Bill," one of the most touted high school recruits ever in a state that's all but blinded by the Friday night lights of high school football. Bradley ended up as a defensive back when Royal's wishbone was born in the 1968 season.

Donnie Little was a gifted athlete who became Texas's first black quarterback in 1978, and he got booed for breaking that barrier as well as being the signal-caller for a stagnant offense. "It was more wide open in the game plans than in the games," Little says. "It wasn't really a conservative offense, but it was run that way." His signature play became the quarterback draw—before he was phased out to wide receiver.

Then there was Rick McIvor. McIvor had an arm damn near twice as strong as Bobby Layne's. "Rick could throw it ninety-five yards," Robert Brewer swears. "I saw him do it in pregame warm-ups before the Oklahoma game in 1980. He came out of the tunnel, took a couple of running steps, and threw it from the goal line to the guys covering the punts at the other end. A guy caught it on the five. I verified that with a trainer."

Brewer sent McIvor to the bench for the 1982 season. Although McIvor remains the last Texas quarterback to throw an NFL pass, he finished his pro career as a backup wide receiver.

Brewer was known as a great finesse passer but says, "They called it touch, but I was winging it. I was throwing it as hard as I could."

In 1984 Texas recruited a blue chip out of Houston, Shannon Kelley, who would marry America's Olympic sweetheart, Mary Lou Retton. Kelley had a promising junior year in 1987 and is listed as Texas's season and career leader in passing percentage.

Kelley, who's in the real estate business in Houston, says, "At Texas there's a pressure that's kind of indescribable. It's a completely different pressure from that at other schools. If you drive down the streets of Houston, at least one out of every four or five cars has a Texas Ex sticker. You're not just playing in the eye of the University of Texas with fifty thousand students on the Forty Acres. You're talking about the whole state of Texas. And the nation. It's a much bigger realm than forty acres."

Mary Lou says, "I don't think Shannon was given a fair shot at Texas. I think politics gets involved, like anything else. I think an offensive coordinator and his quarterback should be like brothers, and it wasn't like that at all."

"I had three offensive coordinators in five years," Kelley says matter-of-factly. "If a company had three CEOs in five years, I guarantee you it wouldn't make much progress."

Kelley had most of his problems with John Mize, a longtime friend of McWilliams, who was later demoted to defensive tackle coach when Lynn Amedee was hired to run his offense at Texas. "Coach Mize and I just never jelled," Kelley says. "He would yell at me and belittle me in front of the whole team. If George Bush yelled at James Baker, would Congress believe in him? How in the world can you be a leader if the coach doesn't even believe in you? If Peter got yanked and never got to play again, where would his confidence be?

"See, I was playing not to lose rather than playing to win. I was just praying to God I wouldn't screw up. He would tell me, 'You're not relaxed.' Well, hell, how could I relax? He was always on my butt. One day he got on me so bad I wanted to quit. I asked myself, 'Is it worth feeling so bad about yourself that you just almost hate yourself?' That's the way he made me feel at times.

"I'll never forget one day in practice before the Baylor game of my junior year. Bret Stafford fumbled a snap, and Mize was pissed off about that. Then I went in and fumbled the snap. And I mean all hell broke loose. He got on me and said, 'This is why we can't play you. If you come in and do this in practice, how can we count on you in a game?'

"I wanted to come to Texas and have the great career. And I really have a hard time believing I didn't have the talent. I don't think they ever would have ever recruited me if that was the case. I could run a four-five forty, and I could throw the ball as good as any Texas quarterback, barring Rick McIvor."

Kelley's speed, however, only worked against him. "I was going to transfer to Mississippi State before my sophomore year," he says. "When I went back in the fall, I was number two behind Stafford. As soon as you report, that's a year of eligibility. After the first day they moved me to receiver. All Coach Akers had to do was tell me in the spring they were going to move me. And I would have said, 'Coach, thanks for being honest with me. I appreciate my time at Texas. My bags are packed, and I'm gone.' But no. One day. That's a year of eligibility. I don't know if he wasn't thinking, or if he de liberately did it."

That wasn't the only incident that had Kelley thinking. Mize would get on Kelley about calling the wrong formations for a play. Kelley later studied a videotape and became convinced an assistant was signaling in the wrong formations from the sidelines. Kelley confronted Mize and Kelley says he was told, "Get the fuck out of my office."

Mary Lou's sweetheart was benched midway through his senior season. "It was a scapegoat thing," he says. "I got moved after the Arkansas game and we won only one game after that, so what did they gain?

"I'm not sour because of the experience, and I want Texas to be successful and wish good luck for Coach McWilliams. But Mize did scar me and he did hurt me, and I'll live with that for the rest of my life. The greatest thing for ex-athletes is the time they had in college, when they played. What do I have to remember?"

Kelley remembers being benched in favor of raw freshman Mark Murdock. Murdock would in turn be replaced by a redshirt freshman named Peter, the baby of the Gardere family.

"We call him the miracle, because we were told we could have no more children," his father says. "He has always been a very precocious athlete, a natural athlete. Peter could dribble a ball when he was barely standing up, just one and a half and he's out there dribbling a basketball. He started playing baseball with the eight- and nine-year-olds when he was seven.

"I guess the thing that helped him develop most was the soccer," his father says. "That helped his quickness and his punting."

At Houston Lee High School, Gardere was a punter and placekicker as well as a passer.

"His freshman year they won a lot of games with his field goals," his father recalls. "They were running a basic T, with some pitchouts. It was not sophisticated at all."

But when the Houston Gamblers, of the upstart United States Football League, coached by Jack Pardee, folded, some of Pardee's assistants found themselves out of jobs. Two of them, Bob Young and Wayne Tedder, latched on at Lee just as Gardere was moving up to the varsity.

They put in a run-and-shoot just like the pros ran, and the rollout offense fit perfectly with Gardere's talents. "I don't think Peter is a natural pocket passer by any stretch," his father says. "He's not that tall and I think he just throws better on the run. I think as long as he can keep moving he's better off."

Gardere's run-and-shoot numbers got him noticed by teams outside of Texas.

"We tried to pick schools that were academically sound and had good football programs, and I think Notre Dame, Penn State, and Michigan are three representative schools," his father says. "We were thinking about going to see Stanford, but Peter would never have made Stanford. His grades haven't been real good. I think that's always been the one short suit in his life, really. He'd like to make better grades. I think he just doesn't know how to study."

When he visited Penn State, some of the first people Gardere talked to were professors. "I think the one school that really appealed to him was Penn State," his dad says. "That's such a beautiful location. Happy Valley or whatever they call it. They were so attentive, but it's just in the middle of nowhere. It's so hard to reach and there's not much around there.

"Michigan is so cold. I was in the stands with another father and I was dying. My feet were so cold. We went out at halftime and bought everything that was maize and blue—blankets, stocking hats, scarves, whatever. The chill factor was ten below zero and a hundred and five thousand people were in the stadium for Ohio State versus Michigan. Unbelievable. The other father and I thought the boys were down on the sidelines. We were very concerned about them. We found out, after the game, that they had gone up to the press box and were living like kings while we were freezing our behinds off down in the stadium."

At Michigan the Garderes had hoped to find out how another Texas player, former San Antonio quarterback Wilbur Odom, was faring up north. "My gosh, he was outstanding in high school," Pete Gardere says, "and you'd ask somebody about him and it was almost like he didn't exist. It was the strangest feeling in the world. It was like they were hiding him. We never did meet him."

Then, there was Texas A&M.

"George Pugh was doing the recruiting," Pete Gardere says. "Unbeknownst to me, he had been working on Peter two, maybe three years at the suggestion of Peter's high school coach. They really had Peter going.

"The day before we go up for the official visit, here comes a Federal Express package. It's a long letter from Jackie Sherrill stating, 'Peter, we welcome your visit, we want you to know we want you to be on scholarship.' The timing was excellent.

"Then we get there and, of course, they have an outstanding cafeteria because they grow most of their own stuff, and it's just super. We went to the dorms, and they're nice. Then, we walk into the stadium and you hear the announcer on the loudspeaker say, 'Welcome to Kyle Field, Robert Wilson of Worthing High School,' as Robert walks out. The kids are really impressed with this, and they do it for every one of them.

"We walk into the dressing area, and I noticed Peter had sort of disappeared. I poked my head into what was obviously an equipment room, and back in the corner, I could see George Pugh. He's measuring Peter with a jersey that has Gardere on the back. I said, 'George, that's a low blow,' and he started kidding about it.

"The next thing, we went up to see Jackie Sherrill. Whatever they say about him, he's plenty smooth and he's plenty well organized. He is a manager, a goddang good one. We walked into his office and there, on the table in front of the desk where we were to sit, is a picture of the new Cotton Bowl ring that he designed himself. He let us know that right away. Three diamonds. Garnets on the side. It's not even subtle. They let you know they've been some place. He said, 'Let me do this. Let me show you some highlights of the last couple of years.' So the highlights come on—he has a television with a huge screen—and he's sitting behind the desk. He's got a tape in there. And here comes Murray, Kevin Murray. The announcer says, 'Murray throws a sixty-yard pass.' It's pretty exciting. Then zip, all of a sudden it's 'Peter Gardere fades back. He throws a fifty-yard pass.' I could hardly believe it. Sherrill had all this dubbed. They had Peter playing about seven or eight plays, even though it was still Murray on the screen."

All the while, however, Pete Gardere was hoping his son would go to Texas, which he pushed as the best school to attend if football didn't work out. He knew just how brief a college football career could be.

Pete Gardere was a defensive back at Texas in 1951, and the son of George Gardere, a 143-pound quarterback who led Texas to victories over Alabama and Rice in 1922 before he suffered a broken jaw against Southwestern. Twenty-nine years later, George Gardere looked at the X ray of the injury of his son.

"First thing that happens, when my father sees the X ray, he faints. He's gone," Pete Gardere recalls. "I thought this must be rough because he's a defense attorney; he knew X rays. They showed him that break and he nearly died. I knew I was in trouble."

"I'd been dumb. I shut my eyes and made a tackle on a guy that was as big as I was. I hit with my head and no shoulders, and I just popped it. It's a wonder I wasn't paralyzed because my neck was broken completely in half.

"I'd gone cross-eyed after the hit. Frank Medina, the trainer, was over there turning my head from side to side, and it's a wonder I didn't die right there or get paralyzed.

"Later, they came up with the idea of immobilizing me with curare, to give me a shot, and the syringe was so big it looked like a damn fire extinguisher. Curare is a South American poison, and it scared the heck out of me because I thought I was dying. I was partially paralyzed, anyway.

"The neurosurgeon started drilling into my head, and it was kind of like you were boring into wood. I had my hand up; I was catching the damn dust coming out.

"Somehow, it all turned out all right. Then Ed Price, the coach, comes up and says that there's some good news, that I'd been given another year of eligibility. My mother told him to get out of there in a hurry."

Pete Gardere's football career at Texas lasted all of one play and eight seconds in the 1951 opener against Kentucky. That, however, is where Peter decided to go, even though Texas was convinced it had already landed its quarterback of the future, Jason Burleson.

"I don't know that any promises were made, but I think they really counted on Jason being their quarterback," Pete Gardere says. "I think Peter was kind of a backup in their thinking. He was a lot smaller than Jason. I don't think they really knew a lot about him. Peter's school, Lee, unfortunately, didn't like Texas to recruit there. I had a heckuva time just getting Lee to send a tape up to Texas.

"Peter was asking me about this guy Burleson. He's six-foot-seven, two hundred and twenty-five pounds, and a junior decathlon champion. My observation was that, other than TCU's Sonny Gibbs, I hadn't seen a six-foot-seven quarterback that had mobility. You got to understand, I'd never even seen Burleson. Then, when I get up there for the first practice, I stand next to Jason and he ain't even six-foot-five. I went, 'Ooops.' I was thinking, 'Uh-oh, this may be a long year.' "

In his redshirt year Gardere stayed even with the scatter-armed Burleson. When Murdock faltered early in the 1989 season, Gardere was given the first shot at replacing him.

A year later, Gardere is trying to solidify his job, after getting knocked around pretty good in his first two games.

His father says, "I can remember before the Colorado game, Lynn Amedee was in the press saying, 'God, Peter's got happy feet. He moves around too much. He can't stay in the pocket.' I think at Colorado he almost stayed in the pocket to his detriment. They broke his nose on one hit because he hung in there too long."

Now, after two tough games, Gardere is getting ready to face Rice, the SWC's best academic school and normally its worst athletic one. Former Texas football coach Fred Akers once said, "Rice always plays us tough," to explain a tight game with the Owls. He was fired that year, even though he turned out to be a prophet. Rice has played Texas shockingly close the past few years.

On an early October night, the Houston air is thick, and it quickly congeals into a carwash of a rainstorm. A lightning show moves the game's starting time back thirty-five minutes. Just before kickoff, a huge rainbow arcs across the sky, planting itself in the far left corner of Houston's shimmering skyline.

Texas receives, moves past midfield, and then stalls. But Alex Waits's punt on fourth-and-one from the Rice 46 is fumbled, and Chad McMillan recovers for Texas at the Rice 19. On second-and-eight from the 17, Gardere finds Johnny Walker near the sideline and he goes out at the Rice 4. Patrick Wilson takes a pitch, rumbles in, and placekicker Michael Pollak hits the point after as Texas goes up 7–0.

Rice's first drive stalls, and Van Malone creates a little Showtime by blocking the punt. Texas takes over at the Rice 20, but can't move. After Gardere is sacked on third-and-seven, the Longhorns are forced to settle for a 41-yard Pollak field goal and a 10–0 lead.

When Rice's quarterback Donald Hollas is intercepted by Willie

Mack Garza, Jimmy Saxton gets his chance. Saxton takes over first-and-ten at the Texas 45. Two sweeps by Adrian Walker net only one yard. Saxton throws an up-for-grabs, incomplete pass that's accompanied by a 15-yard offensive pass interference penalty. Texas ends up facing fourth-and-twenty-four and has to be bailed out by a 53-yard punt from Waits.

On Texas's next drive, Gardere is back and hits three of his four passes. Rice continues to falter on offense. At half, Texas has added two more Pollak field goals and leads 16–0.

Gardere has completed 13 of 21 passes for 159 yards, but Saxton starts the second half first-and-ten at the Texas 31. The Longhorns are flagged for holding and clipping on consecutive plays. With the situation suddenly desperate, Amedee sends in Gardere. Gardere, who completes all four of his passes, marches Texas all the way to the Rice 1, where Adrian Walker vaults in. It's 23–0, and it looks as though the game is over.

After Rice scores to make it 23–7, Mark Murdock gets his turn. On his third play, his first pass is intercepted and returned to Texas's 2. Suddenly it's a game.

Just as suddenly, it's not. Brian Jones, the Texas middle linebacker who was so dejected after the Colorado game, slams into Hollas, who fumbles as he tries to sneak over right guard. Texas safety Lance Gunn recovers. No way Amedee is going to put any quarterback but Gardere in with Texas at its own 4.

Gardere finishes the game, which Texas wins 26–10. "We should have scored fifty on them," Jones huffs. He's right. Texas's offense has sputtered and settled for four Pollak field goals. Gardere, however, finishes with nice enough numbers, 19 of 29 for 241 yards and no interceptions. For his backups, Saxton and Murdock, auditions are over. Undefeated Oklahoma looms ahead of 2–1 Texas, and the Sooners don't take kindly to tryouts.

6

Coming Home Again

David McWilliams pulls a Travis Club Senator from the corner of his mouth and savors the freshly chewed taste of a twenty-dollar-a-box cigar.

"It's just a pacifier for me," shrugs McWilliams, who rarely lights one. "I usually spend about a day and a half per cigar. But Oklahoma, now that's about a six-cigar weekend."

McWilliams is sitting on the edge of his leather chair in his decidedly masculine office. Footballs and trophies are lined up on a window ledge. Mounted bass are frozen in mid-leap on the far wall.

"He's a Texan," says Pat Culpepper, a former high school and college teammate. "He doesn't like to be indoors for too long."

But now, two days before the Oklahoma game, McWilliams is in his office and deep in thought about how to repeat last year's miracle 28–24 win. He's thinking. And thinking some more.

At forty-eight, the always deliberate McWilliams still has days when he looks ruggedly handsome. Other days, he looks paler than Larry Bird, almost haggard. The eyelashes that were once so long that even Darrell Royal noticed them are now overshadowed by the half-moon reading glasses that slope unevenly across his nose.

His salt-and-pepper hair has gone heavier on the salt after two straight losing seasons. His uneven sideburns, looking like Spock's on "Star Trek," curve out of control down the sides of his face. Clarence Beck, who shaped McWilliams's crew cuts for a dollar a trim in the '60s and still cuts his hair today at Wooten's Barber Shop on the Drag, isn't to blame. It's just that McWilliams's hair has no game plan.

His disheveled hair and casual appearance are part of an unpretentious style that borders on indifference. "The only time he's uncomfortable is when he's wearing a tie," one team manager says. "And he gets it off as fast as he can."

McWilliams is as down-home as a dirt road to a fishing hole, as comfortable as an old pair of boots. He wears on you, people say.

His players are likely to walk right in, prop up their Nikes on his desk, and take a bite out of his tuna fish sandwich. Or ask Coach to run get 'em a Coke while they jump on the Stairmaster that McWilliams climbs five times a week.

A player's coach, they call him. And not just one of those modern "player's" coaches who lets his team do anything on and off the field as long as it wins.

McWilliams, after all, played at Texas six years before Darrell Royal got around to loosening up.

"They were at the dining hall one day in 1969," recalls Jones Ramsey, former sports information director at Texas. "James Street came in with real long hair, and Darrell turned to Mike Campbell, and he says, 'Mike, what are we going to do about Street's long hair?' And old Mike, he's eating with two hands, and he says, 'Well, he's our winningest quarterback. I suggest we let him wear it any length he wants.'

"And Darrell got pissed. I mean really pissed. He didn't like that at all. But then Bear Bryant called up Darrell about the middle of the season and said, 'Darrell, what are we doing about all this long hair?' And Darrell said, 'I suggest you let them wear it any length they want it. If they're starters.' "

Darrell and Bear, they were coaches' coaches. McWilliams is almost a players' player.

"I think, more than anything, I want to be friends with them," he said in 1987 before he'd coached a single game at Texas. "You can do that as long as neither takes advantage of it."

Former Texas quarterback Shannon Kelley says, "I love Coach Mac. He's honest. He'll look you in the eye and tell you yes or no. You won't have to read about it in the paper. Coach McWilliams is flat-out fair."

If McWilliams is fair, Fred Akers could be forbidding. "I was frightened to death of him," Kelley says.

Royal's players were half scared of the huge shadow he cast across Texas. Akers sought—downright demanded—control. McWilliams and his players juggle it. It's a risky act, but it's genuine. Under

Akers, players were more regimented, more suppressed—at least publicly.

"Coach Akers didn't want us to talk bad about anybody or say our true feelings," says senior offensive tackle Stan Thomas, who nonetheless staged a one-player protest on the dorm-deserted weekend when Akers was fired. "Coach Mac lets us say what we feel."

McWilliams also listens to what the players say. He heard out tight end Stephen Clark when the senior approached him in January 1990 about helping the team become more focused, more together, more—more of a team.

"He experiments, he thinks about what will work for us," senior running back Chris Samuels says. "If he conditions us a certain way, he might notice that our legs are tired on Friday or Saturday. So he changes. Our diet, our eating habits, our dining hall facility have changed. So has how we practice. Just about everything has changed.

"More importantly, he really cares about us as players, and he'll do anything for us. I really believe that. When you have someone like that encouraging you, it's kind of hard not to give him everything you have. We definitely would like him to stick around for the University of Texas."

McWilliams isn't so much easy to talk to as he is easy to be around. But if you're not around him, you may be out of mind. He's notorious for not returning calls, even from his assistants. His mentor, Darrell Royal, was a master at using the press, and had fun doing it. McWilliams tolerates the media as a necessary evil. But then talking has never been his game.

"David's one of those quiet observers," says Bill Ellington, a former coach and athletic director at Texas. McWilliams's Longhorn teammate Knox Nunnally, now a lawyer, goes a step further. "I didn't know he could talk until he became a coach," he says.

Others still aren't convinced.

"He's just gibberish," Longhorn historian Robert Heard says. "You don't think so at the time, when you're listening to him in person, but you go back and listen to a tape, and he has these incredible run-on sentences. He changes verb tenses, and he has these extraneous matters come floating out of nowhere. He doesn't talk in circles, he talks in spirals that just go spinning out into space."

"He gets excited and doesn't realize it," Stan Thomas says. "He'll say he has one more thing to say and end up saying twenty things. The next thing you know, you're thinking 'What was he trying to say?'"

"But he's more like a father to us. He'll come to meetings and hug you. When Lou Holtz walks into the room at Notre Dame, everybody probably just shuts up. But Coach Mac will talk to you the same way, whether it's in the dining room or on the field."

The talk is usually pretty plain. Royal could describe Oklahoma's Joe Washington as smoother than "smoke through a keyhole" and mesmerize an audience. Or say of a gutty but less-gifted runner, "He doesn't have a whole lot of speed, but maybe Elizabeth Taylor can't sing."

McWilliams, on occasion, will dust off a Royalism or two. Over-zealous alums roared as if he were the second coming of Will Rogers when he told them he'd been picked for the Texas job, "I guess 'cause I done good."

McWilliams, however, quickly found out that even a perfect past tense doesn't get it at Texas, where the emphasis is always on winning now, winning often, and winning big.

When McWilliams and wife Cindy stole out of Lubbock, which was madder than a spurned lover, they flew to Austin on December 5, 1986. Athletic director DeLoss Dodds had a limousine whisk them from the airport to the auditorium at the LBJ Library.

Just blocks from the press conference and booster love-in scheduled to announce the return of the native son, the limousine broke down. Was it an omen that McWilliams couldn't go home again? In the school's savagely proud football history only two Texas letterman had been appointed head football coach, Clyde Littlefield and Ed Price. Both won SWC titles, but were hounded into accepting "reassignments" within seven years.

The nationwide search that Dodds had promised six days earlier —when he announced Akers's dismissal—centered on the Republic of Texas. Only Arizona State's John Cooper, now at Ohio State, seemed to receive serious consideration. Royal, who was on the selection committee, says of the search, "Mine wasn't nationwide."

Dodds started with two dozen names. He gave that list to a head-hunting firm, which gathered more information on the candidates. Dodds then narrowed the field to about five. Bill Curry, then at Alabama, North Carolina State's Dick Sheridan, and Mike Shanahan, Denver Bronco offensive coordinator at the time, were on the short list. Air Force's Fisher DeBerry got a look. So did Arizona's Larry Smith.

"If Texas people had voted," says Dodds, who made the choice, "David would have gotten ninety-nine point nine percent of the votes. It was mandated."

In his only year as a college head coach, McWilliams turned a losing Texas Tech team into a 7–4 squad that made the Independence Bowl.

McWilliams's record during his one-year leave of absence—and that was practically all that his sabbatical at Texas Tech for the 1986 season was—wasn't the reason he endeared himself to orangebloods. No, David is Texas, from the top of his untamed hair to the bottom of his ostrich-skin boots.

McWilliams has the only closet in his upscale Westlake neighborhood that has ten pairs of boots and not a single pair of dress shoes.

When he's not coaching, recruiting, or fishing, he's usually at home, playing with daughter Summer or his three sons, Dennis, Corby, and Hunter. He's more partial to crossword puzzles than books.

Occasionally, he'll put a pinch of Beechnut between his cheek and gum, but wife Cindy is more tolerant of his smelly cigars than she is of the tobacco-splattered plastic cups he leaves around the house.

Offensive coordinator Lynn Amedee says, "He don't even have an ego. His hair's always messed up, he's got one suit, and he remembers where he came from and knows who he is. He's probably the most genuine guy I've ever been around."

Cindy had a crush on David when she was a senior cheerleader at Abilene High and he was the coach. They married twenty-three summers ago.

"My favorite thing about him is his marvelous humility," Cindy says. "He is just so humble."

Royal once said of his former player and assistant, "Any way you turn him, he looks good."

McWilliams looked good as an undersized center and defensive tackle who took on larger players like Oklahoma's 245-pound Ralph Neely. He looked good wearing a national championship ring after Texas's undefeated 1963 season. He looked good as an assistant coach to Royal for seven seasons. He looked even better as Akers's defensive coordinator for four years.

Unfortunately, he also looked better as an assistant than he did his first three seasons as Texas head coach. "Mac was twenty-one and seventeen as a high school coach," a Texas school official says. "Why do we think it will be different in college?"

Having Royal's blessing didn't automatically make him a winner. He entered the 1990 season with a 16–18 record at Texas, and even that unimpressive mark could easily have been worse.

Asked what McWilliams had done right in three seasons, one Longhorn insider says, "Talk about your thin books. He initially had the confidence of the kids because of his background and his way. That's one thing he did far better than Fred or Darrell."

Perhaps he did it too well. McWilliams has been criticized for the same warm qualities that draw him praise. Some knocked him for being too loyal and bringing some unqualified assistants from Lubbock. He has never admitted that making buddy John Mize offensive coordinator was a mistake, but in the spring of 1989 he demoted him to defensive tackle coach.

"What David brought with him is garbage," another Texas follower says harshly. "That's unkind, but true. David wasn't very analytical. It was strictly loyalty."

McWilliams's lengthy delays in making decisions also weakened his support, and his indecision nearly cost him one of the country's top offensive coordinators. When he was shopping for coordinators, he let the process drag on so long that a frustrated Lynn Amedee finally told Florida writers he was staying on Galen Hall's staff.

When McWilliams called the next day to say Amedee was his man, Amedee announced he had been offered more money. Maybe, but word spread that Amedee just didn't know how else to explain McWilliams's foot-dragging. Had McWilliams acted sooner, Texas might have signed highly touted quarterback Donald Douglas of Liberty, Texas, who followed Amedee to Florida. After Amedee left, Douglas transferred to Houston.

Others charged that discipline was lacking on McWilliams's team and his players didn't fear him or losing. "He's not the type of coach that makes your stomach drop when he yells at you," placekicker Michael Pollak acknowledges.

The external criticism has stung, but McWilliams rarely lets on.

"He's an easy person to hurt," Culpepper says. "And expectations are so high at Texas. It was like the Tower of Babel. There were problems all throughout the athletic department. He was a symbol of what was happening at Texas."

Another close friend says McWilliams "didn't come in with guys like Mike Campbell. David had some coaches that weren't ready for that kind of pressure. They were all living off David."

"I guarantee you David didn't know what he was getting into," another longtime Texas observer says. "Tech wasn't that big a job. He could drive around West Texas, play golf a half dozen times, and he'd met the fans."

McWilliams stuck by his assistant coaches. And even his worst critics concede he should be smart enough to handle the job.

He ranked fifth in his class at Cleburne High School and graduated with honors in mathematics from Texas.

"I've seen the guy sit in a corner and work on a math problem for an hour and a half," says Culpepper, a former Cleburne and Texas teammate who coaches at Lufkin in East Texas. "David would be over there like a monk. He just concentrates. He probably would have been a pretty good golfer. He reminds you of Jack Nicklaus."

His teammates picked him as a captain of the 1963 Texas team. At 188 pounds, McWilliams wore out game films to find an edge against celebrated giants like Oklahoma's Ralph Neely and Mississippi's Jim Dunaway.

The 267-pound Dunaway was one of the top linemen in the country in 1961. When Ole Miss faced Texas in the Cotton Bowl on New Year's Day of 1962, the lighter McWilliams certainly didn't look like much of a match for him. Dunaway told McWilliams, "You couldn't make our B-team." But McWilliams kept plugging away in a game that Texas won 12–7.

While growing up in Cleburne, McWilliams was extremely competitive at football and fishing.

"He always wanted to make the last cast," says Culpepper. "He'd fish when there were patches of ice on the river. He liked to be by himself. David enjoyed that."

That, or being with his dad.

Dennis McWilliams left a wife and unborn child when he went overseas to fight in World War II. He was shot down behind enemy lines, and taken prisoner. He was later left in a hospital the Germans abandoned, and found by Allied forces.

After returning home, Dennis McWilliams moved wherever there was work. He finally settled his wife and young son in Cleburne, a blue-collar hub town for the Santa Fe Railroad near Fort Worth. Not until David was six years old did he live in a house. His father took a correspondence course in carpentry and built it himself with lumber scrounged from a deserted boxcar.

Dennis McWilliams worked at an auto dealership and as the veteran's service officer for Johnson County. In between filling out forms and applying for benefits, he sometimes had to talk a disillusioned veteran out of committing suicide. It made Dennis McWilliams appreciate life all that much more.

Finally in 1953, with the help of an eleven-year-old son who passed out campaign fliers, Dennis McWilliams was elected county tax assessor, a position he held for twenty-five years.

Son David made money picking cotton, shucking corn, and even digging up worms. As a fourth-grader, he opened a fireworks stand across from the county courthouse and made forty to fifty dollars a day during Christmas vacation.

"He would do anything to make money," uncle Perry Don Wright says. Although he was Virginia McWilliams's brother, Wright was only four years older than David and became a close friend. "He wasn't no dummy. He'd pick up Coke bottles for a nickel apiece, pick and hoe cotton, haul hay—whatever he could do. Every time he'd make a dollar, he'd save seventy-five cents. For what? I guess to buy fishing lures."

David and Perry Don pulled more yellow catfish out of the Brazos River than they could ever count. At times, the two wouldn't even need a line. They'd block in spawning catfish with sandbags or toad sacks and reach down with their hands, searching for fish protecting their eggs under rocks, and just snatch them.

Big fish, sixty to seventy pounds. Some nights they'd haul in up to three hundred pounds of catfish.

"One time we bought ninety dollars' worth of groceries—and that was a lot of money back then—and we didn't come back for seven, eight days," Wright says.

McWilliams still loves to be decked out in his fishing gear and up to his kneecaps in a rippling cold river in Green Mountain Falls or Toledo Bend.

"Like coaching, he just don't quit," Wright says. "He works it. If you get ahead of him, you're going to stay all night. He's hard to beat. He just has the right touch."

He had it in football as well. From the time he was a fourth-grader at J. N. Long Elementary in Cleburne, McWilliams was always a bit smarter than the rest. That's why a slow, chubby ten-year-old who could barely throw a spiral played quarterback until high school.

When Cleburne varsity coach Brooks Conover wandered over to check on the freshman team one Thursday and spotted the miscast quarterback, he asked freshman coach Aulton "Bull" Durham why McWilliams was taking snaps. Durham shot back, " 'Cause he can remember the plays."

A year later, McWilliams was playing center rather than taking snaps from one. He played that new position well enough for the state cochampion Yellow Jackets that sportswriter Jack Proctor of the *Cleburne Times-Review* called him "one of the greatest centers ever to don football pads."

After graduating in 1960, McWilliams was invited to play in the All-American game in Baton Rouge, Louisiana, featuring many of the nation's top high school players. When McWilliams arrived, the coach of the South squad sized up the 185-pounder and asked what the hell he was doing there.

When McWilliams said he was a center who was going to Texas, the coach laughed, "Well, you ain't going to play ball for me. You're not big enough."

When the squad suited out in pads for a practice, the coach stuck McWilliams at middle linebacker and pitted him against a 215-pound center. When McWilliams flattened him and caused a fumble, the coach called him lucky. On the next play, McWilliams knocked the fullback flat unconscious.

"Hey, McWilliams," the coach called out, "I think you'll play a little bit."

Despite losing 15 pounds in the Louisiana humidity, McWilliams played both ways for all but three minutes of the all-star game and intercepted a pass to set up the winning touchdown for the South.

At Texas, he once played fifty minutes against Oklahoma, one of the schools that recruited him hard. As an all-state center and linebacker, he visited Rice, Baylor, TCU, A&M, Texas Tech, and SMU. He talked to Colorado, and all of the service academies were interested.

On his recruiting visit to Norman, Oklahoma, McWilliams spent almost four hours with a professor of petroleum engineering.

Still, Dennis and Virginia McWilliams liked Royal and top aide Mike Campbell. Friend Pat Culpepper was already at Texas. So it was off to Austin.

As a freshman, McWilliams listened to the 1960 Texas-OU game on the radio and can still remember hearing Longhorn tackle Eddie Padgett rushing Sooner quarterback Jimmy Carpenter into an interception that Culpepper returned 78 yards for the final touchdown in a 24–0 win.

McWilliams, however, had never been to a Texas-OU game in the Cotton Bowl. Little did he know he would be making three trips down that storied ramp to the field as a player and another twenty-and-counting as a coach. The game would become his Christmas in October, and his own measuring stick.

"When I was a little kid, I'd find ways to sneak into the State Fair," he says. "It seems I've spent my whole life trying to get to the Cotton Bowl. Before the game, it was the UT student body versus Oklahoma's. There was probably more hitting in the stands than on the field sometimes."

That's not how he remembers the 1963 meeting. McWilliams, a 188-pound defensive tackle, was forced to line up against the 245-pound Ralph Neely.

"The hardest thing was just seeing around him, he was so big," McWilliams says. "One time they ran a dive play, and the runner just runs right by me. I never made an attempt to get the ball. All I had to do was take one step and he would have run right into me. The coaches asked, 'What are you doing?' I had to say I couldn't see him. I think Neely was surprised I was that small."

McWilliams used his great leg strength and knack for getting underneath bigger players to gain leverage. He held his own in a game Texas won 28–7, a victory that propelled the Longhorns to a number one ranking they would never lose. Texas swept through the season undefeated and was preparing to face Navy in the Cotton Bowl.

As a pregame gift, players on both teams were given commemorative watches. David McWilliams had selected a woman's watch. It was to be a Christmas present for his mother. Four days before the Cotton Bowl game, McWilliams's mother suffered a stroke.

Perry Don Wright, on a troopship in the middle of the Atlantic Ocean with the 24th Infantry Division, received a telegram saying his sister was critically ill, but he couldn't get back home in time. Virginia McWilliams, an attractive, spirited woman who was so feisty at games that she would beat on those sitting by her and who once flung her open purse into the night when her brother scored a touchdown, died at age forty-six.

McWilliams and fellow tri-captains Scott Appleton and Tommy Ford attended the funeral along with Royal and his assistants. When Appleton was fighting bouts with alcoholism after he'd left Texas, it was McWilliams who would get calls at two in the morning and come to his side. But on this day, Appleton and the others were consoling him.

When the hearse came to pick up Dennis McWilliams at their home, he turned to his two sons and said, "Boys, we're just going to have to get the ball and run up the middle."

McWilliams did just that. On January 1, 1964, he played one of his best games and helped hold Heisman Trophy winner Roger Staubach of Navy to a minus 47 yards rushing in a convincing 28–6 win in the Cotton Bowl. "He didn't leave any of it out there," Royal says of McWilliams, whose elbow had become so badly infected during the season that Perry Don says "it almost rotted off."

After the game, Staubach sought out McWilliams and offered his condolences. David saw Perry Don, who had arrived from New York, in the dressing room. He broke down and cried.

Seventeen years later, McWilliams's father would die on the night David was at the Bluebonnet Bowl as a Fred Akers assistant in a 16–7 loss to Lawrence Taylor and his North Carolina teammates. David's oldest son, a linebacker at Texas, is named after David's father.

After that 1963 season, McWilliams left Texas and was hired by the legendary coach Chuck Moser at Abilene.

Within a year and a half, Abilene coach Wally Bullington resigned to go to Abilene Christian, and his top assistant, Ted Sitton, wasn't interested in the head coaching position. So, at twenty-three, McWilliams became the youngest head coach in the state in 1965.

"I was too dumb to be scared," he says.

In four years, his record was an unspectacular 21–17–2, but it came against brutal competition. The winner of the district widely known as the "Little Southwest Conference" won the state championship or played in the finals all four years McWilliams was at Abilene.

Abilene cheerleader Cindy Hacker's parents moved to Iowa, but she returned to attend McMurry College in Abilene. Finances were about to force her to transfer to less expensive Texas Tech in Lubbock, but David, whom she'd been dating while she was at McMurry, intervened.

The night after the high school all-star game in San Antonio in 1967, McWilliams drove back to Abilene. He met his future father-in-law, career military man Ed Hacker, the next afternoon, and David and Cindy were married that night. David met his mother-in-law for the first time at the wedding reception.

"Her dad and I are exactly the same," McWilliams says. "I'm probably neat to a fault. It always drives Cindy crazy. If I'm cooking, I wash the dishes I've already used. I guess by being mathematical, everything has a place."

There's been little question where his place is. Six years after leaving Austin, McWilliams got the call to come home. Royal offered him a position as a freshman coach, and McWilliams bit quickly. For the next sixteen years, he was an assistant under Royal and then Akers until he left for Texas Tech for one year. There, he took the Red Raiders to their first bowl game in nine seasons.

When he arrived at Texas, he was certain he would get the job done. But the spark didn't come until late. Some trace it to the ignominious 50–7 loss to Baylor in the next-to-last game of the 1989 season.

"I think the Baylor game made the Texas staff," Culpepper says. "I think they realized the kind of crap that's going to come down when they play that way. That's one of those dates circled on the calendar. Before that, they were kind of mercenaries. All of a sudden they realized they had a pretty dadgum good job, and they were about to lose it.

"I think the staff pulled very close together. Do we want to go out and get high school jobs, or do we want to make a stand? Maybe Texas can't dominate for six or seven years, but Texas should be able to compete. The whole staff got scared so badly they rallied together."

The demanding off-season program McWilliams put in place also served notice to his players that it was time for Texas to be Texas again.

"I remember last spring he was talking to the Longhorns on a cold afternoon," sports information director Bill Little says. "You could see a flash in those steel eyes. I thought, 'Hey, this guy means business.' He's going to get things done."

But when? Royal confided to president Bill Cunningham in December of 1986 that it might take four to five years to rebuild the program. Texas's rapport with high school coaches, the main pipeline to recruits, had fallen into disrepair under Fred Akers. The stiff-shirt, y'all-should-be-honored-to-come-to-Texas approach had turned off some recruits, and those that did come sometimes left because of academic or other problems.

"You've got to recruit a group and make seniors out of 'em," Royal told Cunningham. "And you've got to have a class backing each one of 'em up."

Earl Campbell, the school's only Heisman Trophy winner, says he noticed the dropoff in talent immediately when he returned to his alma mater two years after retiring from the New Orleans Saints.

"I'm surprised Texas didn't finish at the bottom the last few years," Campbell says. "The program had all the juice sucked out of it. The milk was gone out of that cow. Coach Mac had to start all over again."

And at Texas, the only way to tell if you've made it all the way back is to beat Oklahoma.

7

Bordering on Greatness

At practice before the big game against Oklahoma, David McWilliams looks relaxed. Even more relaxed than he usually is.

The Crude Feud in Dallas may be the game that makes or breaks coaches at both schools, but it's still McWilliams's kind of old-fashioned head knocker. "In most cases they're going to beat us with the fullback up the middle," he says. "The game is played between the hash marks. It's straight vanilla."

But in a rocky-road, double dutch-chocolate setting, Texas vs. Oklahoma isn't just another game; it's a weekend border war hawked by a carnival barker that Dallas just tries to survive every year. It's a throwback to the Prohibition Era that still shakes the glass-and-concrete canyons of the Oz-like city. It's a rivalry that's not so much a football game as a showdown between two states that really don't like each other. The series has been spiced with bottle throwing, spying, and untold gallons of bad blood.

Oklahomans think Texans are obnoxious and arrogant.

Texans think Oklahomans aren't much better than the red dirt they live on.

Oklahomans think they have the better football program.

Texans think that's because Oklahoma loads up with Texas high school stars it paid to get.

Oklahomans think Texas cheats, but just doesn't get caught as much.

Texas sucks.

Oklahoma sucks.

The traditional chant begins Friday night on Commerce Street in the heart of Dallas. Fans act as if Oklahoma still had Prohibition and neither state had any civilization. They crawl by in cars and shout obscenities at folks wearing the wrong colors and hope that maybe two hundred or three hundred people will get arrested the way they did in the good old days.

Hell, in 1968, when most of the country was growing a counter-culture, the mean drunk on Friday produced 653 arrests and had Dallas police processing prisoners in a vacant downtown parking lot that was quickly dubbed the O.K. Corral.

These days, Commerce is a misnamed street where there's hardly a place to buy beer and darn near no place to piss it away.

"Hey, goddamn it!" a husky man in a sport coat screams as he chases through a parking lot after a group of college kids who've just relieved themselves next to his car.

Commerce Street is a mindless, senseless, hoot-and-hollering BYOB tradition flying in the icy-glass face of modern Dallas. The town's tony, redeveloped warehouse district, the West End, is a short walk away. The West End has Cajun food, Dixieland jazz, Aussie beers, upscale chili, and good old-fashioned meat markets for singles, everything that a Dallas yuppie could want.

Despite efforts to move the revelers and their money to the West End, most still cling to Commerce Street as if it had honky-tonks and strip joints the way it did in the 1950s when Candy Barr was peeling at the Colony Club and when Oklahoma was one of two remaining dry states. Back then a weekend in Dallas was an Oklahoman's idea of sin.

For years Commerce Street has been lined with impersonal office buildings that give way to small businesses as you head east, toward the fairgrounds. On Friday night, almost all of those shops are closed, and some are sealed by protective mesh fences that have been pulled down for the night.

People come to Commerce Street not because of what it is, but because of what is has been. It's the place for Oklahoma and Texas fans to yell at one another because . . . because that's what they've always done.

Partygoers are carrying Lone Stars, Buds, Millers, Michelobs, and Coors, swigging while they walk and yell, and they're still moving faster than the cars, which have turned Commerce Street into an exhaust-choked parking lot. Stereos are cranked. Attitudes are adjusted. Tops are down.

"Whooo, Hook 'em Horns," screams a coed who's busting out the sunroof of a slow-moving Toyota.

Oklahoma fans salute her with an inverted Hook 'em sign, which is the international symbol for Hook This, Horns.

"Oklahoma sucks! Oklahoma sucks!" screams a twelve-year-old from the bed of a Chevy pickup. The oversized foam cowboy hat he's wearing flops down and covers his face.

A pickup truck full of Texas alums propped up in lawn chairs inches by. A Camaro in bad need of a muffler growls. In a white Fleetwood Cadillac stretch limo, the high-rolling occupants savor the craziness from behind opaque tinted windows. A couple of street-corner capitalists are scalping six-packs for seven dollars each. Police dressed in enough battle gear to handle a soccer riot line both sides of the streets, where pedestrians are allowed to walk one way only.

The yelling, drinking, and start-and-stop driving goes on into the early hours of Saturday morning. At 10 A.M., Officer D. Pierce of the Dallas Police Department reads the final score. "We had ten Sooners and fifty-one Texans arrested," he says. Yeah, Texas could even party better than Oklahoma.

By that time, the party is moving to the two hundred-plus acres of Fair Park that surround the aging Cotton Bowl structure on the east side of Dallas.

As the game between once-beaten Texas and undefeated Oklahoma nears, fairgoers mill around. They're eating foot-long hot dogs sticking out of buns whiter than Wonder bread, nachos dripping with gloppy processed cheese, french fries fat as fingers glistening with grease, ice cream melting right out of sugar cones, sticky cotton candy, corny dogs double-dunked in mustard and falling off sticks, huge turkey legs almost too hot to hold, funnel cakes snowed under in sugar, apples dripping with caramel, chalupas, chimichangas, burritos, gyros, baklava, strudel, and frito pie. Beer is hawked, sometimes straight from iced-filled garbage cans, on an otherwise sanitized carnival midway.

Twenty-five-cent coupons, not crass cash, are the medium of exchange. Those who don't spend them all on food splurge on the games that line the midway. Fans, a lot of them wearing bright Sooner red, shoot basketballs that look bigger than the rims they're supposed to go through. They try to underhand softballs into milk cans or knock the containers down with overhand fastballs. They play skee-ball, aim darts, and hurl footballs through tires. All for the bright stuffed bears, tigers, lions, pandas, dolphins, raccoons, and knockoff Teenage Mutant Ninja Turtles that dangle above them.

At the midway, the 212-foot ferris wheel, the Texas Star, drips with gondolas as it spins slowly and offers up a romantic view of the Dallas skyline. A mock pirate ship rocks back and forth like a huge pendulum to the squealing delight of its young occupants. The roller coaster, the Zyklon, clatters across its twisting tracks. Teutonic music is oomping and pa pa-ing from the Bavarian Slide.

The fairgrounds are chock full of attractions. Stunt snow skiers are twisting and flipping off a forty-foot ramp. There's a puppet show, sheep dog show, pig and goat races, the music of Billy Roy's one-man band, a bread-baking contest, pygmy goat show, the Kilgore Rangerettes, and . . .

The Texas-Oklahoma football game.

It's just flat different from other football games. The half-Texas and half-Oklahoma crowd makes it rowdy no matter which team is winning. The neutral site has helped create a mean series of streaks. Since there's never a home-field advantage, talent usually wins out. Often the same team wins for several years in a row. And those wins also impress the future talent, high schoolers watching on the sidelines, that both Oklahoma and Texas are likely to be recruiting.

Of the eighty-three players on Oklahoma's roster, twenty-nine are from Oklahoma and thirty-eight decided to become transplanted Texans.

"We hated Oklahoma," says Pat Culpepper, a former Texas teammate of David McWilliams. "We felt it was our bound duty to beat them in football. It was serious with us, we felt we were obligated to beat them."

Bragging rights are at stake. So are blue-chip recruits. And eventually, coaching jobs. Maybe that's why a series between two wildcatting states is played so conservatively. Oil, after all, is just "bidness." Texas vs. Oklahoma is football—the kind of gut-wrenching experience that kept even a bootlegger's son like Barry Switzer from letting it all hang out the way he did against Big Eight rival Nebraska.

Running down the ramp at the Cotton Bowl, that's a larger-than-life experience that sticks with every player ever to take part in the border war.

"The only way I know to describe the feeling you have before the game is that when you walk onto that field there is a force field of electricity," McWilliams says. "You actually visualize streams of electrical current coming off the field. You feel like you're walking a foot off the ground."

McWilliams is getting ready for his twenty-third Texas-Oklahoma game as a player, assistant coach, or head coach. That will tie him with Switzer and Darrell Royal for the most appearances ever in the series.

Royal's last Texas-Oklahoma game was in 1976. It was the game he most wanted to win in his career, the one he'd prepared for all summer, the one that left him retching on the sidelines.

The Texas-Oklahoma series helped make Royal, a former star quarterback for Oklahoma, a legendary coach. Before Royal arrived for the 1957 season, Texas was 1–8 in its previous nine tries against the Sooners, who had a coaching legend of their own named Bud Wilkinson.

When University of Texas regents chairman Tom Sealy first presented Royal to the press, he said, "Now Coach, who's the first team we're gonna beat?" Royal replied, "I think we open with Georgia." That was the first laugh he drew at Texas, where everyone knew he had to beat Oklahoma.

Royal beat Wilkinson in his second year, 1958. He won seven more in a row after that. After 1970, when Texas won a UPI national championship, Royal had a 12–2 record against his alma mater. But he then lost five straight, including three straight to Switzer, the brash young coach who got on his nerves.

It was Switzer, in a thinly veiled reference to Royal, who said that some coaches would rather listen to guitar pickers than recruit. "I know exactly why we had such recruiting success," he once said. "We outwork 'em. I'm young. My staff is young. Our hair is still growing. We can jive with kids, dance with them."

Before the 1976 game, Royal got word that Oklahoma had someone spying on his practices. When the *Austin American Statesman* broke the story two days before the game, Switzer denied all. Fourteen years later in his autobiography, Switzer admitted the unethical ploy. At the time, however, he told one paper, "If they ever catch an OU spy, he's [Royal] got my permission to castrate and assassinate him."

Royal challenged Switzer to take a lie detector test. Switzer declined. And things got even uglier when Robert Heard, then an Associated Press reporter in Austin, quoted Royal as calling the Oklahoma staff "sorry bastards."

"The interview was over and he knew it," Royal says. "I said, 'Frankly, I don't trust the bastards in anything they do.' That's the way I said it. It was after the interview was over, and he said, 'You really are incensed about it, aren't you?'"

On game day the Oklahoma fans let Royal have it as he walked out

75

at the beginning of the game. "I was booed from the chute to the fifty-yard line," Royal recalls. "I walked real slow, too. To let them boo a lot. I wanted to make them yell longer than they wanted to."

Royal and Switzer—frozen in silence—were escorted to the fifty-yard line by President Gerald Ford, who had no idea about the depth of the feud. The following game turned into one of the greatest Texas defensive efforts ever. Texas was leading 6–0 with just 5:23 left when Texas's Ivey Suber fumbled.

"It was a draw play and he was waving the ball around more than he should have," Royal sighs now. "We'd have been better off if we'd run one of those plays right at the line instead of trying one of those offbeat things."

Oklahoma safety Zac Henderson recovered at the Texas 37. The Sooners, who had made only two first downs, then took ten plays to score when Horace Ivory slipped around left end for a 1-yard touchdown. Oklahoma's chance to win, however, evaporated on a high snap as they missed the extra point.

When asked if he felt the game had been a moral victory, Royal said, "If I'd thought we won, I wouldn't be sitting here with my belly about to throw up."

"I was so dejected," he recalls now. "It felt like a loss." Royal looked haggard after that game, the most tense in a taut rivalry. He talked to Texas officials about retiring two games later, while flying back from a 31–28 loss to Texas Tech.

As for Switzer, the coach that Texas supporters say ran Royal out of football, his last effort as a coach at the Texas-Oklahoma game was in 1988. He thumped McWilliams's team 28–13. But Switzer left after the drug-related arrest of quarterback Charles Thompson and after shootings and alleged rapes in the Oklahoma dorms had become a symbol of a football program out of control.

Oklahoma likes to say it now has more character than characters. But at a pep rally before the 1990 game, Oklahoma safety Jason Belser half-mooned the crowd to reveal a message that said, "Tuck Fexas."

Mild stuff, really, compared with what made the Sooners infamous. But then, Switzer's replacement, former defensive coordinator Gary Gibbs, is a straight-arrow disciplinarian his players nicknamed "The Thinker." Gibbs gave the Sooners new marching orders. Go to class. Make curfew. Stay out of trouble. Pick up a diploma. The Boz wouldn't recognize the place.

But Gibbs is still expected to have his players do what Oklahoma does best, which is win football games. Last year, however, his Oklahoma team entered as a 17-point favorite only to be shocked with 1:33 left when Peter Gardere, who was making only his second start at quarterback for Texas, found receiver Johnny Walker for a touchdown. Walker later said Gibbs's first Oklahoma team didn't have the cockiness and togetherness that made Switzer's Oklahoma teams so hard to beat.

This time, in 1990, Gibbs's team is favored again, by eight points.

"I predict . . . " says Switzer, who's standing in the south end zone during OU's warmups and wearing a blazer and a pink shirt, ". . . I predict I'll have a beer before the day is out."

Switzer's replacement has the pressure of being a head coach still looking for his first win in the series. David McWilliams, meanwhile, is finally looking to break even at Texas.

In his fourth year, McWilliams is 18–19 at Texas, where only one coach, Jack Chevigny, ever finished with a losing career record. A loss to Oklahoma, and McWilliams's winning percentage will once again dip below the 13–14–2 record Chevigny compiled from 1934 to 1936.

It's a warm 81 degrees when Texas's Michael Pollak drives his kickoff into the end zone for a touchback to open the game. Oklahoma's attack is based on its two bruising fullbacks, Kenyon Rasheed and Mike McKinley, both of whom average well over five yards and many more headaches a carry. Texas defensive coordinator Leon Fuller fretted late in the week about their fullback tandem. "If the fullbacks get a hundred and fifty yards," Fuller says, "we'll be in trouble." Rasheed, a 6-foot, 238-pound sophomore, has received most of the pregame media attention. But Gibbs opens with McKinley, a 225-pounder who's one of the strongest Sooners.

After a personal foul against Oklahoma, McKinley gets his first carry when it's first-and-thirty-two for Oklahoma. He rumbles for 38 yards and a first down that has Sooner fans roaring. But the drive ends with a 47-yard field goal from R. D. Lashar.

Texas answers with a march that moves the ball all the way to the Oklahoma 8. It's third down. Gardere goes back and tries Texas's best scoring play, a lob to one of the 6-foot-4 Cash twins. No contest. Tight end Kerry Cash jumps up and one-hands the ball over 5-foot-9 left cornerback Darnell Walker. Touchdown. Texas leads favored Oklahoma 7–3.

Now it's all Oklahoma. The Sooners keep hammering up the middle of the Texas defense, gaining yards, controlling the clock. Highly touted freshman quarterback Cale Gundy, who threw for more than

7,000 yards in an All-American high school career, comes in for scatter-armed starter Steve Collins in the second quarter. He doesn't even need to throw the ball on a 58-yard up-the-gut touchdown drive, in which Oklahoma only bothers to go outside once for a 9-yard gain.

At halftime, Oklahoma is up by only 10–7, but the score doesn't come close to reflecting the Sooners' domination. Oklahoma has held the ball for 20:36, while Texas has had it for just 9:24. The Sooners have run 38 times for 179 yards. The Longhorns, who haven't scored a touchdown on the ground against Oklahoma since their last good season–1983–have 13 rushes for 19 yards. Only luck and the confusing punts of left-footed kicker Alex Waits have kept Texas close. But now, safety Stanley Richard reminds his teammates of the vow taken after the Colorado game. "We're not going to lose again," he says as Texas prepares to return to the field. Richard also tells his teammates he's going to smack any Sooner in the mouth who strays into his area, which is pretty much what Richard has been doing while looking like an All-American.

Texas's luck holds in the third quarter when Gundy fumbles on third-and-goal from the Texas 5 and defensive end Oscar Giles recovers on Texas's 12. Once again the Texas offense doesn't respond, but the Sooner turnover that robbed Oklahoma of at least three points could be critical. Texas offensive coordinator Lynn Amedee, who thought about replacing Gardere with Jimmy Saxton in the first half, is blistering Gardere's ears on the headset and cranking up that line of thought again.

When another Oklahoma drive stalls, however, Gardere again comes out. On the third play, though, Phil Brown fumbles and it's recovered by Oklahoma on the Texas 35.

Oklahoma settles for a 26-yard field goal that puts the Sooners up 13–7 just before the third quarter ends.

The game looks as if it's fixing to be over early in the fourth quarter when Kerry Cash fumbles after a 12-yard catch and Oklahoma takes over on its own 42. The Sooners are pounding through the Texas middle again with McKinley when a personal foul stalls the drive. Lashar has a shot at a 49-yard field goal but Texas's 6-foot-6 defensive end Shane Dronett blocks it.

The Longhorns are down by only 6 and start on their own 32. On third-and-six from the 36, Belser appears to Tuck Fexas permanently by intercepting a Gardere pass intended for Johnny Walker. A personal foul, however, has Oklahoma looking at a first-and-twenty-five that's too much for the ground-bound Sooners. When Oklahoma punts, Texas gets the ball back on its own 9. Oklahoma, which has stuffed Texas all day, starts playing cautiously with less than seven minutes left in the game.

And, on second-and-eight from the 36, Phil Brown goes out with an injured ankle and freshman Butch Hadnot trots in.

Brown is the player whom ESPN draft analyst Mel Kiper has rated as Texas's only super blue-chipper, even though Brown is merely a redshirt freshman. The Commerce, Texas, product has attracted national attention with his games against Penn State and Colorado before he started trying to break every play against Rice.

Hadnot has carried only four times for 11 yards in the 1990 season. But the freshman is Amedee's kind of guy. Big. Strong. Tough. Amedee kept on recruiting Hadnot even after he verbally committed to Texas Tech—chalk up one more Tech defector to Texas—and when other schools backed off because of his low SAT scores. They saw a potential academic casualty. Amedee thought he saw the next Earl Campbell.

"I was right there with Coach Amedee when he came here on his visit," Campbell says. "I couldn't believe a kid eighteen years old could be built like that. I mean, I had big thighs and bow legs when I was coming up, but that kid is an exception. He reminds me more of Jim Brown than Earl Campbell. I mean, he's got the whole physique. His thighs are better. Mine were twenty-eight inches. He's got to be close to thirty, thirty-one. Between him and the Good Lord, he controls his own destiny if he's willing to work at it."

Many of the Texas players have been working out in Texas's multimillion-dollar weight room for years. But, when they make their way up the small hill to the facility, it's Hadnot's thigh muscles that pop out. They look as though they belong to a speedskater, not a football player.

When Oklahoma shifts to a nickel defense, Hadnot breaks his first play for 23 yards. He gains 10 more on the next carry, and 5 more yards are tacked on for a facemask penalty. Texas is alive.

Mammoth offensive tackle Stan Thomas comes into the huddle talking about how he's going to drive his man 10 yards down the field. Then he does it.

The Oklahoma players are getting nervous. They know they've been the better team, but now they're worried about losing.

On third-and-eight from the Oklahoma 25, Gardere misses Chris Samuels with a pass. But Samuels was hit early. Pass interference. Texas has a first down on the Oklahoma 19. Two runs by Phil Brown, who's come back in for Hadnot, net only three yards. Then Gardere misses Johnny Walker.

Texas calls a time-out with 2:05 left in the game. It's fourth-and-seven from the 16.

Oklahoma doesn't want any déjà vu. Walker's seen the tape of last year's game twenty-five, thirty times. "I loaned out the tape to teammates to help them get through the spring," the senior split end says. "Time stopped on that play. It seemed like I stayed up in the air for about five minutes." The trip down must have taken even longer for Charles Frank, the Sooner cornerback whom Walker beat on the deciding play.

So when Walker goes out to the right, he draws double coverage. This time, Frank has Keith Cash in one-on-one coverage. He guesses that Cash is going to go for the corner of the end zone and yet another of his patented alley-oops. Cash takes off from scrimmage, and here comes the alley . . . Oops.

After faking for the corner, Cash slants in for a post, freezing Frank. Touchdown! When placekicker Michael Pollak hits the extra point, Texas—outplayed all day—goes up 14–13.

After the kickoff, Oklahoma takes over on its 20 and Gundy comes out throwing. He's just a freshman, but two-minute drills are nothing new to him. Seven out of eight times he scored on two-minute drills in high school, including a win in the state championship game.

There's more than a minute to play, and Oklahoma has moved to the Texas 46. Gundy is thinking pass. Gibbs sends in a run and fullback Kenyon Rasheed picks up a yard going at the middle of the Texas defense. Then, on third-and-seven from the Texas 43, Gundy hits tight end Adrian Cooper for a gain of eight. Fifty-nine seconds left. Plenty of time. Enough time for . . . three running plays? They net only six yards. The crowd is stunned. Texas is stunned. And Oklahoma is stopped. Fourth down.

Placekicker R. D. Lashar is on the sidelines, holding up a "We're number one" finger for the ESPN cameras. He comes in for a 46-yarder into a stiff wind. The snap is good. The placement is good. The kick heads for the middle of the uprights . . . and is blown to the left. Lashar drops to his knees as that end of the stadium, the Oklahoma side, falls into a drop-jaw silence.

The far end of the stadium erupts with the celebrating shouts of Texas fans. Texas players swarm onto the field so fast that David McWilliams first thinks they're going to draw a penalty. He doesn't realize there's no more time left, that the game is officially over.

Even Eddie Day, the unemotional Texas trainer who is always so composed he's almost comatose, leaps high into the air in exhilaration, then calmly walks off the field. An exuberant McWilliams gets a congratulatory hug under the goal post from son Dennis. "It's something I'll never forget," the coach says.

The Oklahoma players aren't quite so sentimental.

"We do have better plays than up the middle," tight end Adrian Cooper snaps after watching his team attempt only 11 passes and complete 4 of them for 57 yards. "The coaches, I feel, should not wait till the crucial moments of the game to pass. There was a time in the first half I wasn't covered by anybody. The coaches saw it, but they never went back to it."

"I'd have preferred to have thrown all passes on that drive," says Gundy, who may have been wondering why he had turned down Oklahoma State, where his older brother Mike had become the Big Eight's all-time passing leader. "It wasn't much of a two-minute drill. I'm just not used to these running plays. I know they've been doing it this way for thirty years and I guess they've been successful, but I was frustrated."

"We should have scored forty on them," Rasheed says after Oklahoma has held the ball for almost two-thirds of the game. Rasheed and McKinley accounted for 132 yards between them and many of tailback Dewell Brewer's 85 yards were between the tackles, but somehow Fuller's bunch had survived.

The Texas players are elated. "We went into the tunnel with our heads up," yells defensive end Oscar Giles. "They went in with their heads down. It was like a fight with about three or four rules. They had us on the ropes. Then we hit them with an uppercut."

"Lightning strikes twice," defensive back Grady Cavness yells.

Texas vs. Oklahoma. It is usually won up the middle. But not this time.

8

We're Not in Kansas Anymore

It's late August 1981, and DeLoss Dodds has the air-conditioning in his Toyota on full blast to soften the searing summer heat. He's en route from Manhattan, Kansas, to his new job in Austin as athletic director at the University of Texas. As he hits Dallas, he pulls over to phone his predecessor, easygoing former Darrell Royal assistant Bill Ellington.

Ellington, who took over for Royal as Texas's AD in 1979, offers some simple advice from his ranch in Quinlan.

"You've got just two problems at Texas," he tells the new AD, who's just about to start sweating. "One is the basketball coach. And the other is the football coach."

Hello, Toto. We're definitely not in Kansas anymore.

It could have been someone other than Dodds cruising down I-35 to Austin that day only to be warned that he'd have to can Abe Lemons and Fred Akers—one of the most lovable characters in Texas history and one of the winningest.

It could have been legendary Dallas Cowboys coach Tom Landry heading to Austin.

Tom Morgan, then chairman of the men's Athletics Council, headed the search committee and was told Landry might consider stepping down as Dallas Cowboys coach. Landry, who has a home overlooking a golf course in Lakeway, west of Austin, is a Texas ex. He played offensive and defensive back in 1947–48 after piloting a B-17 bomber in Europe during World War II.

"Gil Brandt thought Tom might be interested, just to get off the

82

fire," Morgan says. "I talked to Tom a long time on the phone. He told me he still wanted to coach. He thought that being an AD was something he might want to do someday, but he wasn't quite ready for it. Getting Tom would have put to rest the alumni who wanted an orange-blooded athletic director."

Ellington had pushed hard for his assistant, T Jones. Phil "Legs" George, the Angelo State athletic director and former Longhorn basketball player, was also interviewed. Morgan checked out Florida State's Hootie Ingram, Delaware's Dave Nelson, and Penn's Andy Geiger. He kept coming back to Dodds, the AD at Kansas State.

"DeLoss was very reluctant," Morgan says. "He was not very receptive. I think he was worried about the circumstances; it's a highly political job. I'm not sure but he's regretted it a lot since then."

When Dodds and his wife, Mary Ann, left for Japan with the Kansas State basketball team that summer, Morgan was pessimistic about Texas's chances of getting Dodds. Then Dr. Jim Ayres, an English professor and a member of the Athletics Council, phoned Dodds upon his return. The academician's appeal, Morgan says, "tipped the balance."

Dodds seldom made a major decision without consulting his good friend Glen Stone, and the Kansas State sports information director was with Dodds for three straight afternoons while he was wrestling with his decision. Dodds declined the Texas offer twice but finally accepted when it was upped.

"If you go, it'll hurt like hell to lose you, but I'm happy for you," Stone told his boss. "They pay you to go into the jungle, but you never know if you're coming out."

In naming Dodds, an outsider, the school passed over one of its own. T Jones, a former All Southwest Conference quarterback for the Longhorns in 1952, was a former Darrell Royal assistant.

Jones came to the University of Texas from City National Bank of Austin, where he was a senior vice-president. At Texas, Jones ran a tight ship, sometimes checking desks at 4:55 to make sure the school got its full eight hours—from hired help.

On September 1, Betty Corley, Ellington's secretary, gets a call from Morgan. She's told to round up the staff for a 4 P.M. meeting.

Just before four, in strides a tall, dark-haired gentleman with a perpetual five o'clock shadow. The forty-four-year-old Dodds is introduced. Athletic department employees are told Dodds is a former assistant commissioner of the Big Eight Conference and a former athletic director at Kansas State. Few are overwhelmed by his credentials. After all, Manhattan, Kansas, is hardly the Big Apple of college athletics.

Only Cleburne Price, the Texas track coach, knows the former quarter-miler and Kansas State track coach well.

Dodds, however, knows Austin a lot better than it knows him. Since 1956, he's made nearly every Texas Relays track meet. He and K-State assistant sports information director, Johnny Keith, were running buddies, on and off the track.

"He taught me everything about life. That's how bad off I am," Dodds jokes. "He and I ran together for a while. Till he about killed me. And then he left and I survived."

Keith, a skinny version of W. C. Fields known to legions of reporters as "Ranger," never met a six-pack he didn't like. Dodds was more partial to an occasional Jack Daniels. They would go to clubs on Congress Avenue when they weren't coaching at Memorial Stadium or downing nachos at El Rancho's.

As a partier, Dodds calls Keith a "first-team All-American. How'd I keep up with him? I didn't. We'd go out at night and stay out late, and he'd want to get up at five-thirty the next morning and go run. So we'd go out and run."

That's as semi-wild as Dodds would ever get in Austin, where he quickly acquired a reputation as a deliberate, reserved pipe smoker. When Darrell Royal was AD, his idea of hell was having to sit through a meeting with a bunch of pipe smokers. "They spend their whole lives lighting their pipes," Royal says.

Still, Dodds was impressive that September afternoon in 1981.

"I asked Cleburne about DeLoss," Corley says, "and he raved and raved about him. He called him the best administrator and the best track coach he knew. He was the most organized man, and he always knew the rules perfectly."

But what were the guidelines in this job? Where was the manual on how to be an AD at a football power that wants to be number one every year?

Dodds now says of Texas football coach David McWilliams, "He's been a head coach one year out at Texas Tech, and that's good experience, but that ain't being head coach at Texas, and that ain't being head coach at a major program with the kind of visibility and pressures you get at Texas. David's still learning to be a head coach. He's taken a quantum leap this year."

Dodds could have been describing his own early years at Texas, where a lot of people were waiting to see an outsider fall flatter than

Kansas. There may have been little on his resume that prepared him for the powderkeg he was fixing to light.

"DeLoss came in, and for the longest time didn't know where the bathrooms were," one Texas school official says, "and I'm not real sure he does now, that he really understands where he is, what he's doing, and what needs to be done. DeLoss had never been in this kind of position of responsibility and authority."

Dodds was brought in to modernize what Morgan calls "a country-store" operation, but he was also hired to fire coaches.

Basketball coach Abe Lemons was crusty and caustic, but he had more country wit than even Darrell Royal. Lemons, who was partial to unlit cigars and combustible one-liners, would hold court at a downtown Italian restaurant named the Red Tomato and was hugely popular. His high-scoring teams played fast and loose and were the hit of Austin, which was booming from a comfortable college town into a high-rolling, real estate-speculating Texas metropolis.

No cow was sacred to Lemons, and that scared Board of Regents members and school administrators, who grew increasingly worried that his ref-baiting antics and hot-tempered rhetoric didn't fit the buttoned-down, first-class image the university was trying so hard to project.

At the same time, the Fred Akers fan club was having more and more trouble reaching a quorum. His offense was boring. His discipline was lacking. And Fred Akers still wasn't former Royal assistant Mike Campbell. Never would be.

It wasn't the way Dodds had seen Texas from the outside.

"Texas is better thought of outside the state than it is inside the state," Dodds says now after a decade on the job. "And it's thought of pretty well in the state. You get out of the state of Texas, and you talk about the University of Texas, and it means a great deal."

Folks' opinion of Dodds may have taken some reshaping as well in those early years. Even the opinions of his friends.

One year before Cleburne Price's death of a stroke in November 1986, Dodds "reassigned" Price, in part because of Price's deteriorating health, which had not allowed him to attend meetings and many practices. It was a painful experience for Dodds, who hates firing employees. But Lemons said pointedly, "Dodds called him into his office and ripped his buttons off."

Lemons understood. He had a similar summons to Dodds's spacious office on Bellmont's second floor—and lost his own buttons.

"DeLoss wasn't happy about having to do it," Morgan says. "We told him we'd be glad to do it, but he thought it was the responsibility of the athletic director. The Athletics Council was pretty dead set. Abe just was not responsible. We'd tell him not to do things, and he'd go ahead and do them. I sat down with him twice in the two years before that and told him if he didn't change, he'd get fired. He had warnings, and we had it in writing. I wrote him three letters. He wanted to run the basketball program out of his hip pocket."

Lemons's final request was for a glass-bottomed car, so he could see Dodds's face when he was running over him. But Lemons has since backed off that somewhat. "I realize now that DeLoss was just a pawn for other people," Lemons says.

"Firing Abe right off the bat took a lot of guts," says Texas women's athletic director Donna Lopiano, who heads up just one of ten Division I-A programs with separate men's and women's departments. "I liked Abe, but I think that was a pretty good decision. Abe was not attentive to the academic side, but he's a great basketball coach. That was a tough start for DeLoss."

Dodds also attributes much of the animosity aimed at him to the new era of high-finance big business that is college athletics in the '90s.

"I just came at a time when things weren't that good," Dodds says. "When I walked in here, people didn't know what an AD was. Never heard of one. They knew what the football coach was, and the football coach had also been AD. He was doing things, making decisions, but his popularity was based on whether he won or lost. And he was winning. I walk in and I'm an AD, and nobody knows what I do or that I'm here until I do something with Abe Lemons. Then they know."

"People don't like administrators," says Dodds, whose staff has swelled to include one associate athletic director and four assistant ADs. "I don't like bureaucracy either, but when you're in this business, you're eaten up by it. ADs are never associated with good things. I'm not one of those that has my arm around a winner. There's people all over the world that, when somebody wins, boy, they've got their arm around them. I don't feel good doing that."

Almost from day one, Dodds was blindly attacked for being an outsider, a non-Longhorn and a non-Texan in a state that still semi-considers itself a separate nation.

"I think the spirit of the University of Texas is so strong that even if you don't attend here, it envelops you, and you become a part of it," says Roy Vaughan, executive director of the Ex-Students' Association. "Bill Cunningham is from Michigan State, but there's not a more rabid supporter of the University of Texas in the world. DeLoss Dodds came down from Kansas State, but he's as University of Texas as you can get."

Dodds, however, is regularly knocked for not wearing anything orange, not bleeding orange, and not being orange. He's heard it enough times to make him turn K-State purple. It's a patently unfair charge, his many defenders say.

"I'm proud of K-State," Dodds says. "I'm proud I grew up in Kansas. I'm a good person. I think if I didn't have pride in my school, I wouldn't be much of a person. I expect people who go to Texas to have pride about their school. Anybody that says anything to me about not being a Texas ex, I ask them how long they were here. Most of them say four or five years, and I say I've been here ten. Surely I can pick up in ten years what you picked up in four or five. You know, I love this place too.

"If I were that kind of person, I would wear orange underwear. But I'm not that kind of person. I did not wear purple when I was at K-State. I do not like purple. I wear more burnt orange than I do purple. I've got six pairs of boots, six cowboy hats. I wear 'em on my own time, I don't wear 'em on university time."

On or off the clock, Dodds is considered one of the top athletic directors in the nation, an astute negotiator and a shrewd businessman born with a poker face. He has served on most of the NCAA's prominent committees dealing with television and the possibility of a Division I football playoff.

A good listener, Dodds learned well from former Big Eight boss Chuck Neinas, who once told him not to say anything important at a meeting until the end because that's all anyone remembers.

Dodds's sense of humor is about as dry as Austin in mid-July, but Lopiano notices that Dodds has become more relaxed. At games, however, he sits erect in his private box seat, rarely showing his emotions.

"DeLoss sweats blood all over those games," says Darrell Royal, who frequently shares Dodds's private box. "He probably lives and dies with every snap, but pipe smokers don't show emotion."

Dodds smoked his first pipe in 1960 and was still refilling, tamping, and puffing away as the 1990 season began. He smoked Philip Morris cigarettes as early as age twelve after he delivered newspapers on his route. He quit in high school, for athletics.

He picked up a pipe as a twenty-three-year-old platoon leader in the Army. For six months at Fort Knox, Kentucky, Dodds was a lieutenant in charge of five tanks.

"If you got tanks, you've got maintenance," he says. "Ninety percent of the time is maintenance. Officers don't do maintenance. So what do they do? They just go in the corner somewhere and smoke a pipe. I'd rather have been an enlisted man where I could have worked."

As an AD, though, Dodds is all officer, and as serious as any CEO. It's an image that university president Bill Cunningham and the regents appreciate. He is very much in their favor.

"I like him," Royal says. "His department is well organized."

"As long as Cunningham is in power," one school official says, "DeLoss is safe. But since DeLoss came, the department has probably tripled in personnel. Some were uncomfortable hires. People who don't get along with people."

Some, like the ousted Fred Akers, feel Dodds epitomizes the shift to a corporate field where the suits of the players don't have numbers.

"The game has changed a great deal," Akers says. "I don't know if it will ever be the same as it used to be when I first became a coach. The day of looking a guy in the eye and giving him a handshake and telling him something and meaning it, those days are gone. That's uncomfortable when you've been raised to respect your word and mean it when you give your word.

"Today, when you have a meeting, you'd better have fourteen lawyers present. I didn't think that DeLoss had control, I never did when he first came there. He was just following orders. Whose? Whoever *they* are."

Of Dodds's critics, none carries more volume and venom than Robert Heard.

The former Associated Press reporter and author of a newsletter with 1,500 subscribers scrutinizes the Longhorn program relentlessly and has made it a crusade to dump Dodds. He regularly castigates Dodds for what he considers to be a variety of transgressions—for thinking only of the almighty bottom dollar, for overstaffing, for hiring former basketball coach Bob Weltlich, for bringing with him to Austin the Kansas Mafia, but most of all for not being born burnt orange.

"It's not that DeLoss is such a bad administrator, I'm sure there are worse ones," Heard says. "He's fairly good in some areas, and he's pretty weak in some areas. He simply does not love the university. There are some jobs where you need to have it. He has a particularly sensitive one, where he's got to deal with some people who frankly put too much emphasis on sports. They live and die by sports and they want to know that you bleed orange. He doesn't do that. He'll never do that."

Dodds sloughs off Heard, saying, "He doesn't know me from Adam. I had lunch with him once, and he did all the talking." Dodds knows he is not popular with some rank-and-file Texas fans, but he is comfortable with those he hobnobs with at various functions around the state.

"I do very well with the people I know," he says, "and I know a lot of people. We've got those Longhorn Clubs, and I do fine with those people. I think some criticize me because I'm always associated with things that aren't going right. When football wasn't doing well, who were they writing about? They're writing about David and DeLoss. When basketball wasn't going well, who are they writing about? Bob and DeLoss. If baseball wins a national championship, who are you going to write about? You're going to write about Cliff [Gustafson]."

But not Dodds. Dodds's hiring of former Mississippi Coach Bob Weltlich turned out to be as unpopular as his firing of Lemons. Weltlich, a former Bobby Knight assistant who could be as dour and demanding as The General himself, came to Austin with a my-way-or-the-highway approach. Many of Lemons's talented players picked the highway. So did the fans, who bailed out as Weltlich struggled to rebuild the program. By the time Weltlich finally had some decent talent in place, Dodds was ready to make a change. In 1988 Weltlich, now at Florida International, was "reassigned."

Dodds courted Kansas State's Lon Krueger, inciting even more anti-K-State feelings from Dodds's detractors. He spoke with former K-State classmate Gene Keady of Purdue, who's even gruffer than Weltlich.

Finally, Rhode Island's Tom Penders, pushed strongly by assistant athletic director Craig Helwig, became the choice almost by default. In his second season, 1989–90, Penders took the Texas basketball team to the Elite Eight in the NCAA Tournament for the first time since 1947.

Heard grumbles, "He just dumb-shit fell into the Penders deal. The first thing I'd do—and it's so simple—the first thing I'd do is fire DeLoss Dodds and put Donna Lopiano in there, and she'd take it. I'd do that so fast. She's not from Texas. Darrell Royal wasn't from Texas. But they do bleed orange. It's an accountant's job for Dodds.

He likes it, I mean, he likes the perks. But I think to do the best job, you need to love your job."

Heard isn't just a lone voice in the wilderness—or the jungle of Texas politics.

Glen Stone, a former K-State friend of Dodds's who is now Texas Christian's sports information director, says, "A lot of people have told me privately that they have had it up to here with him. He always has been cold and calculating in his dealings, but he has driven a lot of wedges between himself and a lot of people the last couple of years."

The split between Stone and Dodds came in a key 1986 basketball game at TCU's Daniel-Meyer Coliseum. A win over TCU would have given Texas the outright SWC championship. For Weltlich, the game meant everything. It would prove that his maligned program could succeed. For Dodds, who had hired Weltlich, it meant just as much.

Stone left press row early to ready the interview room for Horned Frogs coach Jim Killingsworth. So, he wasn't on the floor when TCU guard Jamie Dixon snake-danced through the Texas defense and nailed a 30-footer at the buzzer to upset the Longhorns 55–54.

Stone heard the crowd explode, but didn't know what had happened. He walked into a tunnel and ran into the players as they were rushing off the court. A uniformed security guard was stopping anyone without proper credentials and had abruptly halted Dodds and Craig Helwig.

Stone patted the guard on the shoulder and told him, "No, no, they're okay." He asked Dodds what happened.

"Fuck you, motherfucker," Dodds uncharacteristically bellowed back while a photographer and a wire-service reporter were still within earshot. "Get out of my face. Fuck you and everybody here."

Dodds stalked off in one direction, and Stone in another. To this day, the two men have never discussed the incident. Or much of anything else, although Dodds tried to speak with Stone the week after the episode. Betty Corley, Dodds's personal assistant for more than nine years, couldn't believe the story about a boss so even-tempered that he never slams a door or even a phone. But Stone swears by his version, as does the reporter who was there.

"Dodds must have been under incredible pressure," says Mike Rabun of the UPI. "It was pretty ugly."

"As far as I'm concerned, DeLoss Dodds died that day," Stone says. "He doesn't exist in my repertoire of friends."

Stone says he saw flashes of that boil-over rage by Dodds at K-State. Dodds had once asked to borrow Stone's car to take his athletes to a track meet, but when Stone refused. "He threatened to whip me," Stone says.

But the scene at Daniel-Meyer was the clincher.

"I was really hurt," says Stone, who has known Dodds for a quarter of a century. "I never had a friend do that to me. I just don't trust him."

That's a side Dodds's closest friends and associates wouldn't recognize. "He's honest, straightforward, well balanced," Morgan says. "I'd grade him high."

Corley talks of the warm family man whose greatest love is playing with his two-year-old grandson, Steffan.

Dodds and wife Mary Ann both grew up in Riley, Kansas, a small town of about six hundred folks just eleven miles from the K-State campus. DeLoss's father, Clarence Dodds, was a high school coach and superintendent until he died of cancer when DeLoss was just eight years old. His death left Elma Dodds with five children from age fourteen to one and a half, four of them girls. The Dodds didn't own their home, and Elma Dodds went to work as a schoolteacher. DeLoss himself worked, both before and after school. While he was a butcher's helper at a grocery store, Mary Ann was a soda jerk down the street at Hassebrook's drugstore.

Dodds liked the work, and he put in a lot of hours hauling and trimming meat until ten o'clock on Saturday nights. The late shifts didn't leave much time for socializing.

"Our dates were not very exciting," Mary Ann says. "Mostly, we just sat on the porch swing and rested."

The death of his father made DeLoss more responsible, more serious. But the tall, thin teenager with oversize ears also loved sports and had a talent for them. He played six-man football for the Riley Wildcats and went to K-State on a football scholarship, although it was in track that he carved out a reputation as a crack quarter-miler.

After graduation, he served six months in the Army before returning to Manhattan as assistant track coach. Two years later he was named head coach, and some, including Stone, think he could have been perfectly content to remain in that position.

"Mary Ann's always been the driving force behind him," Stone says. "He could be happy smoking a pipe and being a track coach, but she's a mover and a shaker."

Dodds almost certainly could have been happy in any of the jobs he held. He didn't so much climb the career ladder as have it placed before him.

"I've never gone after the next job," he says. "I've always been asked. I was an assistant track coach, and I was asked to be ticket manager at K-State. I was asked to be track coach at K-State. I was asked to be an assistant commissioner in the Big Eight office. I was asked to be AD at K-State, and I was asked to be AD at Texas. Never applied for any of them. Never thought about the next job.

"I was twenty-five years old when I got the head coaching job. I decided that I would not coach past forty years old, because I watched a lot of track coaches that were beyond forty, and I thought they kind of quit or kind of lost their fire for it. I didn't want to do that. I wanted to be in it all the way, and then I was going to do something else. At thirty-eight, I went and did something else."

In three years as K-State AD, Dodds buoyed a struggling program that had been swimming in red ink. He brought K-State to the break-even point from a $750,000 deficit, a feat of some doing in such a rural setting. He did it by courting business leaders. Every Monday or Tuesday for a solid year, he would invite a businessman to lunch. Over a salad or a sandwich, Dodds would ask him about his wife, his golf game, or the weather. Not once did he ask for money.

"All he was doing was planting the garden," Stone says. "It was going to get harvested later."

For an introvert like Dodds, the project was a coming-out party. He was always shy, which makes it even harder to believe that he once considered becoming a Presbyterian minister. He is, however, also very competitive.

Mary Ann Dodds recalls her husband's endless Ping-Pong matches in the basement of their Kansas City home with son Doug, now a lawyer in Austin. They kept score domino-style on the cement wall. "After they'd finish dinner, they'd say, 'Let's go down and play one game.' They'd come up hours later."

Dodds looks fit and about five years younger than his fifty-three years. He walks regularly for four or five miles around their home off the fifth hole at Onion Creek, where he works on his 10-to-12 handicap.

For all his enemies who call him DeLOSS or DeLo$$, Dodds has a lot of friends in high places. He has served on major NCAA committees like the Postseason Football Committee that looked into possibilities for a Division I-A playoff. As chairman of the CFA Television Committee, he helped negotiate lucrative packages. It was once thought he was grooming himself to succeed Walter Byers as executive director of the NCAA or become the head of the U.S. Olympic Committee.

"He is the best TV mind in the country and an ace business person," Lopiano says. "Texas is in as good a financial shape as any Division I-A program in the country."

Dodds rarely speaks of himself in any personal terms, and never expresses any ambitions publicly. Totally accessible, he regularly returns reporters' phone calls and generally is well liked by the press.

"DeLoss's posture is to kill them with kindness," one school official says. "He gives the impression when he's around people that he really likes them, so it is hard to trust him. One Big Eight official claims Dodds is manipulative but that can almost be considered a compliment for an athletic director.

Respected by the Board of Regents, appreciated by President Bill Cunningham, tolerated by Longhorn coaches, Dodds appears safe. To many, the Weltlich hire in basketball was his albatross, but he got rid of that bird.

Vaughan says Dodds is "the lightning rod for any criticism," but adds that Dodds also never takes credit for all of the positives of the athletic program. Maybe it doesn't matter. Texas orangebloods can take or leave Dodds, but many will never really take to him.

"Goddamned pipe smokers never make a decision," one veteran UT watcher in Austin groused during preseason. "I'd blame DeLoss for a lot of the alienation of Texas exes—this great, powerful blob out there that's mad, confused, indignant. There are some places I suspect where he'd better not go—some outside of Houston, in Dallas. He's not Texas, and has operated like that. The basketball job comes open, and the first place he goes to is Kansas State, which is understandable because that's what he knows. But people around here are very loyal.

"Of those with the depth of feeling, at least half will run over him if he's in the freeway. There's another thirty or forty percent of them that tolerate him. That leaves ten percent who like him. He's very pleasant to play golf with. As for people with orange underwear, they get indignant as hell because the regents and brass pat him on the back and give him bonuses."

That kind of talk used to disturb Dodds much more than it does today. He's grown with the job.

"It bothered me early on, but it doesn't bother me anymore," he says. "The first time you read something about yourself, it hurts. Next time, you might get a little mad about it. The next time, you say it's part of the deal."

"You can have great loyalties without graduating from a school," wife Mary Ann says. "By pouring your heart and soul into a job, it burns your heart burnt orange."

9

To SEC-ede or Not
to SEC-ede

On a brisk Thursday of Arkansas week, defensive end Oscar Giles is standing outside Memorial Stadium when Texas quarterback Peter Gardere strolls by after practice.

Gardere doesn't say a word to the massive Giles. Instead, he chirps, "Tweet, tweet," and continues on his way, laughing.

Giles is a rock-hard 246-pounder who's one of the early candidates for the Outland Trophy, but he's also known for his perpetual, gap-tooth smile. This week he's been getting a lot of kidding from teammates about the tall tale he made up about the finish of the Oklahoma game, that a little bird with "Whatever It Takes"—Texas's team motto—written on its breast pushed R. D. Lashar's last-second field goal wide to the left.

The Longhorns are still savoring the sweetness, the giddiness of their win over Oklahoma, but now they have defending SWC champ Arkansas coming in to Austin. A win over the Razorbacks, and Texas will be off to a 4–1 start that will almost certainly be 5–1 as soon as SMU comes to town; those football flatliners are still trying to come back from the NCAA two-year death penalty for a major slush fund.

A loss, and Texas's season is still iffy. Texas, back in the AP rankings at number nineteen, would probably fall out of the Top 25 again. Instead of the Cotton Bowl—which desperately wants and needs Texas football to be back—the Longhorns might end up in the Peach, the Independence, or some other place they don't really want to be.

"This is like a hump," Giles says. "We need to get over it."

Giles and the rest of the Texas players want a win. They aren't even thinking of the historic importance of the game, which just happens to be huge.

After two big shootouts in 1969 and 1970 and sixty-nine other bitterly contested games, Arkansas is making its farewell appearance in Memorial Stadium in Austin. The Razorbacks are headed for the SEC, college football's big-time, while Texas remains behind in an SWC that is threatening to become a backwater of college athletics.

It's ironic that the team and state that always suffered from an inferiority complex in this clash is moving on to the superior conference.

No great college football rivalry is as lopsided as Texas-Arkansas. Rice has more victories over Texas than does Arkansas. Entering the 1990 game, Texas leads the series 53–18. When the Longhorns can't find a way to beat the Razorbacks, Arkansas comes up with a way to lose. In the 1987 game the Razorbacks dropped into such a deep prevent defense that they were playing *behind* tiny Tony Jones when he was in the end zone making a winning touchdown catch at the gun. In 1989, Arkansas was at home, armed with an eventual Cotton Bowl team and facing a Texas team that would sink to 5–6. Naturally, Arkansas choked and Texas won 24–20.

"We're like a horse washing out before a race. He's in a cold sweat," Arkansas wide receiver Tim Horton confided before that loss.

Horton watched helplessly on a crucial fourth-and-seven play from the Arkansas 38 as a pass from Quinn Grovey, the school's best-ever option quarterback, sailed over his head and clean over the Arkansas bench right into a suddenly slack-jawed crowd.

"I was trying to throw to the shortest man on the field," Grovey tried to explain. "As soon as I let it go . . . I just watched it go into the fifth row. It was just a weird feeling."

"We were in a daze last year," Arkansas tailback Aaron Jackson now says. "I couldn't figure out why. We were a step behind, a second late. It's like we were moving in slow motion."

Even legendary coach Frank Broyles, now Arkansas's near omnipotent athletic director, admits that Texas arouses different feelings than other foes.

"The Texas game, for everybody in the conference, is as much psychological as it is scheme and strategy," says Broyles, whose own record against Texas was 5–14. "Not just us. Everybody. You can define scheme and strategy, but you can't accurately script morale and attitude in that game."

Broyles was so upset by Arkansas's 15–14 loss to Texas in 1969, the game that cost his Razorbacks the national championship, that he has never seen the game film. "No use in crying about it," he says stoically.

Or in standing on conference tradition in rapidly changing times.

The Big Shakeout in college football began when Notre Dame broke from the sixty-four-member College Football Association's television package and signed for five years with NBC. That prompted Penn State's Joe Paterno to say, "We got to see Notre Dame go from an academic institution to a banking institution."

Penn State, meanwhile, jumped to the Big Ten, severing some of Eastern football's finest rivalries in the process. Then, the Southeastern Conference called the Hogs and some other schools in an attempt to put together a real super conference.

The SWC reaction was swift, if ineffective.

Baylor's Grant Teaff called the raiding SEC "the Iraq of college football."

Teaff added, however, "Had Texas been the champion the last couple of years, or been right in there, there wouldn't have been near the gnashing of teeth, particularly by the national media, and the bashing of the conference when Arkansas left. Arkansas is a loss to us, but I mean it isn't all that big a loss. Good gosh. They'd only won two championships since Heck was a pup."

Actually, Arkansas had done a lot more than just win the last two conference titles. The Razorbacks have a winning record against every SWC team except Texas and have had twenty-three Associated Press Top 20 teams in football while flat-out carrying the SWC in basketball and pouring money into the so-called minor sports.

Arkansas's jump to the SEC didn't surprise Texas athletic director DeLoss Dodds, who predicted realignment years earlier. The Razorbacks had once flirted with the Big Eight. Broyles saw the SEC with its Deep South traditions, large state schools, and huge paychecks from TV as well as the gate as an even prettier opportunity.

In the SWC, Arkansas—the only one of the nine league schools not in Texas—always thought of itself as an outsider looking in.

"I think they felt for a long time that they weren't treated the same as the Texas schools," Dodds says. "They felt the officiating was against them. I don't know if they've ever been a real happy member of the conference. I think they probably didn't have any legitimate gripes, but in terms of dollars, they're much better off in the SEC."

The SEC's expansion mode was triggered by rumors that the CFA's television package for sixty-three of the best teams in Division I-A—excluding CFA member Notre Dame, the Pac-10, and Big Ten—would be struck down for violating antitrust laws. In that case, every conference would have to fend for itself. Leagues with more states, more people, and more television sets would have that much better leverage with TV networks. The SWC, with private schools Rice, Texas Christian, Southern Methodist, and Baylor, would be in big trouble.

So the Razorbacks bolted.

Arkansas shares borders with three SEC states, but has barely 1 percent of the nation's TV sets with 673,100. Was the SEC simply using the Razorbacks as bait to lure in the bigger fish, Texas and Texas A&M, from a state with 6.5 million TV sets?

"You only have to look at the numbers and population base to understand that," Dodds says. "I'm sure they'd rather have a Texas and an A&M than an Arkansas. I'm not sure it turned out like the SEC wanted. Arkansas is a good deal for them, but I'm sure they much preferred ending up with Texas and A&M and Florida State."

Texas and A&M, the two remaining linchpins of the SWC, quietly mulled over their options. They cast longing glances at both the SEC and the Pac-10.

The SEC offered state schools, great rivalries, and the biggest crowds in college football. But the package also included road trips to hard-to-reach places like Starkville and Oxford, Mississippi, and Auburn, Alabama.

"I don't want to be making road trips to West Buttocks, Mississippi," Texas superfan Scott Wilson says. "That's one of the nice things about the SWC, you can drive to most games."

Worse, the SEC's win-at-nearly-all-costs philosophy was the very outlaw image the SWC spent the latter half of the 1980s trying to shake.

The Pac-10 offered big-time football with a more laid-back attitude about winning. Better, more glamorous road trips. For the academicians, there was the prestige of institutions like Stanford and Cal-Berkeley. The lucrative Rose Bowl was another big plus.

Uh, the Pac-10 was offering, wasn't it?

One Pac-10 athletic director was adamantly opposed to annexing Texas and Texas A&M—Stanford's Andy Geiger, who later left for Maryland. Oddly enough, he could very easily have been on the other side of the fence had Texas hired him as athletic director in 1981 instead of Dodds.

Texas A&M alums started pushing for the SEC. That's also where Texas's basketball coach Tom Penders wanted to go because he feared that the time zone difference on the West Coast would hurt basketball. Texas women's athletic director Donna Lopiano, who has the vision but not the voltage of a Frank Erwin, spoke out for the Pac-10.

For lack of a forceful, dominant personality like Erwin, the former chairman of the Board of Regents, Texas stayed put.

"A&M and Texas agreed to go to the SEC," says former A&M coach Jackie Sherrill, now at Mississippi State. "In theory, the president of Texas and the president of A&M agreed, but neither one of them had the balls to do it, especially after [Speaker of the House] Gib Lewis got after it. The first thing [A&M president William] Mobley asked was, 'What's the political drift in Austin?' The guy who used to be the Speaker of the House, Bill Clayton, said it's fine. It wasn't.

"How close were they to joining the SEC? Very close. Frank's [Broyles] smarter than they are because Frank didn't want to get left behind. But the SEC knows they will get one eventually, either one or both."

Donald Zacharias, president of Mississippi State and the SEC, begs to differ with his new coach.

"They didn't [renege]," says Zacharias, who is a former Texas chancellor. "I never had that impression. We tried to be very careful and not set it up where somebody was put in a position of us being interested in someone if they were not interested in us or vice versa. There's been a tremendous downturn in funding. I think there will be more [NCAA] cutbacks, which puts people in a position of looking for ways to increase their resources."

Zacharias, no doubt, knows that his league has much more drawing power than the SWC. His Mississippi State football program was last in the SEC in average football attendance in 1989 with 30,513 per home game. That would have ranked ahead of Houston with Heisman Trophy winner Andre Ware and three other schools in the nine-team SWC.

Some in the Texas athletic department lamented the lack of a Frank Erwin, who undoubtedly could have pulled the trigger.

"If Frank was alive, we'd be gone," one Texas official says. "The Pac-10 is Donna's creation, although our football people didn't want to compete against the SEC. Lynn Amedee wanted to go to the SEC, but David wanted to stay in the 1950s."

When Texas and Texas A&M didn't quickly follow Arkansas, the state's politicians became involved and effectively grounded the pair.

Contrite, if not exactly convinced, the Longhorns and Aggies announced they were staying put. For now.

The two issued a thinly disguised ultimatum to the other six SWC schools. Texas A&M and Texas made "suggestions," like improving football attendance, which the other schools have unsuccessfully been trying to do for years in a state where pro sports have made costly inroads on the college game. They wanted a stronger commitment to women's athletics, which takes money the other schools don't have.

The meter is running.

"I think in the long run the Southwest Conference probably won't survive," says Tom Morgan, former Texas Athletics Council chairman. "There are too many negatives about it. It all depends on what happens with regard to a national championship playoff. That's such a big if that I'd hate to predict. I predicted the demise of the Southwest Conference before, and it hasn't come to pass."

In 1964, after some internal bickering in the SWC, Texas got hit with an NCAA probation and threatened to join a super conference of Southern schools, an idea whose time almost came in 1990.

So, Donna Lopiano, will Texas bolt for greener pastures?

"I hope so, but that's Bill's call," Lopiano says, deferring to president Bill Cunningham. "I made no bones about it. I think Texas needs to be with more like institutions. I think Texas and A&M have outgrown their compatibility with the other SWC schools. I don't particularly like the SEC. I don't like their academic reps and the ability of the schools to control their athletic programs. I like strong president-controlled schools like in the Pac-10 or Big Ten."

Dodds says the Big Ten holds the cards because its current deck of eleven schools isn't practical. Might Texas even long-jump to the Big Ten, as geographically crazy as that seems?

"I don't think you preclude anything," Dodds says. "You've got to stay viable. I don't think the Big Ten's happy with eleven. I think they'll go to twelve or fourteen or even sixteen. I think Notre Dame will have to get in a conference. The independents—Florida State, Miami, Penn State—are gone. Those things will eventually cause Notre Dame to do something. The Big Ten is where they fit."

Sherrill concurs. He predicts the Big Ten could become the Big Sixteen by adding Syracuse, Pittsburgh, Missouri, Nebraska, and, ultimately, Notre Dame.

"Right now academically Texas will probably go to the Pac-10," Sherrill says. "Reason I say that is Texas right now feels they can dominate A&M. They crushed A&M in basketball and baseball, and now football has come back. They weren't as dependent on A&M.

They'll both leave the conference at the same time, but A&M will go to the SEC and Texas will go to the Pac-10 next year. I think it will come to a head in the summer of 1992, because that will be the year the SEC has its playoff. That's when it will all unravel because everybody will see the public interest that a playoff can generate."

Arkansas, meanwhile, has been playing as though it was embarrassed to be leaving the SWC. In home games against TCU and Texas Tech, Arkansas yielded a staggering 103 points in two games, more than Lou Holtz's 1977 Arkansas team allowed in an entire 11–1 season.

If Arkansas has anything going for it, it's timing. As usual, Arkansas catches the Longhorns one week after Texas's emotional meltdown in the Cotton Bowl against Oklahoma. Rarely can the Longhorns work up the same kind of hate for the Razorbacks that they have for the Sooners.

"A lot of people in Arkansas dislike Texas," says Aaron Jackson, who played his high school football in Denison, Texas. "I don't think people in Texas dislike Arkansas. A lot of people here put too much emphasis on this game. It does have an effect."

New Arkansas coach Jack Crowe is very skeptical of his team's chances. Maybe it's because he senses the paranoia that Razorback fans feel about Texas and somehow transmit to the players. He says the Razorbacks seem to "change their personality" for this game. He becomes the first Razorback coach in history to close the team's practices.

"We became tentative because of whom we were playing," he says of the 1989 game, when he was Arkansas's offensive coordinator. "It was like we were walking in sand.

"I think I know that this game is important to the people of this state. I don't need any sixth sense. Every conversation I'd hear every week would be: 'Congratulations. We're behind you. Beat Texas.' There'd always be those two words thrown in at the end of the exchange."

Crowe, a former co-offensive coordinator at Clemson, has been the Arkansas coach for all of ten months. Former coach Ken Hatfield stunned the state with his resignation after he had taken his last two teams to the Cotton Bowl, only to lose to UCLA and Tennessee. Hatfield, a former star punt returner for the Razorbacks from 1962 to 1964, had openly feuded with Broyles. When Broyles announced in 1989 that he would remain as athletic director for another five years, Hatfield decided to take a leave of absence—a permanent one. He left Arkansas for Clemson at the height of recruiting season.

A devout Christian who would suspend Arkansas players for as little as having empty beer cans in their dorm rooms, Hatfield had never really been embraced by the Razorback faithful—or faithless. They booed him unmercifully when Tony Jones and Texas shocked Arkansas 16–14 in 1987.

When Hatfield decided he'd had enough, Broyles was caught unprepared to hire a new coach. Former Razorback Fred Akers, trapped in a losing situation at Purdue, phoned Broyles to press his case. But Crowe, who had come from Clemson as Hatfield's offensive coordinator only one year earlier, was named head coach to stop the bleeding midway through recruiting season.

Ten months later, Arkansas has only seventy-six scholarship players, nineteen shy of the allowable ninety-five. Crowe's first Arkansas team is quarterback Quinn Grovey and not much else. Even Grovey heard the boos when Arkansas lost to TCU 54–26, and then dropped a thriller to Texas Tech, 49–44.

After the Tech game, vandals broke into Grovey's 1986 gray Oldsmobile Cutlass and ripped off a radar detector and a portable stereo. Grovey's happy to be on the road. Arkansas has won the last two contests in Austin's Memorial Stadium. What's more, as Grovey says on Monday, "At least if we get booed down there, it'll be by the people who are supposed to boo us."

Grovey is conscious of the psych job that Arkansas does on itself preparing for Texas, but says, "I always thought I'd have a psychological edge because I'm from Oklahoma. I'm not going to have that jinx on me."

Broyles is so distraught over his team and the furor over Arkansas's departure from the SWC that he's dropped ten pounds in two weeks and lost his taste for his favorite butter pecan ice cream.

"We've had a run of bad luck," Broyles says. "People recognize in today's parity if you get a run of bad luck, you fall off dramatically. We don't have the speed we've had, and we don't have the experience."

Crowe is making his first return to Austin since he was an assistant on the 1984 Auburn team that starred Bo Jackson. That game is notable not so much for Texas's 35–27 win, but for the most famous play of Jerry Gray's college career. Gray, now an All-Pro defensive back with the Los Angeles Rams, ran down Jackson from behind and savagely threw him to the artificial turf after a 53-yard gain, separating Jackson's shoulder.

"He didn't just tackle him," Crowe winces in reflection. "He body-slammed him. But you know what? I think this guy Stanley Richard is better than Jerry Gray."

Richard, Texas's fastest player, is already known for hitting harder than Gray ever did. "He's an octopus," marvels Charlie Weatherbie, Arkansas's quarterback coach. "He just swallows you up like he's got eight arms. You can't get away from him."

As if he doesn't have enough to worry about, Crowe is fretting over the type of reception the Longhorn fans have planned for Arkansas. He rolls his eyes and asks, "They still ring those cowbells, don't they?"

That they do. Glenn Richter's band loves nothing more. The band director estimates 275 of the 340 band members have them.

"They can make a lot of racket," Richter says. "Bear Bryant hated those things. Barry Switzer hated them, Jackie Sherrill hated them. The band would look for ways to aggravate those guys."

Richter has more than bells in store for the departing Razorbacks. The Longhorn band experimented with a Looney Tunes routine during the Rice halftime and has received permission from the Texas administration to repeat the show, which chastises Arkansas for leaving the conference.

"They said, 'Okay, just don't pick on Gib Lewis.' That was the only requirement," Richter says, referring to the Speaker of the House who had led the charge to stop Texas's and A&M's flight from the SWC.

Almost like the Cotton Bowl a week before, the crowd is electric. A bright sun washes down on the tents atop Neuhaus-Royal for the bigwigs and deep-pockets. The Blazers, the bowl reps from the Cotton, Peach, Liberty, John Hancock, and All-American, are pressing the flesh and getting ready to size some of it up.

On the field, the Longhorn band struts in front of the Arkansas contingent. Arkansas drum majors lead obscene cheers in response. "Texas sucks," they yell. "Eat shit,"

Texas is pumped. Arkansas hopes it is.

"Memorial Stadium is intimidating with the twin-deck stadium," Arkansas offensive lineman Mark Henry says. "You hear those cowbells right behind your bench. Texas is our biggest rival. Most of us have grown up to hate Texas. It makes our year to beat Texas. To the fans, this is the only game of the year; it determines our season."

Arkansas has the option to start the game and picks defense. Crowe knows that Texas's offense ranks last in the league. Midway through the first quarter, Texas is on the move. Butch Hadnot steps off 10 yards. Phil Brown runs for 5, and Hadnot picks up 8 more. Chris Samuels follows Hadnot's block on a pitch left, running for 16. Guard Duane Miller and center Todd Smith clear a path, and Samuels has 19. Five plays later, Texas's 6-foot-4 flanker, Keith Cash, runs a simple down-and-out at the front of the end zone in the right corner and, shielding 5-foot-11 free safety Richard David from the ball, hauls in Peter Gardere's pass for an easy six.

It takes Arkansas just four plays to answer. From 33 yards out, Grovey fakes an option and, with strong safety Van Malone blitzing, finds a wide-open Tracy Caldwell down the middle for a tying touchdown.

Twice in the second quarter, Gardere connects with Johnny Walker, once for 27 yards and again for 22. Both set up Michael Pollak field goals, and Texas takes a 13–7 lead into the locker room.

During intermission, the Texas band parodies the conference realignment. One band member dressed like a Baptist minister runs around with a clipboard and sneakers, satirizing Baylor's Teaff. Another, decked out like the Razorback mascot, gets flattened by an SWC locomotive. Two other Texas band members representing Texas and A&M seem to be destined to live happily ever after as the band strikes up the "Wedding March."

The crowd roars in approval. Who needs the Razorbacks anyway? Let 'em go.

The Razorbacks will not go quietly, however. Arkansas scores first in the third quarter on Todd Wright's 50-yard field goal. Texas comes back strong and drives 80 yards in 11 plays. Gardere scrambles twice, finally scoring on an 8-yard run for a 20–10 lead.

Arkansas is in danger of letting the game slip away. The collars are tightening. Derek Russell, the silky senior split end who is averaging 109 yards a game, is getting antsy. The third quarter's half over, and he hasn't touched the ball.

Coming into the game, Russell's 544 receiving yards were third best in the nation, even though he was playing for a 2–3 team.

"If they come out in man-for-man coverage," Russell had said at midweek, "I can smile all day. None of their defensive backs impresses me a whole lot. I don't want to be arrogant, but I don't think anyone can cover me one-on-one."

Finally, he gets to show why he averages about twenty yards a catch. On second-and-eight from the Arkansas 22, Russell lines up on the left side and starts his fly pattern. He is shadowed by cornerback Grady Cavness. Tracy Caldwell, lined up inside Russell, squares off his pattern and cuts to the outside. Mark Berry, the other corner, sticks to his side but collides with Cavness, knocking him to the turf. Russell snares the ball in stride and prances to a 78-yard touchdown that brings the Razorbacks to within 3.

"We got picked, Ref," Texas defensive coordinator Leon Fuller screams on the sideline, unaware that Cavness was decked by his own man.

Four plays later, disaster strikes again. Gardere can't find anyone on second-and-six. Turning to run, he's separated from the ball by Arkansas linebacker Ray Lee Johnson. Scott Long recovers for Arkansas at the Texas 30.

On first down, tailback Aaron Jackson tries the left side, but runs into Brian Jones. The Texas linebacker, who sealed the Rice game by causing a fumble, splatters Jackson. The ball pops directly into the arms of Texas linebacker Winfred Tubbs.

For Arkansas, the fire is gone. Later in the third quarter, Grovey tries an option play for one of the few times all day. Like ten other third-down plays in fourteen tries, this one, too, fails. Richard, the player Crowe's staff feared most, all but decapitates Grovey.

Spurred on by the adoring crowd of 72,657, Texas pours it on in the fourth quarter. Adrian Walker somersaults over the pile for a 2-yard touchdown. Hadnot piggybacks the 196-pound free safety, Richard David, into the end zone from the 4 for another. Backup quarterback Jimmy Saxton and sophomore split end Darrick Duke practice the Gardere-Cash fade route from the 6. Touchdown.

The Texas players are up 40–17, but they want more. They line up in their usual swinging-gate formation for the conversion. The center, holder, and kicker line up conventionally, but the other eight players converge near the left hash mark. If the opponent doesn't adjust, the center snaps the ball sideways to a teammate for an easy two points.

Arkansas is slow to react. Defensive end Oscar Giles is on the sidelines screaming, "Go for two!" Center Turk McDonald hikes the ball as a long lateral to Kerry Cash, who runs it in for two points.

"If we had gone for one, I would have been disappointed," Giles says. "No, I would have been mad."

When fullback Patrick Wilson scores the game's final touchdown with 1:04 to play, Keith and Kerry Cash race toward the middle of the field, face the east side of the stadium, do an impromptu dance, and whip the crowd into a full-throated frenzy to climax a 29-point fourth quarter. Texas 49, Arkansas 17.

Texas athletic director DeLoss Dodds emerges from his private box during the Longhorns' fourth-quarter spree to refill his pipe. Looking at a fun season for the first time in years, he smiles and says, "Don't we deserve a little bit of it?"

Upstairs in the press box, Jim Williams, the chairman of the Cotton Bowl board of directors and a former All-SWC tackle at Arkansas in 1964–65, knows it's the best thing for the Cotton Bowl that Texas is 4–1. "Oh, yeah, there's a lot of mouths watering for Texas," Williams says, motioning to the happy blazers sitting to his left. "The greatest thing we can have for the conference is for Texas to be back. We need Texas to be back."

As for Texas quarterback Peter Gardere, he's a little relieved. The Posse from San Antonio Holmes—receivers Johnny Walker and the Cash twins—had been the center of much attention immediately after the OU game. Privately, they chafed a bit at the credit Gardere received when he was later named the SWC Offensive Player of the Week. When they got on him about that in the dressing room before a practice, Gardere didn't know whether to be indignant or just insecure.

Against Arkansas, however, Gardere flashes some of his old magic. Although he completes just 15 of 24 passes against the Razorbacks, he is 6 for 9 in the pivotal second half.

Walker, meanwhile, looks like the second coming of Lynn Swann. He catches passes over the middle, in traffic, off his fingertips, and even jukes safety Kirk Collins out of his cleats. He grabs five passes for 104 yards and looks as though he's poised to have a big season.

The fans sense that the whole team could finally have that kind of year. Few have budged or tried to escape the traffic. They chant "SEC, SEC, SEC," then break into the lyrics from Steam's number one hit song of 1971, "Nah nah nah nah, hey hey hey, good-bye." Sixty thousand are still around to sing "The Eyes of Texas" louder than it's been sung in years.

Texas coach David McWilliams, whose last seven wins were by an average of 6 points, is asked if he was trying to run up the score. He arches his eyebrows and says innocently, "I just haven't had much experience in this situation."

This year is showing signs of being different.

"All season, we needed to put somebody away. We'd forgotten how to do that," Oscar Giles says. "Arkansas was the first step. SMU will be the next. If we don't make the Cotton Bowl, it will be a disappointment. The Cotton is what we want."

10

Monday Night Football

Welcome to Monday night football, Cajun style.

It's almost 6:30 P.M. and Louisiana-bred Lynn Amedee is getting ready to hold court for more than a hundred of his rowdy friends at the Lakeview Cafe, a trendy Tex-Mex and seafood Austin restaurant west of downtown.

The seventy-five-minute talk show, a lead-in to KLBJ-AM's radio broadcast of "Monday Night Football," is being piped out from the main room to the overflow of fans out on the deck overlooking tranquil Lake Austin.

You wonder why they bother with the electronic amplification. Amedee's deep voice sounds as if it could carry halfway to Waco, or to College Station, where he helped put Texas A&M in three straight Cotton Bowls.

The roundish, big-jowled offensive coordinator is seated with hosts Bill Schoening and Ed Clements at a table near the fireplace in a room that resembles a large, lushly paneled den. The crowd facing the trio is pumped with the unexpected success of the Texas football team. So is Amedee. He gets his palm greased with about fifty bucks a week for being an entertainer, but it isn't the money that brings him to Lakeview each Monday. It's showtime.

Amedee doesn't so much answer callers' questions as bulldoze right through them, syntax be damned. Amedeese, they call his free-wheeling speech, in which this, that, and those become dis, dat, and dose. The "tendencies" that callers keep talking about—and that Amedee keeps insisting don't exist in his varied offense—come out sounding like one of the states where he's coached, Tennessee.

Of course, it's not just how Amedee says things that will have the *Washington Post*, of all papers, writing that he has one of the liveliest coach's call-in shows in the country.

It's what he says. A year ago a caller challenged, "It's fourth-and-goal at the eight, what do you do?"

"Shit, I don't know," Amedee replied on the air with the benefit of a few of his beloved Buds. "You make the call."

"You never know what he's going to say," says Schoening, who does the remote show without the aid of the seven-second delay button they have in the studio. "He doesn't just talk about football. He's always talking about Cajun food and when the Bud Girls come in, he always pretends to lose his train of thought and starts flirting with them."

Tonight's hot topic is freshman running back Butch Hadnot, Amedee's prized "pup," which is what he calls his young football players.

"If I liked boys, if I was that kind of guy, I'd like Butch," he says and keeps right on talking before listeners even have a chance to wonder, What did he say?

Amedee's enthusiasm for Hadnot, however, is semi-understandable. You could put a bag over Hadnot's head and still recognize him coming up the small incline to the Texas training and dressing room. As long as he was wearing shorts, revealing his huge thighs, that is.

Hadnot's legs carried Texas to the Sooner-stunning win over Oklahoma when he was brought in for the final drive. He showed more promise against Arkansas, picking up 52 yards and a touchdown in 12 carries. A baby bull, Amedee calls the 6-foot-2, 210-pound rookie.

That, and the missing piece to his offensive puzzle. To be able to do dis and dat in his balanced offense, Amedee needs a quarterback who can zip the out pattern to the sideline and a big, mobile tight end. He also has to have a power back, one who can neutralize linebackers, who in turn become more concerned with him than with those sleek wide receivers tiptoeing through the middle.

"We couldn't even run the sweep last year," Amedee says. "Chris Samuels, we hammered on him. We benched him because he wasn't tough enough. Phil Brown's good, but he's not the answer."

With Hadnot around, Amedee is able to make better use of a much-improved Samuels as a punt and kick returner and a slashing runner on sprints and draws.

"So how do you think Hadnot is coming around?" a talk show caller inquires.

"Butch Hadnot has handled this situation very maturity-ly . . .

maturity . . . mat . . . how many beers have I had?" Amedee shrugs off the fumble with a booming laugh.

Just three, but who's counting? At the commercial break, he raises his Budweiser and salutes the crowd. Then, he turns to the show's hosts and asks, "What was the word I was trying to think of? Maturity?"

No matter. At that, the forty-eight-year-old coach with the touch of white intruding around his temples asks the whereabouts of the local Bud Girls, who are absent on this night. Amedee is feeling no pain, and why should he? The Longhorns are 4–1 and have just climbed to number thirteen in the nation in the volatile AP poll. Eight Top 25 teams were beaten over the weekend, and two others suffered ties.

Could we be talking Texas's first national championship in two decades?

"It might not be out of the question," David McWilliams had said in his office the day before.

Amedee has been as responsible for the rise of Texas as any of McWilliams's assistants, even though his offense was ranked dead last in the league before the Arkansas game because of Texas's tough nonconference schedule. Lord knows Amedee has gone to great lengths to learn about offense.

His resume includes one high school post, ten college stops, one NFL job, and a stop in the now defunct World Football League. As for houses, he says, "My wife Judy is a heckuva real estate agent." Best he can remember, his wife of twenty-nine years currently has him paying on only two mortgages.

He coached in professional football for a pair of one-year stints. There was a two-year disaster as head coach at Division I-AA Tennessee Martin. "A glorified high school job," he calls it now that it has become a good trivia question on his radio show, one that lets the old quarterback show off his arm by slinging a free T-shirt to the man who provides the winning answer.

For the large majority of his career, however, Amedee has been an assistant coach in college. An assistant coach with a head coach's mentality, drive, ego, and charisma.

He's paid his dues. And he's picked up a little something at every stop.

In his three years of Canadian ball at Edmonton, where he played with Jim Finks, now general manager of the New Orleans Saints, Amedee gleaned the motion offense that came with that league's wider, longer field and use of twelve players. He jumped to the National Football League for a season with J. D. Roberts and the New Orleans Saints. The Saints went marching out with a 2–11–1 record, and so did Amedee and Roberts.

From there, he joined Jack Gotta in the World Football League in 1974. The staff took Birmingham to a 19–5 record and a championship win over Jack Pardee's Chicago club. For their efforts, the coaches didn't get paid for six months. No worry. Amedee says Gotta was offered the Chicago Bears job but turned it down, secure in the knowledge that Birmingham would become an NFL expansion franchise. It's still waiting. In July 1975, the WFL folded.

"We were totally out," Amedee now can say with a laugh. "My wife really liked pro football then."

Charlie McClendon called from Louisiana State, and Amedee went home to Louisiana. Lynn Amedee had played alongside the eventual Mr. LSU, Billy Cannon, at Istrouma High in Baton Rouge, Louisiana's answer to Texas high school powerhouse Odessa Permian. Fourteen players from Amedee's state-championship team, including Roy Winston of Minnesota Vikings fame, went on to play for major colleges.

From McClendon, the winningest coach in LSU history, Amedee learned the art of organization. He hasn't forgotten McClendon's meticulous practice schedules. Or the pressure.

Midway through his third season at LSU, the Tigers were losing 21–7 at the half to 13-point underdog Ole Miss. Star running back Charles Alexander had 16 yards rushing on 14 carries when Amedee headed for the locker room.

"We rode the stadium elevator down, and when we got to the bottom, the governor of the state was there," Amedee says. "He asks, 'How's it going, Lynn?' I said, 'Pretty tough.' He said, 'I'll tell you how tough it's goin'. If y'all lose, y'all are fired.' "

McClendon wasn't any happier.

"If we don't start throwing the football," he warned Amedee, "your ass is fired."

Replied Amedee, "Charlie, I got news for you. If we lose this game, we're all gone."

LSU rallied to win, but a year later, McClendon did get the axe, and Judy Amedee was back in the real estate business.

Johnny Majors brought the Amedees to Tennessee, where Lynn got a chance to work with receivers like Willie Gault and Anthony Hancock. In Knoxville, Amedee picked up the sprint draw and the veer, and learned more about how to get players who could really make those plays pop.

"Johnny Majors is probably the best recruiter I've ever been around," he says. "He doesn't forget a name."

Unfortunately, no athletic director seems to be able to remember Amedee's when he applies for a head coaching job, and that irks him.

After Tennessee beat Purdue in the 1979 Bluebonnet Bowl, Amedee seriously thought about leaving coaching and taking up with his second love. He lived next door to a vice-president of Budweiser, who offered him a job as a salesman.

"I really thought about getting out," Amedee says. "I really got frustrated and hey, I've been going with Budweiser longer than I've been going with Judy."

John Majors said, "Lynn, you love football too much. You'd miss it."

So he stuck with it and became a head coach at tiny Tennessee-Martin. While there, he learned mostly how to scrimp. There was no recruiting budget to speak of, no coaches' cars, no nothing. He was, however, schooled in the art of hiring and firing, budgeting, and scheduling—skills he still hopes to put to the test.

Ten years later, he's still looking. "I'll never, ever deny I want to be a head coach," he freely admits.

The few head coaching jobs that have come his way, however, he has rejected.

"I've turned Tulsa down once before . . . Iowa State," he says. "If it's a good school, especially if it's in the South somewhere, in a pretty good conference, then I'd like to take a shot at it."

He loses more in board rooms than he does on football fields. At Texas, he's shooting for a fourth trip to the Cotton Bowl in five seasons as a Southwest Conference offensive coordinator. At Texas A&M, where he helped to get the Aggies to Dallas on New Year's Day for three straight years, loyal friends still have him on a short list of potential successors to R. C. Slocum, should the Aggies start stumbling. Amedee is a bayou boy who doesn't burn bridges.

Still, he can't prop his feet on the biggest desk in an athletic department.

He lost out to Larry Smith for the Tulane job.

He lost out to Curley Hallman for the Southern Mississippi job.

He lost out to Jack Pardee for the Houston job.

He lost out in Lubbock to David McWilliams. "The Texas Tech deal really upset me," he says. "It was the week of the Texas game, and Jackie [Sherrill], he didn't hold me back, but he wouldn't let 'em talk to me."

He didn't argue when LSU, his alma mater, hired Bill Arnsparger off Don Shula's Miami Dolphins staff.

But when LSU rejected him for Mike Archer, he was miffed. Archer had been called a boy wonder, but Amedee was a proven home boy who'd been a star quarterback and kicker for the Tigers in the early '60s. He'd been chosen the Most Valuable Player in a 13–0 Cotton Bowl win over Texas in which David McWilliams was just another losing Longhorn.

Archer was already in trouble at LSU, while Amedee was beginning to enjoy his perks at Texas.

"If the LSU job comes open—but I don't believe it's going to come open," Amedee says. "Unless he loses the rest of his games, they'll give him another opportunity."

Amedee, meanwhile, has a job that most men would kill for. He's pulling down more than $100,000 at Texas, if you count his $78,000 salary and perks. He's playing enough rounds of golf at two prominent Austin country clubs that, as a long-off-the-tee six handicapper, he's considered the best golfer in the athletic department this side of the golf coach.

His radio show is dynamite for the radio station and the Lakeview Cafe. Monday used to be slow at Lakeview, but now fans are showing up as early as 4:30 to get a ringside seat.

But what is it? Why doesn't his phone ring from that Division I athletic director in a major conference?

Is it his drinking?

"One night Craig Helwig and a couple of other people from the Texas athletic department came to the show," Bill Schoening says. "They were just about wearing trench coats. It was like the SS. During a break, Amedee turned to me and said, 'They're spying on me.' He's pouring his Bud into a cup under the table. He calls it his orange juice."

"I don't have any DWIs," Amedee says in defense.

He's also a lunchtime jogger, extremely competent coach, and proven winner. Texas athletic director DeLoss Dodds fielded some calls from starched alums who thought Amedee wasn't up to the Texas image and then declared him part of Austin, where loving fun is every bit as valued as loving the university.

"I've got no NCAA problems," Amedee adds. He's been at A&M, which was socked with a two-year probation after he left for Florida. There, head coach Galen Hall ran into troubles, including allegations about $11,000 that Amedee was getting as supplemental income from a booster fund rather than from the athletic department—an NCAA no-no. But, officially, Amedee has a clean blotter with the NCAA, while head coach David McWilliams was once cited for making penny-ante loans to players when he was an assistant coach at Texas.

So what gives? "He tries too hard," says one Amedee friend. "He politicks for jobs instead of relaxing."

"Amedee could fit in with some of those huge egos at Texas," says an assistant coach at one Southwest Conference school. "At the coaching clinic in San Angelo one summer, somebody went up to Lynn and said, 'Hey, that's a good-looking pair of boots.' Lynn went, 'Yes, and I've got twenty-seven pair.' Well, who cares?"

Says a former Texas assistant coach, "Amedee thinks he'll be the next head coach at the University of Texas. I hate it for David."

Critics think Amedee oversells himself, comes on too strong. He's not humble enough, they say. Not everyone at Texas, outside his listening audience on KLBJ, has a love affair with the former Aggie. Some appreciate his entertaining offense, but wish he would be a little less flashy off the field. Others suggest he might make more rounds in recruiting and fewer in golf.

"My handicap is about fifteen if Jim Bob Moffett is listening," winks Amedee, referring to one of Texas's richest alumni.

More than anything, though, detractors say Amedee needs to remember his place.

"It's not Lynn Amedee's offense," says Pat Culpepper, McWilliams's former high school and college teammate. "It's David McWilliams representing all the exes of Texas."

"The old guard has nothing to do with Lynn," one longtime school official says. "Nothing is ever his fault, according to him. He is not very popular."

Even Darrell Royal, who rarely criticizes anybody, adds, "I read the papers, and I don't know if David's coaching or not."

That may reflect as much on McWilliams as it does Amedee. He certainly gives his top offensive aide enough latitude to operate on and off the field. It's the same kind of style that Amedee hopes to employ when he does get a head coaching job.

"There are coaches that call me every day hoping Lynn Amedee gets a job," he says. "We'll have a good staff. I've got guys that are pretty damn good coaches, that are around this country that know who I am, know how I am. They would like to be part of it. I'm an assistant coaches' coach. I let them coach. I don't take my job home with me. It's never been work."

Amedee brought his entertaining style to the Southwest Conference in 1985. In his second season in College Station, the Aggies, who'd been known as talented underachievers, became the first team in league history to average more than two hundred yards passing and two hundred yards rushing. Amedee ran the offense, although Jackie Sherrill's on-field interests lie exclusively in the same area.

"Jackie wouldn't call the plays," Amedee maintains. "All he wanted to do was holler. One time we were playing TCU at Kyle Field. We're driving, and we get flagged when Jackie walks onto the field to argue a call—he likes to intimidate officials. Anyway, he says on the headset, 'I think we got ourselves a penalty.' I said, 'I don't think there's any *we* in it.'

"I tell you what, I learned how to be a tough guy under Jackie. He likes to say, 'When all the alligators pop up, you'd better have a tough skin.' You learn what pressure is."

Like in 1989, Amedee's first season at Texas, when the Longhorns bogged down after electrifying wins over Oklahoma and Arkansas.

"The players griped about some of the things they were going through," Amedee says. "I told 'em, 'You hadn't had any pressure yet.' I said, 'You ever been fired by the governor of the state?' "

When Amedee has had talent to work with, there hasn't been that kind of pressure. At A&M he had Kevin Murray, the best quarterback in the Southwest Conference for two of Amedee's three seasons in College Station. Murray's reputation for being difficult to deal with was whispered as one reason no pro team drafted him after an outstanding college career. Amedee was Murray's biggest supporter. Amedee also had an all-star supporting case. Big backs like Anthony Toney and Roger Vick. Fast backs like Darren Lewis and Keith Woodside. A powerful tight end with speed in Rod Bernstine.

In 1989, his first season at Texas, Amedee had an underachieving offensive line and an inexperienced quarterback incapable of exploiting some of the best wide receivers in the nation in Tony Jones, now with the Houston Oilers, Johnny Walker, and the Cash twins.

"You wish that Tony Jones was back another year," Amedee says. "Last year we came in here and tried to do this stuff, and all of a sudden we couldn't get him the ball. I mean we had nobody to get him the dadgum football. Now, he'd probably catch a heckuva lot more."

So would Eric Metcalf, the darting scatback with hummingbird moves who left for the Cleveland Browns the year before Amedee arrived.

"I think Amedee's style really could have exploited Eric's talents," says former Texas quarterback Bret Stafford.

Amedee doesn't have anyone with the explosiveness of Metcalf, but he has much better depth than Texas had in 1988. The emergence of Hadnot and Phil Brown, coupled with the speed and cutting ability of Adrian Walker and Samuels, excites him. For Arkansas, Texas switched from a one-back set to a two-back set and pounded the Razorbacks into submission.

Only at quarterback is Amedee less than satisfied, and he is intent on improving Gardere if it kills him. Kills Gardere, that is. Although he didn't make it public at the time, Amedee twice considered pulling Gardere in the Oklahoma game.

"Once early in the first half, we came close," he says, "and once early in the third quarter. I was going to go with Jimmy Saxton. I told Jimmy twice to get ready."

Gardere is hardly immune to Amedee's mood swings. An intensely emotional person, Amedee is the antithesis of Gardere, a calm, even-keeled personality who appears so subdued he could be on tranquilizers. During the Oklahoma game, Amedee became so upset with Gardere that, had the Texas offensive coordinator been on the sidelines where McWilliams originally wanted him, Gardere and Amedee might really have gone at it.

"I was really getting on him," Amedee says, almost proudly. "He was about to take the headsets off and I said, 'You take those headsets off, and I'll drill you.' He knew I was mad."

Some Texas school officials wondered if Amedee wasn't beating down Gardere, robbing him of the magical instincts he had demonstrated the year before. Amedee was convinced he was giving Gardere just what he needed.

"Lynn Amedee is probably his worst critic," Pete Gardere says of his son, "and I'm probably his second worst. I think his relationship, what Lynn has taught him, has worked very well. Lynn does become negative sometimes and he's very hard on him. It's kind of like having a nagging wife. You heard it once, you don't have to hear it twenty times. But I think they have an understanding, a commitment that they're going to work together and make it work. When he's critical of Peter, Peter takes it as constructive criticism.

"A lot of stuff has been made about Peter being on the headphones and telling Lynn 'Shut up, let's get on with something else.' Lynn made that up. That's a big bunch of horse manure. But I think what happened is that Peter took the headset off before Lynn was through."

For all the stinging words his son has to put up with, Gardere Sr. would rather his son hear them from Amedee than someone else.

"I think he really knows offense," he says of Amedee. "I would hate like hell to lose him. I think he's very, very effective."

"It gets his attention," Amedee says of his one-sided shouting matches with Gardere. "It's not like I'm abusing him. I ain't doing that. I just belittle him sometimes. I rip him a little bit. But he understands where it comes from, and he can take that. Peter's a plugger because he doesn't have the great gun. He knows I'll get on him and ring his bell. A lot of quarterbacks can't handle that. You can destroy some egos. I couldn't do that with Kevin Murray. But Peter and Saxton, you can get on their case."

Craig Gatewood, the owner of Lakeview Cafe and an ardent Longhorns supporter, heard it for himself. Invited to watch the Arkansas game from the coaches' box in the press box, Gatewood came away with buffeted ears and an expanded vocabulary.

"He's in a world by himself," Gatewood says of Amedee. "He was screaming from start to finish. I haven't been able to hear since."

It's a small price. Business has picked up at his restaurant on Monday, a night so dead after big football weekends that a lot of restaurants close. Gatewood, in fact, even wanted KLBJ to switch to Wednesday nights, thinking the station would have a bigger response at midweek.

"It was like an echo chamber last year," Gatewood says as Amedee's voice booms in the background. "We'd get no more than twenty-five people in for the show. Now we're getting a ton of calls all day before the show."

They come to watch the entertainer. See him throw an orange spirit towel at one of the winners of the radio station's giveaway trivia quizzes. Listen to him barbecue the English language, Cajun style.

Gatewood interrupts the proceedings to offer Amedee some of his special Razorback red nachos—red chips with pork sausage. It isn't long before Amedee revs up again, though.

"Yeah, when I was coaching at the other school," Amedee says, using his pet name for the Aggies, Texas's top rival, "I always wrote down what happened in our staff meetings. Now Jackie [Sherrill] is one of those guys who talks faster than he thinks."

Another caller inquires about recruiting. Amedee says Texas's priorities will be offensive linemen, wide receivers, and a tight end from junior college. But especially wide receivers.

"We've had some four fours," Amedee says, referring to the receivers' 40-yard dash times. "I want a four one."

"I've dated some four ones," interjects Ed Clements, "and it's not pretty."

The crowd breaks up.

A few moments later, Amedee is off the air. A small child asks for an autograph. Amedee is still raving about Hadnot. "Butch Hadnot in four years can be as good a back as Texas has seen in a while. He can be big-time."

Can Amedee, a lifelong assistant?

A man in a business suit and a dark tie nods in Amedee's direction. "That guy right there is the best coach in the world," the admirer says. "Yes sir, the best coach in the world . . ."

11

Living Off the Land

After emotion-charged border wars against Oklahoma and Arkansas, Texas coach David McWilliams thinks he's looking at a breather in SMU.

SM-whew. The Mustangs have beaten just one Division 1-A team in the year and a half since they returned from the NCAA dead, and that was the scholar-athletes of Vanderbilt. The once mighty Mustangs, who were hit in 1987 with the first-ever NCAA death penalty for a host of recruiting violations, are now little more than a glorified jayvee team.

McWilliams's Longhorns, meanwhile, arc riding sky-high after mauling Arkansas. They've jumped to thirteenth in the nation, their highest ranking since 1984, when they occupied the number one spot early in the season.

Even the bad news doesn't seem all that bad. At first, anyway.

A week earlier, police searching Texas sophomore Alan Luther's Jeep during a routine traffic stop had found a syringe and a small vial of liquid labeled "epitestosterone." They let Luther go while they studied the matter.

Now, McWilliams gets word Luther has been arrested and charged with possession of a controlled substance.

Maybe it's okay. Luther's what, a third-string offensive tackle? No sweat. Luther, a Houston Kinkaid product, is no big name. He's simply . . .

The son of Homer L. Luther. Homer Luther is a visiting professor at the University of Texas, where he teaches a class on entrepreneurism. He's a contributing member of the Longhorn Foundation. He's also a former emissary to China who developed business ties with that nation during Ronald Reagan's administration.

This may not be that easy. Disciplining players at Texas, Fishbowl U., never is. Fred Akers found out the hard way six years ago and McWilliams, Akers's defensive coordinator at the time, remembers that lesson.

At midweek after a win over TCU in 1984, Texas's starting middle linebacker, Tony Edwards, was arrested long after curfew and charged with assaulting a police officer outside an Austin bar.

"Fred told us he had gotten an anonymous phone call from someone who said they were there and that Edwards was innocent," former Akers assistant Scott Conley, now at Arkansas, says. "That may have been when the players began to question the discipline."

Three days later, Edwards started at middle linebacker against Baylor. He wasn't enough help. Six Texas turnovers, including an interception returned for a touchdown, led to 21 points in the Bears's 24–10 upset of the sixth-ranked Longhorns in Waco.

When Texas returned to workouts to prepare for the Freedom Bowl almost three weeks later, Akers finally disciplined Edwards and the other curfew violators. He ran them after practice.

The Baylor loss and the 55–17 Freedom Bowl blowout loss to Iowa sent Texas on a downward spiral that lasted for the rest of the decade. Irate fans not only complained about the losing, but they harped about what they perceived as a lack of discipline.

"It wasn't tight supervision," says Donnie Little, the school's first black quarterback, who played under Akers. "You were your own person, pretty much. I remember Fred told the whole football team one time that we're not going to make that dorm a whorehouse. We were going to the Cotton Bowl one year, and we had snakes in the elevators. Everybody's stereos were jamming all during the night. It was like one big party over there when school was out. We were on top of the world.

"It's good in that you're responsible for your own actions. You've got to mature and grow up and get your ass to class. It was a coed dorm, so . . . it's not like girls were always sleeping in the dorm, but there were always females around. You find athletes; you find females. Some guys were shooting out porch lights with deer guns. Just about everybody had a gun to go hunting."

Not your tightest of reins, but Texas was winning.

"At the University of Texas, as long as you win, as long as you keep turning in the ten-and-twos and keep all the administrators in jewelry with conference championship rings, you can do whatever you want," says one offensive starter. "You can tear the dorm down. You can burn it down practically."

What was considered recreation in 1980 isn't all that different from the players' hobbies in 1990.

"Golf is pretty big over there with guys practicing their golf swings in the hallway," the starter adds. "They practice their driving there, too, so it's always good to kind of peek your head out to see if anything's flying your way. There's a little glass on the door leading to the stairwell, so if you can break the glass, then you're doing pretty good. Last year they turned the study lounge into a basketball court. We set up the chairs so we could watch the games. We had a little hoop de' doop contest.

"Guns? Yeah, I'd say many of the players have them in their rooms. One guy had an arsenal. The difference between Texas and OU is that Texas hasn't got caught."

Not that any college program is immune to discipline problems.

In '84 athletic director DeLoss Dodds did not intervene in the Tony Edwards affair but says, "On some discipline things Fred and I, I'm sure, didn't see things exactly the same. I also think steroids had a lot to do with the discipline side. I think steroids impact you emotionally. . . . Steroids were a problem back then, I think, for every school."

In the spring of 1989, the *Austin American-Statesman* reported that as many as twenty-five Texas football players had used steroids after 1986 and that some players continued to use them during the 1989 season. Then, as in the 1990 season, Texas had one of the most extensive, expensive drug-testing programs in college athletics. The players were all passing. Everything was fine, wasn't it?

McWilliams wants more facts before he rules on Luther.

The first test at the Texas Department of Public Safety Drug Lab indicates the vial contains testosterone, a controlled substance that is illegal without a doctor's prescription. A second test, however, later shows it contains not testosterone, but two-tenths of a gram of epi-testosterone, which is not listed as an illegal, controlled substance.

When McWilliams learns the results of the first test, the inaccurate one, he suspends Luther for breaking team rules.

Steroids are synthetic derivatives of the male hormone testosterone, which, when injected or ingested, allow athletes to develop muscle mass and strength more quickly during their weight training.

The often ugly side affects of the drug are mysterious and can be fatal. Acne. Hair loss. Shrunken testicles. Overly aggressive behavior. Maybe heart disease and liver cancer.

Meanwhile, experts tell Suzanne Halliburton of the *Austin American-Statesman* that epitestosterone is not available by prescription and has no medical use. The substance's primary use is as a masking agent for drug tests. Dr. William Taylor, a spokesman for the College of American Sports Medicine, who specializes in anabolic steroids, says an athlete can inject epitestosterone even an hour before a drug test and receive a negative result for steroids use.

Luther proclaims his innocence and insists he was given the prescription to treat lingering pain and inflammation from a shoulder operation he had more than a year before. Taylor tells Halliburton there's no medical use for epitestosterone and he has never heard of anyone using it for pain and inflammation. Luther, however, goes before his teammates to defend his use of epitestosterone. The Austin police drop all charges against Luther, who will be reinstated to the team in a week.

Steroids were a foreign substance to McWilliams, the player.

"I'd never heard of steroids," McWilliams says. "Maybe I was naive, but it was the mid-to-late seventies before I'd ever heard of steroids."

"This is not an epidemic," Dodds maintains. "We've tested the first and second team twice, and no one was positive."

The previous spring, however, some players said the steroid users at Texas referred to the practice as "living off the land." They said steroids were supplied by other players who occasionally sold the drugs to teammates. Underclassmen said they were told taking steroids "was the only way you'd play here."

They said teammates, most of them linemen, kept their steroids in open view on dresser tops and there was little attempt to hide them.

Dodds doesn't say the Texas football program has always been clean of steroids. In fact, he readily concedes that many college players, including Longhorn players, took them in the early '80s.

"It was just a given that kids were taking steroids," Dodds says. "I think there was heavy steroid use back then. I think it was big.

"It was kind of then that we were finding out what it was doing to kids. Shortening life expectancy. Liver problems. Those things, we were just learning about them. I think it was just then that everybody started reacting to them, too late, obviously. They haven't gone away today and they're just the tip of the iceberg with these growth hormones and all this stuff that's out there right now. The drug testing isn't keeping up with it."

Jeff Leiding, a linebacker at Texas from 1980 to 1983, said he took steroids in his three seasons with the Indianapolis Colts, but never in college. He witnessed Longhorn teammates taking them, though.

"It was there. When I was there, I would say it was isolated to the large-weight humans," says Leiding, who works for a food-service company in Kansas City. "From what I saw, I would probably say less than twenty percent of the players used them." Most of those, Leiding says, were linemen. Pills, syringes, you always knew just who went to the pharmacist. There were various doctors, various connections, you name it. Steroids weren't even brought up by the coaches. We were winning. Winning at all costs. Who cares?"

Former Longhorn and Lombardi Award winner Tony Degrate, from Snyder, was too small-town, West Texas naive to realize what steroids could do for aspiring linemen.

"I didn't understand why guys would go from real big to real small," Degrate says. "They'd be two hundred and seventy pounds during the season, and when the spring would roll around, they were two thirty. I asked guys how they would get so big, and they would just laugh. It was obvious. It was pretty prevalent back then. DeLoss was telling the truth."

In 1990, Dodds puts his faith in Texas's drug-testing policy, which was one of the first in the country and one of the best, according to Frank Uryasz, NCAA director of sports sciences. Texas is also a leader in demanding in game contracts that opponents test their athletes for drugs.

Steroids, according to Dodds, are under control in McWilliams's regime, as are the players.

"I don't think kids want to cross him," Dodds says. "That's one thing I've seen in David the last year. He's tough, strong."

Strong enough to suspend Luther quickly, decisively.

Some of SMU's undersized players, though, scoff at the steroid talk coming out of Austin. SMU quarterback Mike Romo reads Dodds's statements that steroids are no longer a problem. "Sure, humans grow that big naturally," he says, arching his eyebrows.

Griz Zimmermann, SMU's thirty-three-year-old strength and conditioning coach, saw little game-day action as a tight end at Michigan from 1981 to 1983, but he saw enough of Bo Schembechler that he and his Wolverine teammates knew steroids would not be tolerated.

He recalls, "When I was a freshman at Michigan, there was a rumor that a sophomore was taking steroids. He was off the team in two months. Bo wouldn't allow it. It's the same way here. If somebody tests positive, it's bye-bye time. It's not a part of our program and never will be.

"Bo prepared me for my interview down here," Zimmermann adds. "He told me Coach Gregg can be gruff. So I said, 'Right, he's just like you.' He says, 'Yeah, a real son of a bitch.' "

Vince Lombardi once called SMU alum Forrest Gregg, a perennial All-Pro tackle at Green Bay, the best player he'd ever coached. That was strong praise from a granite block of a man who'd coached Bart Starr, Paul Hornung, Jim Taylor, Willie Davis, and a host of other stars.

But now Gregg's making his first return to Texas's Memorial Stadium since he was a senior at SMU in 1955. A long, tall lineman from Birthright, Texas, Gregg had never even considered becoming a Longhorn. He never even crossed paths with a Texas recruiter.

"I guess they didn't think I was any good," says Gregg, a National Football League Hall of Famer. "When I was in school, I thought they [Longhorns] were arrogant."

The trench-tough, Packer-proud Gregg, who took the Cincinnati Bengals to a Super Bowl as a pro coach, was brought in from Green Bay to sandblast SMU's tarnished image and to find a way to win without cheating.

Back in the early 1980s days of Eric Dickerson and the Pony Express, SMU would just line up the best ball players it could buy and stuff it right down the throats of the big public schools like Texas.

After Linebacker David Stanley revealed to Channel 8 in Dallas in November 1986 that he received illegal payments from boosters, SMU was buried under an avalanche of NCAA violations. The most damning concerned a slush fund that slipped monthly cash payments to as many as thirteen SMU players in 1985. The Texas-size scandal reached all the way to Texas governor Bill Clements, who as chairman of the SMU Board of Directors told SMU athletic director Bob Hitch to gradually phase out "wind-down" payments to almost a dozen players rather than stop them immediately.

When the NCAA finally moved, SMU was suspended from football for a year. It was the first-ever "death penalty," sanctions put in place by the NCAA at a special convention in New Orleans. It was deserved, though, in that SMU had been one of the most penalized schools in NCAA history. One of the NCAA investigators on the case was Butch Worley, who now serves as an assistant athletic director at Texas.

The school opted to take the second year off just so it wouldn't have its red, white, and blue butts kicked all over the playing fields of SWC schools just dying to get even with SMU.

Texas certainly wouldn't mind repaying SMU for some of its 1980s extravagances that kept at least two Longhorn teams out of the Cotton Bowl.

"I can't imagine athletics being important enough that it can bring discredit to an institution of higher learning," says Roy Vaughan, executive director of the Ex-Students' Association at Texas. "I think what happened at SMU is absolutely tragic. I don't think it will ever happen here. One reason is they don't want to discredit the university. The other reason is the leadership.

"I think it's part of the culture. When TV revenue got so big, athletics had to either stay a part of the educational process or it would collapse and be a farm system for the pros. All the signs I've seen are very, very healthy. With the scandals at SMU, you think the whole outfit is rotten, but a lot of people care a lot about academics. If you can find one who doesn't, it's in the headlines. All you've got is a wart on a rhinoceros when you examine the whole process."

Of course, SMU backers protested that Texas has as many warts as they do, and is every bit as guilty of blind booster ambition. Former Mustang wide receiver Ron Morris, who admitted taking payments ranging from one thousand to ten thousand dollars, said Texas, Texas Tech, and TCU also paid him as a high school recruit.

In 1987 Texas was placed on probation for the third time—but the first time with sanctions—for thirty-eight rules violations. Only one was termed "significant" by the NCAA, and that was small cash payments and benefits given to Tony Degrate by a longtime family friend, who was also a Texas season ticket holder.

Several former Texas players, though, say the school's boosters helped them out from time to time during their careers.

"Texas is nowhere near SMU," says former Texas tight end Lawrence Sampleton, who played from 1978 to 1981. "No slush funds, no payments. I think if anything were to fall upon UT, it would be for basic necessities."

"It was very moderate," Jeff Leiding adds. "If you're grading it on a one to ten, a three. A two or three. As far as outright flashing of automobiles, credit cards, and gold chains, I'd say most of that came later on from sports agents. I don't think it necessarily came from within the UT system."

Donnie Little, the quarterback whose last year was 1981, says Texas exes would routinely buy him dinners. Leiding says the same.

"After late games, we'd be at Coco's or something, eating breakfast," Little says. "Some alum would recognize me and the next thing we knew, the whole deal was paid for. That happened to me a lot.

"But cash? Not much at all. I wish it would have," he adds, laughing.

"Most of what I received was from restaurants, bars," Leiding says. "I'd run a tab, and they'd say forget it, which isn't uncommon, I don't care where you go. As far as being handed cash, I could probably count 'em on three fingers on one hand when that happened. You're not talking hundreds and thousands of dollars, just overexuberant people when you're walking from the locker room back to the dorm. 'Here. Great game. Go out.' People I'd never even met before.

"Players were taken care of. I never saw any major things. You would wonder where certain things came from, or how this poor kid from West Texas continually would have money in his pocket. If a guy had three hundred bucks to take everybody out one night, shit, don't ask questions. Just go.

"That happened, but sugar daddy isn't a good term. Most of the guys that I knew who were involved in that had genuine guys who were concerned about them."

In town, living can be easy. Leiding says, "If beer cost a buck and a half, sometimes they'd only charge you fifty cents. Some people would cover their costs, some people would just say the hell with it, it was for guys who were playing."

Many of Texas's players sold their complimentary tickets. Little says the practice was widespread.

"That was the only way to survive, man," he says. "You'd do it on your own. Actually, it should be legal. It's unfair for everybody else. You'd have a friend, meet somebody, and have him sell 'em for you. It'd just depend on the game. If the game was big and the records were good, you could get anywhere from a hundred to two hundred dollars for your tickets if it was the OU game or if the Houston game had some significance. That's why they need to pay the kids."

Of course, there were other ways to make money.

In late October 1989, an obscure senior deep snapper Tal Elliott suddenly quit the team, citing "personal reasons." Not until three months later was it charged in stories in the *Austin American-Statesman* that Elliott had served as the team's bookie for betting on professional and college sports.

The Texas athletic department was told by the vice squad of the Austin police in late October that Elliott's name had surfaced frequently on betting slips seized by the police during raids on an off-campus bookmaking operation. Texas athletic director DeLoss Dodds said assistant athletic director Butch Worley investigated the matter in late October.

However, the name of a Longhorn baseball player also appeared on the betting slips, but he was never interviewed by Worley until February, *after* stories about Elliott appeared in the *Austin American-Statesman*, which was four months after Worley was given copies of the betting slips. As it turned out, the baseball player was not involved but merely had the same name as another Texas student who had placed bets.

There seemed little doubt that Elliott was handling bets of his teammates as well as Longhorn athletes in other sports in clear violation of NCAA rules. A teammate of Elliott's once confronted him about the gambling in 1989.

"I told him Florida got in trouble for this," the teammate told him. "He said, 'Yeah, I know. I've got to stop.' He'd bet on anything. He'd bet on pinochle."

One student manager who knew Elliott says the player "used to come in the locker room with money. He'd have it all wadded up, and he'd say, 'I've got to pay off some bets.' Usually, he'd take bets on NFL games, but he even had an over-under on how many people would get killed on Labor Day."

A former player says, "Tal was right next to my locker. I guess pretty much the whole team came up to him. I won't say specific names, but if you want to get to the nitty-gritty of it, pretty much everybody bet with Tal."

"Swimmers, basketball players, football players," another says, "they all bet with Tal."

On most occasions, the amounts wagered never exceeded $100, and some were as low as $2.

But Texas's own in-house investigation by Knox Nunnally, a former Longhorn football player, turned up little information, and no football players were ever suspended. Nunnally conceded that Elliott would not grant him an interview. Messages for Tal Elliott were left with Elliott's father by the authors, but Tal Elliott apparently declined to be interviewed for this book.

William Graham, a free safety at Texas from 1979 to 1981 who played for six years with the Detroit Lions, talks about sugar daddies.

"Nobody would confess it, but there were certain guys who would pop up with certain things," says Graham, who says an A&M booster during recruiting gave him six tickets to the Aggies' Bluebonnet Bowl and a hundred-dollar bill clipped to each. "Like in players' dorm rooms at Texas, they'd have the really nice televisions and the real nice stereos. They'd say, 'I got it from my summer job.' Yeah, right. It was understood. Everybody in a sense had a sugar daddy, but it wasn't always something you flaunted. If you needed to go home and had no money, there was a way to go home. There were certain people you could call.

"My senior year, when everything started to take off, people were approaching me with 'What do you want, what do you need?' I don't want anything. I don't need anything at this point. I was a little bit bitter. Oh, *now* you want to do something for me? What about when I was a freshman and sophomore? I'd been through the hard times."

In 1990, SMU is trying to get through the hard times it has brought on itself. It's also trying to low-key its preppy, fresh-starched image. President A. Kenneth Pye, who came to SMU by way of Duke and Georgetown, points out that Porsches and Mercedes are registered to fewer than 15 percent of the student body and faculty.

Hey, that's a start. Although its $15,504 rate for tuition and room and board brings SMU the bluest blood in Texas, almost 60 percent of the 8,798 enrolled receive some form of financial aid.

SMU adopted some of the nation's toughest admissions standards, which cost the school Dallas Skyline basketball superstar Larry Johnson. Any athlete who scores between the NCAA-eligibility minimum of 700 and 900 on the Scholastic Aptitude Test is considered a risk and must seek admission on a case-by-case basis.

The death penalty, academic restrictions—those are the long odds facing Gregg, who has decided to buck SMU's tailback tradition for the radical run-and-shoot, the same pitch-and-catch offense that brought Houston back from 1–10, the offense that has frustrated Texas's man-to-man defense.

Friday night the Texas players gather in the ballroom of the Doubletree Hotel in north Austin. The featured attraction is a clip specially prepared by team film-man Mike Arias, "Captain Video," as the freckle-faced redhead is called.

Arias shows highlights of the 1975 Pittsburgh Steelers, with Mean Joe Greene and the rest of the Steel Curtain splattering opponents. "Three-fourths of the players wanted to stay and see it again, so we did," Arias says. "Brian Jones wanted a copy of it."

Not everyone is having a good time, however. Lynn Amedee, Texas's offensive coordinator, stalks out of a meeting with his players.

"The coaches were upset because we had a horrible week," split end Johnny Walker says. "Me and Keith and Kerry Cash never practice that hard. It wasn't that we were overconfident. It's just that you don't have to sprint downfield a hundred times. We were horseplaying around. Some people think you have to have a game face on twenty-four hours a day. Some of us don't think that way.

"I think everybody's cocky, but it's a mature type of cockiness. In all honesty, you see the SMU game as a statistics game. You want to build up your stats."

SMU wide receiver Michael Bowen counters, "If we play error-free football, we *might* have a chance."

Maybe he's right. The Mustangs, who have only sixty-five scholarship players on the roster—thirty under the maximum allowed—led TCU 21–14 in the fourth quarter, before losing 42–21. The Mustangs fell to Houston by only 44–17. That sounds bad, but it's a 47-point improvement over the 1989 debacle. Maybe they do have a chance against an obviously flat Texas team.

For the first time all year, the Longhorns don't charge onto the field jumping, pointing, and yelling. There's no real effort to pump up the 65,128 fans. That's far under capacity but still 10,000 more fans than Texas averaged in 1989, when it ranked only twenty-fifth in the nation in attendance.

There's no real reason for Texas to consider this anything more than a glorified scrimmage against a Division I experiment.

A victory should be a lead-casket cinch over the team that suspended football for two years, except that SMU plays the run-and-shoot, which can cause trouble for the Longhorns.

The cloudless day feels hotter than the announced 72 degrees, and the wind snaps the stadium flags a little harder than the official reading of seven miles an hour when the 4–1 Longhorns take the field against the 1–5 SMU Mustangs.

Texas struggles in the first quarter but scores on Michael Pollak's 23-yard field goal. With just under four minutes left in the period, the Longhorns drive to the SMU 39, where they're staring at fourth down. Pollak, standing near McWilliams, wants the chance. Fifty-six yards is within his wind-aided range, he feels, and what better time to show some leg? It's early in the fight, but SMU is just a punching bag.

McWilliams says no. In comes Alex Waits for the punt.

No matter. Slowly, methodically, the Longhorns take control. Butch Hadnot's 7-yard run and Adrian Walker's 1-yard touchdown give Texas a 17–0 halftime lead.

Hadnot, gaining confidence and experience with every handoff, eventually rips off 97 yards and scores on a 65-yard option pitch from backup quarterback Jimmy Saxton. Nine Texas receivers catch a pass.

The Mustangs total a paltry 143 yards on 71 offensive plays, just barely a 2-yard average. Romo spends the day running for his life. He is sacked 8 times. It feels like 88.

"It was like drowning in an ocean of orange," he winces after completing just 11 of 29 passes. "It felt like I spent the whole day on my back. I could tell you what the cloud configurations looked like in the sky."

Romo really is dazed after a 52–3 Texas win. There wasn't a cloud in the sky. Or one on the horizon for a 5–1 Texas team looking like a Texas powerhouse straight out of the glory days of the 1960s.

12

The Suits

Hippies are hanging from the pecan and live oak trees across from his beloved football field, and Frank Erwin is pissed.

It's October 22, 1969, and Erwin, the most feared man ever to prowl the Texas campus from burnt-orange sunup to burnt-orange sundown, is surveying a construction site with plans to add a $15.6 million upper deck to Memorial Stadium. In Erwin's voracious mind, a street has to be altered, a creek has to be redirected, and some trees that have been growing in the wrong place for more than a hundred years have to be cut down.

No big deal.

Nothing to twist arms about over Scotch.

No need to call in any of the hundreds of political favors he's owed.

After all, Erwin is on Forty Acres of his own personalized turf. He's a lawyer and all-powerful member of the Board of Regents who will boast, Texas power-politics style, "Whatever you say anywhere on the University of Texas, you are saying on my territory. I've got your balls in the palm of my hand. If I don't like what you say, I'll squeeze. And if you don't shut up, I'll rip 'em off."

For all his bluster and his cold-hearted politicking, Erwin has never quite outgrown being the jock-sniffing undergraduate who wrote in his 1937 Texas yellbook, "A university is a benevolent association for the preservation of football."

He still thinks universities need football. But, damn it, they don't have to be benevolent. Not when a bunch of "dirty nuthins," as he'd dubbed student protesters a year ago when they got on his good buddy Lyndon Baines Johnson, are standing in the way of progress and a better football stadium.

The dirty nuthins are ringing the trees. They're climbing up in them, hanging on the branches, and yelling at the police. The police are scaling a 75-foot fire ladder borrowed from the fire department and using the front end of a bulldozer like an elevator to get up and yank the longhairs out of the trees. They're barely controlling what's threatening to turn into a riot.

Worse, there's a rumor that a court order is coming down to keep the trees in place. Erwin, a University of Texas Law School grad, wants none of the legal process. He grabs the construction foreman and tells him to get as many power saws as he can find.

According to researcher Deborah Bay, who wrote a doctoral thesis on Erwin's effects on higher education in Texas, Erwin then applauds as the stately trees fall with a sickening thud that rises over the chorus of chain saws. When the restraining order, sought by a group of students and faculty members, arrives forty-five minutes later, the tallest trees have already been reduced to stumps and scrap lumber for the Thanksgiving bonfire.

The carnage is worse than planned. "Unfortunately, there were some great trees with yellow ribbons around them to be saved," a longtime Texas official recalls. "But the kids took them off because they thought they had been designated to be cut down. So there was random whacking. Some of the trees we lost were hundreds of years old."

Later that night, according to Bay, after twenty-six tree-loving protesters had been arrested, Erwin sat in the Forty Acres Club drinking even more than his usual prodigious allotment of Cutty Sark Scotch. He hummed along to the jukebox as he played Frank Sinatra's "My Way" and Peggy Lee's "Is That All There Is?" over and over again.

Was Erwin—Frank Vermin to the protesters—having second thoughts?

"He loved that deal, he just loved it," says Nick Kralj, one of Erwin's closest friends. "The more shit he could get into, the better he liked it. He wasn't anti-environment, but he enjoyed the publicity. That was good at the time, dirty nuthins. He used that to his benefit. He'd go over to the legislature's budget board meetings and say, 'I'm the guy protecting our kids in the university from those communist dope dealers,' or whatever ploy he was using. There was Frank standing out there for what we thought was great in

Texas. But a lot of it was posturing because he had a pretty liberal philosophy.

"He knew what he was doing. He'd end up with the money and build some great monument over there. He used flattery, intimidation, any tool he could to get the money. His theory was that the university had a right to the money, and he wanted all of it. If you ever chronicled it, it's hundreds of millions of dollars that went to the university that he was directly responsible for. If he was selfish, he could have made a jillion dollars for himself with the connections he had."

Erwin was never just a "Suit," as faceless administrators at Texas now are called. He was The Chairman. He cruised campus in the ugliest car in Texas, a black Cadillac he had spray-painted screaming orange just to let campus radicals know they couldn't intimidate him into anonymity.

He could drink more than any man alive and proved it almost every day. "A quart would not get Frank drunk, it would take a quart and one-half," says Kralj, whose Quorum restaurant was Erwin's favorite hangout. "He had four Cutty's and sodas an hour and he'd go at it hard for eight hours. Sometimes, when we stayed up till five or six in the morning, he'd have fifty or sixty drinks.

"Some nights he'd say, 'Gimme all those tickets. Give me everybody's.' There'd be fifty to one hundred people in the restaurant and he'd pick up everybody's bill. Anybody that he thought could help the university, 'Gimme that ticket.' He ran the restaurant like it was his, and that was fine with me. He certainly was a drawing card."

Erwin even prepared his own wall map of the Middle East to help him hold court for legislators, lobbyists, and journalists at the Quorum. He stuck pins in at the major oil fields so that he could highlight them with a flashlight pen.

"The pacifists always irritated him," says Ray Mariotti, former *Austin American-Statesman* editor. "He kept trying to explain why we had to go kick the shit out of them over in the Middle East because they were going to cut off the Strait of Hormuz and we wouldn't have any oil. He could sit in his chair and point to various pins and show how the tankers couldn't get through. There could be thirty, forty people in that bar, and when Erwin decided he was giving an international lecture, everything stopped."

"He was always God, till he died," says Jones Ramsey, former sports information director for Texas.

That happened on October 1, 1980, when Erwin suffered a massive heart attack in Galveston. His funeral drew 2,000 to the Frank Erwin Special Events Center, where mourners sang "The Eyes of Texas" as though it were a dirge.

"I went to his funeral," says Darrell Royal, who had several serious turf battles with Erwin. "You can bet your ass if I didn't like him, I wouldn't have been at that funeral. I told him once, 'You know, there were times when I thought you were a real chickenshit and times when I thought you were a great guy, but if I had to grade you, I'd grade you a big plus.' I'm glad I told him, I really am. I did feel that way about him, and I think he felt the same way about me."

"Frank was never able to dominate Darrell like he wanted to," Kralj says. "He wanted to push a button and have Darrell jump, and Darrell wouldn't do that. Darrell had so many other powerful allies. He had a presence of his own. Frank admired him and liked him, but I think he resented the fact he couldn't tell him what to do.

"Of course, all you had to do was lose one quarter of one game and Frank would want to fire your ass. You were supposed to win all the games by thirty or forty points."

One of Royal and Erwin's biggest face-offs came after the 1974 Gator Bowl, when Auburn trounced the Longhorns 27–3.

"The team wasn't in shape," says J. Neils Thompson, a Texas professor of engineering who was also the president of the SWC then and chairman of the Athletics Council. "The proper atmosphere hadn't been set. Darrell's teams initially were fairly well disciplined, but he slacked off and he let that one get away from him. Frank was embarrassed by the show we put on. He went over there on our plane, but he didn't come back on it."

"Auburn kicked the shit out of us," Ramsey recalls. "That was one sorry game. They had split crews and Darrell said, 'The Southwest Conference officials, bless their hearts, busted a gut to help me out. But they couldn't overcome those bastards from the Southeastern Conference.'

"Those officials fought each other all during the game. They were throwing flags for spite. They have neutral crews now, probably because of that game. Frank was in the stands just talking. He was real loud, 'cause he didn't care who heard. He said—I don't know what he called Darrell—but he said he was going to get him fired. Edith (Royal's wife) hit the ceiling.

"After school started Darrell came into my office, the hair on his neck standing up like when Navy's Wayne Hardin said 'We're number one' before the Cotton Bowl. He wanted me to drive his car down to the Headliners Club. I dropped him off there and all he did on the way over was cuss Frank Erwin. He said, 'That pus-headed booze bastard isn't going to get me fired.' He met with some Board of Regents members who were in Austin. He got a ride back with someone else. The next time I saw him, I said, 'How'd it come out?' He said, 'I won. That sonofabitch is not going to get me fired.' "

Erwin didn't lose many battles or skirmishes in the twelve years he served on the Board of Regents. He was chairman for five years, but the title didn't really matter much. When he was on the board, he was the board.

"When his wife died, he married the university," says Robert Heard, publisher of *Inside Texas* and a former Associated Press correspondent. "He did a superb job of preparing himself. When he went to a regents' meeting, he knew everything on the agenda. If somebody objected or said, "Don't we need to do this?" he had the answers. He knew more about everything that was going on than anybody else, and he just dominated. He wanted to make Texas the greatest university in the world."

"He knew everything about the university from the tunnels underneath it to the top of the Tower," Kralj says. "He knew the history and the people. He'd enjoy talking to a professor about music as much as he'd enjoy talking about football, but he knew what people in Texas wanted to talk about in those days—money, power, politics, and football. He played politics the old-fashioned way."

"He acquired his influence over a period of time by doing favors for people," says Dr. Tom Morgan, a chemistry professor and former head of the Athletics Council at Texas. "He had little piles of power sitting all around him. There was a void that had to be filled, and he was capable of filling it. He was the ultimate inside person."

Erwin cultivated a political network that stretched all the way to the White House. With the help of Texas's huge oil-based monetary reserve called the Permanent University Fund, he was able to match funds to get all kinds of government monies for his beloved university.

While he was alive, Czar Erwin, as he was sometimes called, was hated by the progressive students. He was justifiably feared by academicians and administrators. Erwin, after all, liked to quote Machiavelli's advice to the Prince, "It is better to be feared than loved."

He was able to force out a rising academic star who was dean of Arts and Sciences at Texas, John Silber, who would become president of Boston University and then run for governor of Massachusetts.

In a state that loved hardball politics and its university, Erwin set the standard. "He was the benchmark that hasn't been matched," says one Texas administrator. He was called the Big Orange by fraternities. The regents honored him as "a man of many parts, all of which are orange."

When factions wanted something done at the university, they knew that he was the ultimate authority. A lot of Texans like that better than dealing with a de-personalized bureaucracy.

"It's harder and harder to do that," Morgan says of Erwin's flamboyant style. "Everyone is too visible. That's one of the reasons we don't see Frank Erwins today. He came out of an era where the regents were very politically active in the business of the university. Now we have such divergent groups that it's hard for anybody to have that kind of a dominant position."

"There is a void," says one longtime employee in the Texas athletic department. "No one is there exercising power. That's in the whole university. The monster grew so big that it doesn't have a head. No one wants to be in charge. We got rid of Long John and put Silver in charge."

After Erwin's death and without his fierce personal passion that once dictated how the university operated, money became a more important factor in decision making. The bottom line became the opening line, the final line, the only line.

"We can't buy a pencil without six requisitions," one Texas official moans. "We had to bid for jocks for the baseball team. One company got the bid for the mediums, and one got the bid for the larges. One company gets the jerseys and another got the bottoms. They say The Hill made them do it."

That may be a slight exaggeration, but sporting goods stores do submit itemized bids for different sizes of jocks.

The Hill is Texas slang for the administration. It's headed by the university president, Bill Cunningham, a former marketing professor who still holds the university's James L. Bayless Chair for Free Enterprise. Cunningham is a pleasant, sensitive individual who plays well in most gatherings, although his name wasn't on the original list of candidates for university president until Amarillo lawyer and former regent Wales Madden offered it. Cunningham was eventually picked for the job over serious-minded chemistry professor Gerhard Fonken—the faculty's favorite—on the weight of his more outgoing personality and his ability to pull in a buck. In three years he had increased the business school's endowment from $12 million to $32 million and the faculty chairs from seven to nineteen.

"He brings a combination of reality and capitalism to the university," says Donna Lopiano, Texas women's athletic director. "In good economic times, you could have an academician run the show. But in bad economic times, you'd better have a good business mind. Fonken is his academic ace. He oversees that side of it for him. It's like GM—it has a design department and a sales department."

Although Cunningham will occasionally show up at sporting events proudly sporting a ghastly orange tie, his B.A, M.B.A., and Ph.D. degrees are from Michigan State. He's known more as a supporter of women's athletics than he is of the men. His wife, Isabella, has served on the women's Athletics Council.

"I've known Bill since he was chairman of the marketing department, before he became dean of business," says Roy Vaughan, executive director of the Ex-Students' Association. "He's very positive, energetic, and hands-on. I don't care if it's a problem that's never been solved, that maybe never will be solved. He wants to grab hold of it, get all the information that's there and solve it. He's very, very open. That's probably the thing that's his Achilles' heel.

"He easily has attended more Texas Ex events than any other president, and I've been here through nine presidents. Cunningham's energy level, I don't think there are many people who can keep up with him. He has a breakfast meeting almost every morning at seven or earlier. He has at least one or two events every night, and they go to ten, ten-thirty. I've flown back in with him at midnight and been with him at a breakfast at seven the next morning many a time. He believes in what he's doing so strongly. When you work as hard as he's worked to try to solve some of the problems society hasn't solved yet, and you make some real strides forward, and you get burned, it has to hurt."

Under the meticulous Cunningham are The Suits, headed by athletic director DeLoss Dodds and the so-called Kansas Mafia. Doug Messer, the man with his hands on the athletic department purse strings, served at Kansas. Craig Helwig, who came from Kansas State, was in charge of the fund-raising operation, the Longhorn Foundation, before he left. And those were only two of the five assistant or associate athletic directors in an ever-burgeoning athletics department.

"We must have four administrators for every coach," one head coach grumbles. Sportswriter Mark Rosner noted that Texas has one of the nation's best weight rooms and one of its biggest "dead-weight rooms."

The Texas bureaucracy is compounded because, unlike most universities, Texas has a completely separate department for women's athletics. The women's programs, however, are partly funded by profits from the men's football and basketball programs.

When Erwin headed the Board of Regents, he pretty much ran the university. When Allan Shivers held that post, he had enough clout to completely cut the hugely popular Royal out of the process to name his successor. Now the regents are headed by . . . hey, just who is head of the board these days, anyway? Louis A. Beecherl, Jr., if you must know.

And how about those Big Cigars? That's what Texas's brassy, big-buck boosters were called in the days before Texas oil, real estate, and savings and loans all went belly-up and left them little more than glorified cigarillos.

Perhaps the wealthiest Texas booster is Nassar Al-Rashid, who has his name on the Texas weight room in the Neuhaus-Royal complex. Rashid flew Royal out for Rashid's wife's birthday party in Monte Carlo. According to Royal, he's currently building a $150 million yacht that will have a thirty-two-man crew. The University of Texas engineering grad is tied to big-time oil money. But it's Saudi oil. He's based in Riyadh and is more of a fan than a university politician.

"He always wants to talk about football," Royal says, "and I want to talk about the Middle East."

Now when Texas needs a favor, it's usually provided by just one man, Jim Bob Moffett, of New Orleans–based Freeport-McMoRan, one of the world's largest natural resources companies.

When there's wives and dignitaries to be flown to the Penn State game, it's Moffett who provides the jet. When the university needs to set up some kind of chair for additional income for coaches, Moffett is the Texas ex who steps forward.

And when the Longhorn Hall of Honor adds a member, it's Moffett who gets in and leaves a lot of more talented former Texas players wondering if a place in the Hall is up for sale.

"It makes you wonder what the hell is going on," Lombardi Award winner Tony DeGrate says. "I mean, who was Jim Bob Moffett?"

A product of a broken home, Moffett once sold dog food door to door in Houston. He's a former Texas football player and one-time teammate of McWilliams.

The nation's fifth-highest-paid CEO isn't a frustrated nonjock. He has a friendly agenda and isn't embittered or enraged by Texas losses. He knows what it's like to build. Moffett saw one Longhorn coach, Ed Price, hung in effigy after a 1–9 season in 1956, and he doesn't want to see such a sight again.

"You can't win with controversy, whether it's corporate America or athletics," Moffett preaches. "That breeds defeat. Unity breeds success. We lost that chemistry, that unity, and that led to our demise. Everyone has to rally around; we have to support the program.

"You don't want to lose your pride, but I'm not looking for us to win every year. If it's not an All-America season, no one will be upset."

Those used to be fighting words at Texas.

The history of meddlesome boosters and bureaucrats at Texas can be traced all the way back to H. J. Lutcher Stark, who served as a student manager of the 1910 team.

Stark practically lived on the Board of Regents, serving there from 1919 to 1945. He's unofficially credited with the scalps of three former Texas football coaches.

While Stark's passion was football, Erwin's interests were more wide-ranging.

"That's the thing people don't know about him," says Erwin friend Larry Temple in a deep bass drawl. "Yes, he was interested in athletics, but he was interested in a lot of things. He was a Phi Beta Kappa, even though he didn't go around flashing his key. That burnt orange Cadillac he used to drive wasn't really Frank. He was a Renaissance man, he was very knowledgeable about the opera and the symphony. When you went over to his house, he would have his stereo on full blast, like a kid today with a boom box, only it would be an opera."

His friends say he would have preferred the Performing Arts Center rather than the basketball arena be named for him. There was only one thing that Erwin liked better than sitting in his book-lined, paneled den and downing Cutty Sark to the strains of the masters.

That was being the master, the undisputed boss at Texas.

Former Texas history professor Joe Frantz wrote in *The Forty Acre Follies* that Erwin "never learned the difference between broad policy and daily operation. A regent set policy; Frank Erwin set policy . . . but he interfered in the president's office, in the deans' offices, in the chairmen's offices, in the professors' operations, and, for all I know, in the way the janitors mopped the floors."

Erwin grew up in the North Texas town of Waxahachie, where Frank Erwin, Sr., was elected county clerk of Ellis County in 1934. Texas's greatest athletic booster wasn't much of an athlete in high school. Instead, he was editor of the school paper and a trombone player who won a student conducting contest.

At Texas, the young Erwin became the ultimate frat rat, a Kappa Sigma who served as president of the Inter-Fraternity Council. Later he plugged young frats, like Kappa Sig and future Quorum club owner Nick Kralj, into his high-voltage political network.

Ben Barnes, the boy wonder of Texas politics who became Speaker of the House at the unheard of age of twenty-six, was Erwin's friend. John Connally, who was governor of Texas the day John Kennedy was shot, was the man who first got Erwin on the Board of Regents in 1963. LBJ, who brought the science of Texas-style arm-twisting to a new level when he became President, was an ally.

Erwin, who graduated from Texas's law school in 1948, was with the Austin firm of Hart, Brown and Sparks.

"I'd say the very best lawyer I ever knew was Jay Brown," Temple says. "He could do more things well—try lawsuits, draw up a contract, negotiate a deal, whatever—better than any lawyer I've ever seen. Jay Brown once told me the best lawyer he ever knew was Frank Erwin."

In 1954, Erwin married June Carr Houston, a vivacious, red-haired divorcee with two children.

"I really liked June," Darrell Royal says. "She was a jewel. She was as tough as he was, a courageous lady. She fought that cancer right up until the last. When she lost her hair, she just put that wig on and kept going. I got pissed off at Frank some times, but not at June."

"She had chemotherapy, radiation treatments, surgery, just every kind of bad thing that can happen to you when you have cancer," Kralj says. "I think that had a lot to do with his drinking, when he saw her suffer. He'd just get real drunk and cry about it.

"He always had a great love for the university, but I think he focused completely on that to distract himself from his unhappiness, his loss. It was almost an obsession. I'd say, Frank there are other things. 'Not for me,' he'd say."

June Erwin preferred that her husband concentrate on his law practice. After she died in 1967, however, Erwin spent most of his time on the university. He was able to feed that passion in part because of the university's extraordinary fund that changed the way the university looked at itself—and every other university in the world.

Governor Miriam Ferguson once said of the Texas campus, "To the average man who sees the miserable-looking buildings at the University, it would appear that the state is making an effort to store up hay instead of knowledge."

But in 1923, oil was discovered on a barren tract of West Texas land that had been set aside for the university. The prospects for this piece of real estate were so bleak that Texas A&M initially didn't concern itself with the parcel used to establish the Permanent University Fund. But after oil was struck, A&M scrambled to get in on the gusher. Texas tried to hang on to as much as possible, without calling the whole arrangement into question.

In 1931, Texas and A&M struck a deal that would give Texas two-thirds of the oil money while cutting A&M in for one-third. That cemented the hierarchy and the envy.

The fund, which could be tapped for buildings, was made to order for Erwin. He was the hard-driving force behind the upper deck expansion at Memorial Stadium. That project encountered more problems than just tree-loving longhairs.

"The architect screwed up the photo level," Jones Ramsey says. "Frank, he visited everything that was ever built. He slept at the stadium. He went walking up there one day after they'd finished the upper deck. The beams were in place and he couldn't see the other sideline because of those beams. He didn't say anything to me, but he went to that architect and—that architect died in about three weeks. He had a heart attack."

No one knows for sure if Erwin's wrath contributed to the architect's death, but . . .

Of the photo deck, Ramsey says, "That was an eighty-five-thousand-dollar goof. It would have been about a million these days. That's why they have that scoreboard on the track; that's for the Big Cigars on the ninth level."

J. Neils Thompson says the eighteen-inch girders that hang too low and block the view partly resulted from Erwin's near-impossible deadline, one that didn't allow for many checks. Instead of a photo deck, Texas uses the ninth floor for the well-heeled boosters and had to quickly add an impromptu photo deck underneath the press box.

There were other snafus on a project that had a $15.6 million price tag placed on it for public consumption.

"I forget what Frank said it really cost, but it was some obscene amount of money," Kralj says. "He chastised me, 'Don't ever mention that figure around people. They'll hang me if they know how much we spent there.' It was a hell of a lot of money."

Construction on other projects went a little smoother. Erwin pushed for the $33.8 million Super Drum for basketball and entertainment, for the $7.2 million Texas Swim Center, and for the $2.7 million Disch-Falk Field for baseball.

Baseball fans knew how important Erwin was. Texas's most boisterous contingent, the Wild Bunch, used to stand and toast, "Hey, Frank, it's the bottom of the fifth." Erwin, who was seated on the third-base side, would sometimes stand and tip his paper cup filled with the libation of the day.

"Most people believed that whatever happened around here, Frank did," Roy Vaughan says. "There has never been anybody of all the Texas exes, past, present, and maybe future, who loved the University of Texas any more than Frank Erwin. He didn't do things that hurt the university. But he did it in ways that sometimes hurt people. A lot of people thought Frank was all just bluff and bluster and raw power. He was an incredibly intelligent person, a man of high IQ.

"There was a controversy once over whether the outgoing or incoming governor should appoint a regent. He did a quick brief on that. It was about an inch thick. It went back to the founding of the state of Texas and all the regents who had been at the University of Texas. He did that in a matter of days."

In 1975, Erwin's second six-year term on the board was about to expire, and he realized that Governor Dolph Briscoe would not reappoint him. Board members, however, still wanted him handling their sensitive legislative programs, so they hired Erwin as the University of Texas system special counsel for $1 a year.

By the time Fred Akers was hired in late 1976, regents chairman and former governor of Texas Allan Shivers was running the show. Other than a deep passion for the university, the only thing Shivers and Erwin had in common was a love for power. Where Shivers was smoother than mink, Erwin was as subtle as a bulldozer.

Joe Frantz recalls the time the University of Southern California sent a delegation to talk with Texas officials about establishing a Richard M. Nixon presidential library on the Southern Cal campus. Frantz shepherded them around to the university administrators and then went to see Erwin, who convinced LBJ to put his library at Texas instead of his alma mater, Southwest Texas State.

"They wanted the library, but they didn't really want a museum," Frantz says. "Museums are expensive, they require expert staffing, and they cause parking and security problems. If they had to have a museum to have a library, they preferred to place the museum separately, perhaps twenty miles outside of Los Angeles."

Erwin offered his expert opinion on the complex matter.

"Goddamn," he began, "if you don't put a museum with that library, you don't have shit!"

Shivers had a different modus operandi.

"He was handsome," Frantz says. "Women swooned and men envied. Shivers could take care of you without even lifting an eyebrow. You'd probably never know how it happened. He could have cut me in eighty pieces and I never would have bled. I probably would have said, 'Thank you, Governor.' "

When Shivers was chairman of the board, Erwin was far enough out of power that he didn't even know who was going to be the next coach of his beloved football team. He still had some clout, however.

Darrell Royal, whom Erwin once wanted to fire, says, "What I agreed to resign with—and it was totally my proposal—was totally rejected by Frank Erwin. My proposal was much less than what I got. I was going to take three-quarters pay and be on a nine-month basis. He said no, that's not the way it's going to be. You're going to be full-time, and you're going to have a secretary and a nice office. He's the one that got me the office over in the LBJ Library. People think we were real big enemies, but I think Frank had a respect for me. I don't think he felt I was a nerd who didn't know how to handle the job."

"When we played Boston College in 1976, John Silber came to our party," Vaughan says. "One of the comments I can remember him making was, 'I really need a Frank Erwin on my board.' "

Since Erwin's death, however, Austin and its university have changed.

"It's a different town, a different time," Kralj says. "It was a lot wilder then. We did whatever we wanted, and we had a lot of fun. There was more drinking, fighting, and hellraising then.

"The university used to be more colorful, too. We had some good bullshit going on. It wasn't everybody always watching himself like they do now. 'Oh yes, but . . .' Frank would say, 'The hell with it. Fuck you.' It was real."

The landscape has changed.

The power in a faceless, corporate university has shifted from a singular person and a strong Athletics Council to a smooth athletic director and a more hands-on university president and his underlings.

"I'm afraid it's necessary," Frantz now says of the need for a more buttoned-down university.

But in 1983, he wrote, "As the corporate university takes over, individuality seems to be blanched out of the professors. With a few bright exceptions, professors resemble bright CPAs, bright loan officers or bright computer scientists. Gone is memorable freakishness, gone are anecdotes, gone are tales of monumental goofs and infernal rages and erratic behaviors that would spice life on a vital campus."

And in its place you've got Texas Inc.

13

Lubbock or Leave It

Dusk is descending on a Friday night in Lubbock. Jerry Stelter stands outside his house in the exclusive, staid neighborhood of Rushland Park, where many of his neighbors have lived for more than a decade. Stelter glances over at the still-vacant home next door, where David McWilliams lived during his one-year stay at Texas Tech.

"If he'd just thought for about thirty seconds, he could have made it so smooth, so cool," Stelter says. "It just seemed like they were rubbing it in your nose."

"After that, most of Lubbock wanted them to get gone quick and get out of their lives," wife Mary Kay adds.

Next door to the Stelters is the most visible evidence that the McWilliamses were ever in Lubbock, an empty ranch-style house with white trim and a shake roof.

"Go ahead, look inside, everyone else has," Stelter says.

In the front yard, floodlights are tucked under a couple of the lot's bigger trees. There's a basketball hoop at the back of a long driveway. A big, decked birdbath is in the back. The 5,400-square-foot house also has an island kitchen, and plenty of Mexican-style tile in the living room, kitchen, and den.

"They tore out carpeting—perfectly good carpeting—and put in that tile," Jerry Stelter says.

"I think that tile is the reason it hasn't sold," Mary Kay adds. "It gets cold here—a lot colder than it does in Austin."

Downright icy, as a matter of fact, when the natives are spurned.

When the McWilliamses arrived from Texas, Lubbock was as open to them as the West Texas plains. They were a picture-postcard family from the heart of Texas. David was an ex-football player who had yet to be aged by the demands of being head coach at the University of Texas. Cindy was blond, friendly, pretty, and a photographer who grew up in Abilene. She and David had been at Texas. They oozed the charisma of winners. Lubbock thought it had, at long last, found Camelot.

In Lubbock, winners usually leave and losers are likely to go 3–8 or worse. The town catches the reflection of the bright Friday night lights that burn in Odessa, Midland, and other football hotbeds in West Texas. But West Texas high school players win with heart and oil-field toughness, not with the size and speed of big-time college prospects. West Texas football is 130-pound cornerbacks and 180-pound linemen who hit as though they weigh half a hundred pounds more, knowing full well that playing high school football may be the most glamorous thing they do in their lives.

Worse, Lubbock isn't lively or diverse enough to attract many players from other parts. The town's streets are wide, but they roll up quick. When Texas freshman running back Butch Hadnot, whose cousin James Hadnot played for Tech, arrived for his recruiting visit as a high school senior, he decided, "It's so small, there's really nothing up there. Besides, it's too cold up there for me."

Imagine what players from Texas's big cities think. Hadnot is from Kirbyville, which is just a 3A school in a state that now has super 5A playoffs for teams that have outgrown the regular 5A classification.

In the heart of high school football territory, Texas Tech doesn't ache to be number one in the country or even in the Southwest Conference. After all, the school has never been to the Cotton Bowl as the SWC champion. Although it's one of the conference's state schools, Tech just wants to be respectable in football and have *Sports Illustrated* retract the article that called Tech the ugliest campus in America. That, and Tech wants to beat Texas in football every now and then.

McWilliams, who left his defensive coordinator's post at Texas to advance a career that had slowed along with the Longhorns' football fortunes, did that in the oddest of ways.

In 1986, his first and only Tech team was about to lose to Texas. That, as things turned out, would have made Texas coach Fred Akers very hard to fire after yet another winning season. With a win over Tech, Akers would have finished 6–5 instead of 5–6.

Without a win over Texas, McWilliams's first Tech team wouldn't have attracted much attention from the bowls, or maybe from any search committee if Akers were fired.

Fate, and John Hagy, intervened. Hagy's tough-guy attitude has taken him all the way to the NFL's Houston Oilers, where he's now a safety. Coming out of high school, however, he wasn't considered a real blue chip.

"I was turned down by Texas," Hagy says. "Fred said they didn't have a scholarship. I committed to Southwest Texas; I was ready to be a Bobcat. Coach Mac [then UT's defensive coordinator], he recruited me, he got me the scholarship to Texas."

Hagy was a starting defensive back for a 3–3 Texas team that went out to Lubbock in 1986 with a lot of pressure. "We were aware Fred's job was on the line that season," Hagy says. "But that never factored into our performance. We wanted to play as hard as ever.

"Tech was a weird game," he recalls. "I got a couple of penalties. I was getting clipped and said something to an official. I got a penalty—and then I got clipped again. I complained about it again, and I got another penalty. It's not as if I was being stupid. It was blatantly obvious that I was getting clipped. Fred was pretty understanding."

Hagy's penalties kept a Tech drive alive and allowed a McWilliams team that had suffered some embarrassing defeats early in the season—including a 61–11 debacle at Miami—to sneak off with a 23–21 win that had Tech fans spilling onto the field.

Little did they know that that one win would be essential in making McWilliams the leading candidate for the Texas job. When Texas fired Akers and started looking, Tech fans were worried.

They became downright livid when Cindy McWilliams arrived with David in Austin and flashed a spontaneous Hook 'em sign to the Texas boosters in the auditorium of the LBJ Library. They were back home in Austin! They didn't fully realize they'd never be able to call Lubbock home again.

McWilliams, at first, entertained the idea that he'd coach his 7–4 Tech team in the Independence Bowl. The players voted overwhelmingly not to have him. Lubbock was pissed that McWilliams had left it.

Texas recruiting coordinator James Blackwood recalls, "He took the job on a Friday, and we flew back up to Lubbock on Monday. We hid out in a hotel and flew back Tuesday morning. They wanted everybody gone. When we drove out to the airport Tuesday morning, we saw this huge billboard. It said, GOODBYE MAC, AND T TOO."

T Jones, the Tech athletic director who'd hired McWilliams, and a former Longhorn player and assistant himself, also felt Lubbock's chill.

"It felt like an Air Force mission to sneak McWilliams out of Lubbock," says former Texas manager Jim Shelly, who was a copilot on a booster's plane sent to airlift McWilliams out of Lubbock. "We go to the hotel to register, and Blackwood pulls out his credit card. The guy behind the counter says, 'Oh, you're from UT?'

"Yeah, we're doctors from the UT medical branch in Galveston," Blackwood ad-libbed.

"We got up at five-thirty in the morning, and David's father-in-law drove him to the Lubbock airport," Shelly says. "The whole atmosphere in Lubbock was really vicious."

The Stelters felt, there went the neighborhood. Or at least the neighbors.

"I think they called once," Mary Kay Stelter says of her former neighbors. "After they left for Texas, they never came back. Cindy stayed in a motel when she was here. She called a neighbor to go into her house and get a curling iron."

Tech fans complained that there was an unwritten agreement between conference schools not to hire away coaches. Texas athletic director DeLoss Dodds counters that there never was such an agreement, never will be.

Some Lubbock residents also quickly assumed McWilliams's one-year stint was a done deal as an apprenticeship for the head coaching job at Texas. All parties at Texas deny it; but even the closest neighbors of the McWilliams family were suspicious.

"When six or eight months passed and they hadn't put up drapes, we knew something was going on," Jerry Stelter says. "They spent a lot of money on the house and then they just quit. They never even put up drapes in the front."

"Cindy was kind of embarrassed," Mary Kay adds. "She said the drapes were on order. But not to have drapes? In this neighborhood?"

Jerry casts a glance at a yard that's cut short but full of bare spots and weeds and says, "I wish they'd sell this place; it's an eyesore. In the summer, a woodpecker knocked a hole in the roof and they had a swarm of bees in the attic. A big swarm, I mean hundreds of thousands of bees. They had to get an exterminator. They've cut the grass now, but it used to be high, and all the weed seeds used to blow into my yard."

Actually, McWilliams quietly sold the house a year earlier to

New Orleans lawyer John George Amato, general counsel of Freeport-McMoRan. That's the company headed by Jim Bob Moffett, McWilliams's old teammate and Texas's biggest booster. Amato said he was acting as an "agent" in the purchase but declined to reveal his client. The purchase never changed the for-sale status of the house, it was listed at $280,000.

When McWilliams first returned to Tech for the 1988 game, it was a big deal. A ramp at the stadium had to be covered so that fans couldn't pelt him with anything more than verbal abuse. There was a lot of that after a 33–32 Tech win.

As the 1990 game approaches, there's still some animosity in Lubbock. At breakfast Friday, DeLoss Dodds's waitress bad-mouths McWilliams and the whole Texas administration, unaware of whom she's serving.

Most of Lubbock, however, has mellowed. Tech supporters think they got the better part of the deal. When McWilliams bolted, good old boy defensive coordinator Spike Dykes was named head coach at Tech.

When he was beginning his nomadic coaching career, Dykes told his wife not to plant any trees. In barren Lubbock, where cotton is about the tallest thing growing, it looks as if everyone has followed Spike's advice.

Friday, Dykes would rather spin tales about the first time he coached against McWilliams than talk about his lean prospects in the coming Texas vs. Texas Tech game.

"I've known David since 1967," Spike drawls. "When he went to Abilene, I was the head coach at Big Spring. When we went down to play them, two moving vans were parked near the stadium, so I told my players, 'Men, every stick of furniture I own is in those vans. If Abilene beats us, those vans go east. If we win, me and my family can stay.'

"You know what? Those idiots believed me. We won that game. I've still got former players who come up to me and want to talk about that game. They're grown men, and they still haven't figured out I just made the whole thing up."

Dykes is now perfectly happy in Lubbock, where the sun shines most of the time. But when it doesn't—look out.

Out here they say that the only thing standing between Texas and Canada is some barbed wire fence.

That can't stop a cold front that plunges into town on a slate gray Saturday. At game time the temperature is a see-your-breath 43 degrees and the 24-mile-an-hour wind is merciless, especially when it gusts into the 30-mile-an-hour range.

At first, the Texas Tech fans try to shrug it off and tailgate the way they do in warmer sites like State College, Pennsylvania. They munch on fajitas as they stamp their feet and huddle around pickups—and more pickups. Suburbans, Broncos, and Cherokees—Lubbock must have more trucks than Montana.

To protect themselves against the biting cold, Tech fans have brought plaid wool stadium blankets, hooded sweatshirts, raincoats, and the heaviest jackets they can find. Inside the stadium, near a corner of the end zone, the Texas band has donned its bright orange rain slickers.

They're about the only ones who cheer the Texas football team, which enters to a chorus of heartfelt boos. When the Longhorns win the toss, the choice is easy. They want the biting wind, not the ball.

Texas kicker Michael Pollak gets one up in the frigid jet stream and it sails out of the end zone.

Tech strikes quickly, shockingly against the wind. On third-and-nine from the Tech 21, Tech quarterback Jamie Gill spots his favorite receiver, Rodney Blackshear, all by his lonesome over on the left side with Texas cornerback Willie Mack Garza, who has looked downright awful at times this season.

Garza tries to jam Blackshear, but can't keep him from sliding past to catch Gill's floater at the 50. Garza slips trying to catch up, and is lucky he doesn't pull a hamstring trying to catch Blackshear, who pulls away for a 79-yard touchdown.

Only 54 seconds have elapsed, and already Texas is down 7–0 in a wind-whipped game that has Tech fans chattering about an upset. After all, it was Tech that ruined Texas's season right in Austin in 1989. That's when cornerback Paul Behrman took flanker Anthony Manyweather's fake and stunned his own coaches and teammates by coming up on a third-and-twenty-six from the Tech 35. The result was a 65-yard Manyweather fourth-quarter touchdown that put Tech ahead to stay in a game it won 24–17.

Tech's opening touchdown provides the same kind of jolt and a chance for the huddled Tech fans to get into the frigid game. Texas quarterback Peter Gardere does little to silence the crowd. The wind is behind him, but Gardere misses his first six passes in a quarter where the teams do little more than exchange punts.

It ends 7–0 and Texas, outgained 145–35 in the first quarter, now has to head into the wind.

Texas coach David McWilliams shakes hands with Penn State coach Joe Paterno after Texas's season-opening win. *(Photo by Susan Allen Camp)*

Middle linebacker Brian Jones wears a reminder of the team's goal. *(Photo by Smiley N. Pool*, Austin American-Statesman*)*

Texas legends Earl Campbell and Darrell Royal. *(Photo by Larry Pierce)*

Offensive coordinator Lynn Amedee (center) shares a laugh with KLBJ radio personalities Bill Schoenig and Ed Clements. *(Photo by Ralph Barrera, Austin American-Statesman)*

Receiver Johnny Walker makes a diving catch against Texas Christian. *(Photo by Smiley N. Pool*, Austin American-Statesman*)*

Walker goes high for a pass against Colorado. *(Photo by Susan Allen Camp)*

Texas's Alex Waits prepares to punt against Rice. *(Photo by Susan Allen Camp)*

Safety Stanley Richard delivers a high, hard tackle against Texas A&M. *(Photo by Smiley N. Pool, Austin American-Statesman)*

Texas students camp out for tickets to the Texas A&M game. *(Photo by Ralph Barrera, Austin American-Statesman)*

Tight end Kerry Cash one-hands a touchdown pass against Oklahoma. *(Photo by Smiley N. Pool, Austin American-Statesman)*

Texas running back Phil Brown (29) swivels through the Colorado defense. *(Photo by Larry Pierce)*

Texas athletic director DeLoss Dodds. (Photo by Larry Murphy, courtesy of the News and Information Service, University of Texas at Austin)

"The Chairman," Frank Erwin. (Photo by Frank Armstrong, courtesy of the News and Information Service, University of Texas at Austin)

Safety Lance Gunn and cornerback Mark Berry team up on a receiver. *(Photo by Smiley N. Pool*, Austin American-Statesman*)*

Texas running back Phil Brown (29) hurdles for a gain against Oklahoma. *(Photo by Larry Pierce)*

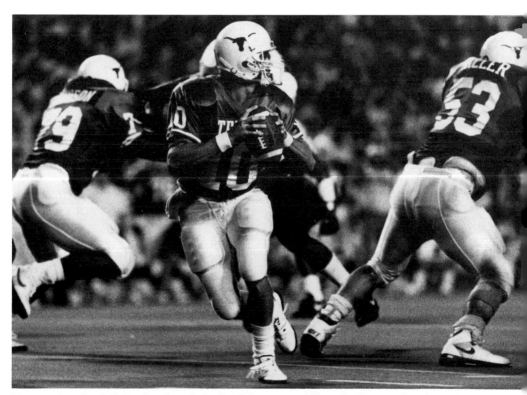

Texas quarterback Peter Gardere fades back for a pass. *(Photo by Susan Allen Camp)*

Texas fans whoop it up. *(Photo by Smiley N. Pool,* Austin American-Statesman*)*

Texas cheerleaders form a pyramid. *(Photo by Larry Pierce)*

Texas defensive tackle Tommy Jeter (99) and defensive end Shane Dronett (81) are pointing for the Cotton Bowl after a win over Baylor. *(Photo by Susan Allen Camp)*

All-American safety Stanley Richard (18) celebrates a Cotton Bowl-clinching win over Baylor. *(Photo by Susan Allen Camp)*

Texas kicker Michael Pollak accepts congratulations. *(Photo by Susan Allen Camp)*

Texas quarterback Peter Gardere (10), coach David McWilliams, receiver Johnny Walker (1) and receiver Keith Cash (11) watch contentedly as the clock ticks down against Houston. *(Photo by Susan Allen Camp)*

"Inside Texas" publisher Robert Heard (far right) listens to Texas offensive coordinator Lynn Amedee (nearest door). *(Photo courtesy of University of Texas sports information department)*

Texas running back Butch Hadnot (40) breaks loose against Texas Tech. *(Photo courtesy of University of Texas sports information department)*

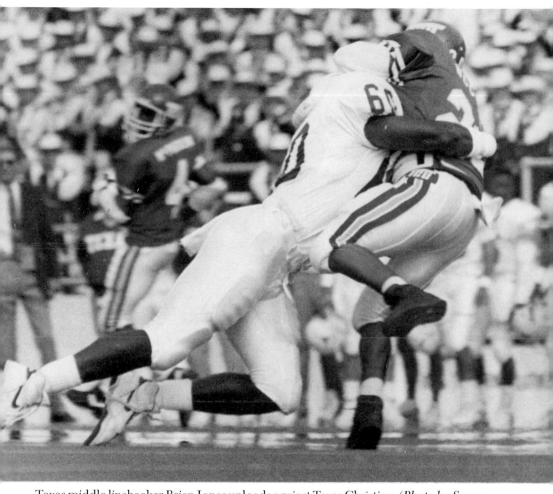

Texas middle linebacker Brian Jones unloads against Texas Christian. *(Photo by Susan Allen Camp)*

Texas players give the Hook 'em sign. *(Photo by Susan Allen Camp)*

On its first drive of the second quarter, Texas takes over first-and-ten at its own 33. The ball goes to running back Butch Hadnot, who is about as popular in Lubbock as McWilliams.

When Hadnot was a high school senior, it was reported that he was headed for Tech. He now says, "I said I was going to Texas. I told Texas that I was going to take my other visits."

Looking at Hadnot, it's hard to believe he wasn't recruited hard by every school in the country, or that he wasn't considered a Top 10 prospect in his own state.

Hadnot comes from a family with a history of severe kidney problems; both the grandmother who raised him and a cousin are on dialysis machines. Hadnot, however, has been an extraordinary physical specimen ever since he was a 6-foot, 180-pound sixth grader.

He has 10.5 sprinter's speed in the 100 meters and close to a 400-pound bench press. He gained 2,144 yards and scored 24 touchdowns in his senior year at Kirbyville, where he once carried 45 times in a single game. "That's a national record," Hadnot, a quiet, religious person, says without boasting.

As a freshman, Hadnot arrived at Texas so ripped that there are those who believe he could become the next Arnold Schwarzenegger if he so wished. The only problems with Hadnot were his scores on standardized admission tests. Rumors were that he was dyslexic. He denies them, because he's not. He took the test orally, critics say with a wink. Not so, Hadnot says. But what did happen? "The Lord opened the door," he says, somewhat cryptically. His academic schedule includes two developmental classes most would consider on a remedial level.

On the field, Hadnot has no problems. He just goes about his business, which in this case is ripping off a 22 yard gain.

"Can't anyone tackle that damn guy?" Dykes moans on the sidelines.

Texas quickly marches to the Texas Tech 9, but the third-and-two move Gardere pulls has Texas offensive coordinator Lynn Amedee hotter than Cajun food.

In Amedee's offense, on anything inside a third-and-three, the quarterback is supposed to do as he is told. No questions asked. No audibles called. Gardere looks over the bunched-up Tech defense and decides to check off the run. He has superglue-fingered receiver Johnny Walker isolated over on the right. He tries to hit him in the end zone.

Instead of lofting one up and letting the two-sport star make the play, he throws a flat pass that falls incomplete and leaves Texas with a fourth-and-two. When Hadnot is then buried for a 3-yard loss, the Longhorns slink meekly off the field with no points.

Amedee gets Gardere on the headphones and lets him have an earful. "Do what you're supposed to do on third-and-two!" he screams at his quarterback.

Amedee's fury quickly subsides when Tech quarterback Jamie Gill rolls right and has a pass intended for Anthony Manyweather picked off by Texas's hard-hitting safety, Stanley Richard.

Even after the break of the game, Gardere is still struggling. On his first play, from the Tech 43, he's sacked and almost fumbles. Then, on second down, he gets lucky. His pass for Walker is thrown right to Ronald Ferguson, who knocks it away, only to have the ball bounce off the Tech defensive back right into the hands of Walker for a 14-yard completion. From there, the Longhorns stuff it in to tie the score.

Near the end of the second quarter, Gill suffers a broken hand when he's sacked by Texas's emerging star at left defensive end, sophomore Shane Dronett. At 6-foot-6 and 258 pounds, Dronett was initially recruited as a tight end out of Bridge City in Orange, Texas.

Other Texas players call him 'Gator' because he's been on alligator hunts. He's also chased other Texas players around the dorm when a stun gun found its way into his hands. Some of his teammates think he's a little off-center. They respect that, because they also think he's gifted.

On the few times when the first teams went head-to-head, Dronett vs. Big Stan Thomas was the matchup in Texas scrimmages. The two even came to blows in one early practice.

Dronett isn't as strong as right defensive end Oscar Giles. He's probably not as fast. He just has the knack for football.

After Dronett's latest sack, the injured Gill leaves the game. His replacement, Robert Hall, completes his first pass for a 26-yard gain to Rodney Blackshear, but Richard forces him to fumble.

Texas is soon on Tech's 3 and Amedee is chanting anxiously into the headphones. "He's got Johnny Walker in the middle! Don't throw an interception!"

Instead, Gardere throws a touchdown to Kerry Cash to make it 14–7 just before the half ends.

It's so dark that the stadium lights have been turned on, even though most of the announced crowd of 50,276 fans have seen enough.

Tech's rallying cry for the year is "Tell Spike I'll be there." No one ever said for how long.

The cold was bad enough, but now it's drizzling. Even fans with rain ponchos and umbrellas beat a retreat to the nearest exit to watch what's left of the game on TV.

In the third quarter, the teams keep sparring in the rain. Tech hits a 35-yard field goal. Texas marches back and has a second-and-thirteen from the Tech 22 when Amedee calls on his baby bull, Hadnot.

Not everyone is convinced that Hadnot is Texas's next Heisman Trophy winner. When Darrell Royal is asked if Hadnot reminds him of Campbell, he says, "Nope. When Earl ran, the snot flew. I haven't seen any snot fly."

Maybe not, but when Hadnot slams off left tackle, he splatters tacklers for a 9-yard gain that has Amedee sounding like Officer Toody on the old "Car 54" TV series. "Oooh, oooh, oooh," he croons.

Now it's third-and-four and Texas is confused. "Goddamn it, fellas!" Amedee swears. Gardere is sacked trying to pass, and draws a flag as well. "What?" Amedee bellows through the press box walls. "They're going to call us for intentional grounding? What a horseshit call!"

The Longhorns settle for a 42-yard field goal that barefooted Michael Pollak kicks in the cold to put Texas up 17–10, but Amedee wanted the touchdown and wants to know how and why his quarterback was sacked on the crucial play.

"You got Samuels?" he says to the sidelines. "Let me talk to him. . . . Who'd you pick up?" he demands of running back Chris Samuels.

As the quarter winds down, Texas has a chance to up the lead. On third-and-goal from the Tech 8-yard line, Gardere hits Kerry Cash for a 7-yard gain.

It's fourth and a long one at the Tech 1. What will McWilliams do? "Field goal, Coach!" Amedee pleads. "Field goal, Coach. Don't call a time-out! It's a little over a yard. You've got to go for the field goal here. You can get it up to ten!"

Texas is hit with a 5-yard delay of game penalty while deciding what to do, but Pollak then nails a 23-yard field goal to make it 20–10, Texas.

So much for offense. The defenses are about to take over and wake up a sleeper of a game.

The Texas defense strikes first in the fourth quarter when slow-but-heady linebacker Boone Powell picks off a Robert Hall pass and rumbles 26 yards for a touchdown.

Later, down 27–10 and seemingly out of the game, Tech's Stephon Weatherspoon crashes in on Texas's Alex Waits as he's attempting a punt on fourth-and-ten from the Texas 31.

"I thought I could get it off," Waits says. "But he was a big guy, a quick guy, and he made a hell of a play. I tried to kick it around him. He just moved over and swatted it. He didn't just close his eyes and go up to block it. I think he made a helluva athletic play and got the punt."

Tech cornerback Scott Allen recovers and runs it in for a touchdown.

Texas safety Lance Gunn later answers with a 23-yard interception return as the score mounts to 34–16. Tech gets as close as 34–22, but when Hadnot busts a 5-yarder for the final score, it's Texas 41, Tech 22.

Hadnot finishes with 95 yards in 23 carries. Dronett records an unbelievable total of 5 sacks.

"I don't know what we've been feeding Gator," says middle linebacker Brian Jones, a former high school star in Lubbock who has a team-high 9 tackles. "Maybe he's been eating gators."

As the Longhorns savor the win, a Hail-with-Texas storm hits Lubbock. The marble-size hail makes an awful clatter in the empty stadium and covers the field with a thin layer of ice. It can get cold in Lubbock, but if you're from Texas, nothing beats leaving Lubbock with a win.

14

Strangers in the Night

Undefeated Houston is heading for Austin and the Big Run-and-Shootout with Texas. The Longhorn press release says, "You can date the beginning of the current Houston Cougar success run to a fateful night in the Astrodome in 1987. Texas was 4–3 and 3–0 in Southwest Conference play, and Houston and its new offense was a floundering 1–6 overall and 0–4 in Southwest Conference play. Texas took a 2-touchdown lead at 34–20 midway through the third quarter, and still had things under control at 34–29, when . . ."

Actually, things couldn't possibly have been farther out of control that week for Texas quarterback Bret Stafford, who ended up getting hurt in the 60–40 Houston win that was the turning point for a Cougar program struggling with its radical new offense and the effects of a two-year NCAA probation. Stafford's week was even more bizarre than the game, one of the wildest contests in NCAA history.

Stafford, Texas's all-time leading passer, is a snuff-dippin', dove-huntin' country boy from Belton, Texas. He relates his story as he outs the throttle of his loaded 75 mile an hour competitive bass boat that he stores near Lake Belton in central Texas.

"I've still got the last letter he wrote me," Stafford drawls. "It's signed 'Stranger in the Night.' I got it the night before they staged the rape. That happened on the Wednesday night before the game."

The rape? Stranger in the Night?

Stafford thinks his problem began three years before the 1987 Houston game.

"I started getting letters in my freshman year," he says. "The first

153

one was about three pages, and said he'd heard what type of person I was and the kind of character I displayed. I mean it just went on and on. I couldn't help but write this guy back and say I appreciated the letter. I usually did that when I got a nice letter.

"The first several letters were very nice. But when he started calling me, I could sense he was gay. He wouldn't sign his name to anything and I was real skeptical. I'd get letters two pages long, and one paragraph would be so sloppy you couldn't read it, and the next paragraph would be like a writer. I mean, the guy was psycho.

"He'd call me up at two in the morning crying. I'd hang up and unplug the phone. He said he graduated from UT and played sports. I imagine he was in his early thirties. We'd talk thirty minutes, an hour, an hour and a half. And I'd just sit there and listen. I have a hard time being rude to people. I guess that's just the way I was raised.

"He'd ask to go out and eat supper or something, but he knew I was engaged. I was real leery of going out.

"In my mind, I was wondering if this was some guy who was trying to get us in trouble with the NCAA because of all the money involved. He'd send a hundred-dollar bill every two weeks, or a fifty. It started after the third or fourth letter. He'd say, 'You and your buddies go out and have a good time.'

"We'd all like to say we have enough character that we would send back a hundred-dollar bill, but that's tough. You get a hundred-dollar bill, and no one can trace it. But it scared me. If I would have known the NCAA wouldn't have known, I would have kept the money. At that time, I was worried about somebody setting us up. He probably sent me about a thousand dollars. Sometimes it might be twenty, sometimes it might be fifty."

Stafford says he took the money over to the business office at the university, got a receipt and a cashier's check, and then mailed the check back to the post office box that was listed as the return address of his secret admirer.

He adds, "I kept the receipt, so if the NCAA . . . at the time, the NCAA was really hard on our tails."

Money wasn't all Stafford received.

"The guy would also send me Mickey Mouse statues, key chains, and candy," he says. "The guy was weird. I threw all that away. The last letter I got was signed 'Stranger in the Night.' "

That came on the Tuesday before the Houston game in 1987.

"Then the next night, about two-thirty in the morning, I'm awakened by a call from my girlfriend—at least I think it's my girlfriend. It sounds just like her to a T. She's crying. She says her apartment has just been robbed while she was studying in the lounge in her complex. They've spray-painted the walls and her clothes black.

"She said nobody was there. Then she said she was going to call the police on the other phone. While I was on the phone, a police operator clicks into my telephone line. So I start telling the police operator what's going on. Then my girlfriend comes back on the same line and says, 'There's somebody in the apartment with me.'

" 'Are you sure?'

" 'Yes, I see him in the other room.'

" 'Do whatever they say.'

" 'He's coming in my room!'

"Then, he starts raping her while I'm listening on the phone. I've got no salvation because I can't get to her before the police get there. Meanwhile, the police operator said, 'I understand what's going on. We have a police car en route. Stay in touch on the line in case I need more information.'

"I'm going crazy. While all of this is going on, we get disconnected. I call back my girlfriend—I think I'm calling her back. A guy answers the phone. I sit there and . . . what do you say? What are you doing to my girlfriend? He might kill her. I finally just asked if she was there.

" 'Fuck you.' he says.

"When he does that, I basically go into shock. I'm running, screaming, and yelling to my roommate, Rob McManis. I dial the operator. I'm talking to the operator and while I'm talking, I get a call waiting. I click over, and it's the police operator who's been helping me all this time. She says, 'We're going to kill you.'

"The police operator says that. Surely, it wasn't a police officer. But it sounded just like a dispatch. You could hear her talking to patrol cars.

"At that time, I realize it's a prank. So I try to call my girlfriend. It's now about three-thirty A.M. She answers the phone like nothing's happened. You can imagine what she thinks. I'm hysterical, I'm going crazy. After I finally calm down, I call an operator and tell her somebody has played a prank on me and that it was a police operator. She said, 'Sir, you're crazy.'

"I'm still very nervous because whoever did this, they now realize where my girlfriend lives and they know she's alone. That's because I told that police operator every detail about my girlfriend—her phone number, her address, how to get there. So I'm fighting time before they get there.

"I call her. We both call the police. Then, me and my roommate run out of the dorm to get my truck. It takes a while, but I finally get the UT police to let me in the parking lot at the stadium. Then I drive over to her place. The first time she heard the whole story was when I was explaining it to the police in her apartment."

Why did Stafford's first return call to his girlfriend go to an "intruder," while the second one was routinely routed to her apartment? How could the pranksters make it sound as though they were the police dispatcher?

"The police couldn't even figure it out, how the whole thing worked," Stafford says. "They think somebody got into my phone system. I'm sure the police thought I was on drugs and the phone operator thought I was spaced out. My girlfriend came back to the dorm with me about five A.M. She stayed there for a while and I didn't go to class that day. I went in and told John Mize, my coach, the next morning, because Mize and I are pretty close. He goes, 'This is worse than a Spielberg movie.' His eyes got real big. He says, 'You need to go talk to the police on campus.' They said, 'We'll put a trace on your phone.' Nothing came of it.

"I'm sure the guy that was writing me the letters was involved, because the letters stopped right after that. But I never met him, I don't even know what the guy looks like. He could be anyone. After that, I was walking around campus paranoid. People would recognize me, and if I didn't know them, I would stare at 'em, thinking, 'Don't look at me like that.' I'd stare 'em down."

Things didn't get any better for Stafford that week. Two days after his early-morning ordeal, he was face-to-face with the Houston Cougars, who were struggling to find an identity in 1987. Future Heisman Trophy winner Andre Ware hadn't even established himself as the quarterback; he was still alternating with David Dacus.

When Texas jumped out to a 24–20 halftime lead, it looked as though the Longhorns were in good shape. But Stafford recalls, "It was a nightmare. My elbow was injured."

Stafford hit 15 of 23 passes for 238 yards and 3 touchdowns in the half. He was heading for the best passing day in Texas history. "Bret played a good game until he got hurt," says Shannon Kelley, who replaced him for the second half. "Then came the onslaught. I set a school record for completions, twenty-three, and I only played one half. But I had three interceptions returned for touchdowns. It started to cave in, and it just got worse."

The Houston program had fallen so low that Texas fans outnumbered and outcheered Houston fans in the Astrodome that night. Until the fourth quarter, that is, when Texas fans quieted and then started to slink off in disbelief as the Cougars outscored the Longhorns 31–6 in the final quarter. Houston defensive back Johnny Jackson, who picked off a Stafford pass and turned it into a 31-yard touchdown in the first half, grabbed two more of Kelley's. He topped his 53-yard TD interception with a 97-yarder for the very next score—an NCAA record—to put Houston up 60–34 before Texas added a final way-too-late touchdown.

Houston, with just 13 first downs, scored 60 shocking points. Texas outgained Houston 601–352 in total yards, and lost by 20 points in a drawn-out night game that was one of the strangest ever played in NCAA history.

The Cougars' bizarre win over Texas was just the jump start their program needed. They didn't lose another game that year, winning two and tying one.

A year later, Houston, the school labeled Cougar High by its detractors, took apart the football team of The University with ridiculous ease, 66–15. In 1989, the 47–9 game wasn't much closer. A team that was 1–10 and all but out of major college football in 1986 had become the biggest, and potentially most embarrassing, challenge on the Texas schedule.

Since that wild game in 1987, the Cougars had become Texas's worst nightmare.

15

Law and a New Order

It's three days before the showdown with big, bad Houston, which is scoring points faster than John Jenkins can talk about why his undefeated team deserves to be number one in the nation. Texas defensive coordinator Leon Fuller, the man who has to come up with a way to stop the Cougars' dreaded run-and-shoot, is taking his lunch break in the office of Jim Fox.

Dr. Jim Fox.

Fuller has a much bigger problem than Jenkins's space-age offense, bigger than the critics who say his own man-to-man defense is outdated.

Leon Fuller has cancer.

Nothing major, Fuller told himself when he first heard the news from Dr. William Ramsdell fifteen days ago. But, hell, Fuller had just wanted Ramsdell, a dermatologist, to take a look at some growths on his neck, face, and arm. They weren't big and they weren't very bothersome. Then Ramsdell looked at them and his face wrinkled up.

He said he didn't like what he saw. He didn't elaborate.

A biopsy revealed that a patch of skin the size of a quarter on Fuller's neck was cancerous. It had to come off, which is why Fuller was seeing Fox, a plastic surgeon.

"Pam cheered me up," Fuller said of his wife of twenty-two years. "She told me, 'Only the good die young.' "

Reminded that he's fifty-two and not all that young, Fuller's face suddenly goes blank. He sighs, then laughs. "Hmm. I didn't think about that."

When Fuller learned he had cancer, Pam had calmly suggested that maybe it was time for him to look for an "inside job."

"What's that?" Fuller replied curiously. "Coaching basketball?"

Most of Fuller's fifty-two years have been spent playing or coaching football. After his parents separated when he was twelve, he was all but raised by Bum Phillips, the Nederland High School coach who later became the hugely popular coach of the Houston Oilers.

Recalls Fuller, "If you've ever been kicked in the rear by a pair of sharp-pointed cowboy boots, you'll know the difference between right and wrong."

Fuller, who weighed all of 126 pounds as a high school linebacker, picked up more than western-style discipline from Phillips. Bum was a proponent of the 4–3 defensive alignment that the driven, soft-spoken Fuller would eventually make the foundation of his coaching career.

As a 152-pound junior college transfer, Fuller talked his way into a scholarship at Alabama. He made his mark for the Crimson Tide when he was most valuable player of the 1960 Alabama team that played the Longhorns to a 3–3 tie in the Bluebonnet Bowl. Bear Bryant called him "the little man with the big heart."

Early in the 1990 season, Bum Phillips, guesting on an Austin radio talk show, went the Bear one better. Bum allowed that Fuller "was the best football player I ever had at any level."

Fuller beamed when he replayed a tape of Phillips's comments in front of his wife and youngest daughter, eleven-year-old Brooke. A puzzled Brooke walked over to her dad and asked, "You think he forgot that he coached Earl Campbell?"

Shortly after his playing days, Fuller began a coaching career that has lasted more than thirty years. He made whistle-stops at places like Oklahoma State and Kentucky until he finally landed the defensive coordinator's job at Wyoming. There, the star of young, positive, well-dressed head coach Fred Akers was rising fast.

After two years on the tundra, Fuller came with Akers to Texas and stayed for five largely glorious seasons.

Three times his defenses led the Southwest Conference. Twenty-one Longhorns who played on Fuller's Texas defenses, including defensive backs Jerry Gray and Johnnie Johnson, went on to National Football League careers.

"Coach Fuller was the greatest guy in the world as far as listening to his players," says former Texas safety William Graham, a former Detroit Lion. "That guy will take an average athlete and make him a good athlete. If he's a good athlete, he'll make him a great athlete, because he was so detailed about making sure you understood."

After the 1981 season, when Fuller's defense was the nation's second best, he left to become head coach at Colorado State. A great choice if you're a skier, a lousy choice if you're a Texas-bred football coach. Out of 104 Division I-A schools, CSU ranked 104th in terms of spending money on football, Fuller deadpans.

"We worked darn hard," says Sonny Lubick, Fuller's offensive coordinator, who now is the defensive coordinator at Miami. "I remember working on Easter Sunday. After a while, you get tired of beating your head against the wall."

In seven seasons, with the help of an involved booster network, Fuller built the school's first two weight rooms. Recruiting went well in his last two seasons.

There was, however, little success on the field. His last two seasons were both 1–10, and he never had a better record than 6–5. Finances were always tricky. "Our recruiting budget was not as big as UT's phone bill," he says.

Once, when Fuller and his staff were ready to go out recruiting, he was told by the athletic department there was no money. Fuller borrowed $5,000 from a local bank and doled out $750 to each assistant.

"Don't go so far that you can't get back," he advised. At Colorado State, his health deteriorated with his won-lost record. In his fourth year, Fuller's left arm would go completely numb during games. Finally, when he was persuaded to see a doctor, he learned it was stress—and his way of handling it.

While Texas offensive coordinator Lynn Amedee downs Bud Lights, flirts with the Bud Girls, and spins yarns on the radio, Leon Fuller is at his office, usually studying film.

Insecure by nature, he never thinks he's going to win a game. "He would just about have a nervous breakdown two weeks before every season," Pam Fuller says. "One day he walked out of the house, laid down his briefcase behind the Jaguar, and then backed out. He sent his briefcase flying fifty feet into the air. Papers were scattered everywhere."

Fuller got the axe after seven years at Colorado State when the school bought out the final year of his contract. The only thing good about his firing was its timing. Paul Jette, a former Longhorn defensive back, had stepped down as David McWilliams's defensive coordinator.

Despite Texas's mediocre record the previous three years, it was as if Fuller had never left. When he returned to his spacious office on the second floor of Bellmont Hall in January 1989, Fuller was jolted by what he saw.

There, sitting on the desk was an orange-and-white Longhorn figure made of taut telephone wire, the same figure that his then-eleven-year-old daughter, Kelly, had made for him almost a decade ago. In his haste to move to Colorado State after Texas's 14–12 win over Alabama in the 1982 Cotton Bowl, Fuller had neglected to pack it.

He opened the sliding cabinets against the wall and discovered all the game films he had left behind. He looked in the right drawer of the desk and found even more memorabilia he had left.

"It was the eeriest thing I've ever experienced," he says. "I mean, I'd been gone seven years, and they'd had two defensive coordinators in that office . . . it was like walking back in a time machine."

Leon and Pam Fuller moved back into their same house in Oak Hill in southwest Austin. On two occasions, renters had offered to buy the house from the Fullers, but Pam had told her husband, "When they throw you out of coaching, we're going back to that house to live."

Ken Dabbs, assistant athletic director at Texas, told him, "You come back. You get the same job, the same office, the same desk. You live in the same house. Hey, it was like we redshirted you for seven years."

In that span, however, the Southwest Conference had changed, mostly because of Houston, which started throwing the ball like crazy in a ground-bound conference where teams once paid top dollar for stud tailbacks.

Texas, led by Fuller's defense, had squeaked past Oklahoma, thrashed hapless Arkansas, and left Lubbock with a win over Texas Tech. But this is "Ha-Ha-Houston," as Amedee calls it in a voice trembling with mock fear. Amedee's offense will be facing six freshman starters and one of the weakest major college defenses on the planet. Fuller, however, is drawing David Klingler, Chuck Weatherspoon, and the real run-and-shoot. The one ranked first in the nation in passing, total offense—in about every category that would keep Fuller, or any other defensive coordinator, wide-eyed awake at nights.

And here Fuller is in a plastic surgeon's office getting a chunk of cancer scraped off his neck. Relatives asked him if he wanted to postpone the procedure a week. He had the growth removed over lunch and was back at practice that same Wednesday afternoon.

After all, when Houston comes to town, there's hardly a lunch hour to waste. The Cougars scare and frustrate everyone on the Texas coaching staff. Houston doesn't play real football, where players just line up and go at it.

"The Oklahoma game, that's played up the middle, between the hashmarks, in the trenches," Texas coach David McWilliams says. "You could close your eyes and know that Texas was playing Oklahoma just from the sound of the hits.

"The Houston game is played thirty yards downfield, on the sidelines. You might go the whole game and not see a real hard hit. It's like a track meet."

Oklahoma and Texas A&M might be able to beat Texas by outrecruiting the Longhorns. Houston flat embarrasses Texas with a better system.

The last three years the Cougars have beaten the Longhorns 60–40, 66–15, and 47–9 with the pass-happy offense that former coach Jack Pardee brought to a 1–10 team. Pardee's Cougars ran up a lot of those points behind Andre Ware, the 1989 Heisman Trophy quarterback. Texas had wanted Ware, too, and recruited him hard—to play defensive back.

Pro scouts think Klingler, Ware's successor, is even better. Houston's offense is so high-powered it scares Amedee, who doesn't even have to face it.

"The thing that you always worry about when you play Houston is that you'll go out there and try to do things that you don't normally do," Amedee says. "If you think you've got to score on every play, the rhythm of the game will get out of hand. We're a possession football team and we've got to stay within that. We've got to move the chains and take our time and not turn the ball over. We've got to be patient. Against this group, ten points is nothing."

Amedee has played and coached in the Cotton Bowl, coached in the WFL championship game, and knows what a big game feels like.

"This is Big Time," he says. "Here we've got a chance to win this son of a gun, and now we're gonna be in that Top Ten. I don't think the national championship is out of the question. Not if we win Saturday. All of a sudden, people better start looking out. You win the rest of them, you're ten and one and playing in the Cotton Bowl, and you're going to be in the top three or four. I've seen stranger things. It's not out of the picture."

When assistant athletic director Ken Dabbs comes to the office Friday, it's a cold, raw morning. Dabbs, who is in charge of the facilities, is fretting that the yardlines on the field need another paint job for the national TV cameras.

"I asked the band to stay off the field last night," Dabbs sighs. "Of course, they don't. I've got a national TV game out here with lines that look like something we had in high school in forty-nine."

Everybody's a little uptight. With good reason. This is as big as it gets. Big-time football, Craig Helwig would say.

On Saturday, 82,457 rowdy fans shoehorn themselves into Memorial Stadium on a gorgeous but chilly evening, the second largest crowd to attend a sporting event in the state's history. Scalpers outside the stadium are asking—and getting—as much as seventy-five dollars a pop.

Texas fans have not only turned out, but they've come to cheer. Longhorn supporters are notorious for arriving late, leaving early, and using their hands as seat cushions in between. Tonight, however, the noise rolls down in booming waves from the loudest crowd ever at Texas, one intent on disrupting the signals of Houston quarterback David Klingler.

The noise, however, can't stop the Cougars from talking a little trash to the Longhorns. In pregame warm-ups, Jamie Mouton, a sophomore cornerback, walks by. He used to be Peter Gardere's favorite target as a receiver at Houston Lee. Now he's playing in a decimated Houston secondary that will start two true freshmen and a junior walk-on.

"He was taunting us while we were stretching," Texas split end Johnny Walker says. "He was saying we weren't ready for them, that we shouldn't be on the same field with them."

"Last year we were intimidated," Texas linebacker Brian Jones concedes. "I know I didn't feel comfortable. Last year we were trying to put in some new defensive stuff."

The stuff other teams have tried in the 1990 season hasn't worked. The 8–0 Cougars are ranked third and have the best passing offense in the nation. Houston hasn't gone more than five consecutive *possessions* without scoring this year. In preseason, Houston's biggest problem was deciding which Heisman candidate to tout as a successor to Ware. Klingler had awesome potential, but built-like-a-manhole-cover running back Chuck Weatherspoon, who'd run for 379 yards in two previous games against Texas, was the player many opposing coaches feared most. Then there was Manny Hazard, who caught an ungodly 142 passes in 1989 to give Houston the NCAA's pass-receiving leader for the third year in a row.

Houston's offense, which uses only one running back, no tight end, and the four fastest receivers the team can find, has worked so well that Jenkins doesn't have to search for plays that work. Instead, he retools his offense by throwing out plays that don't work big. For the 1990 season, Jenkins has jettisoned the little behind-the-line, looks-like-a-hand off shovel pass to inside receivers that always seemed to be good for seven yards.

Seven yards? Jenkins thinks he's got a lot of plays that work better than that. Plays designed to go for touchdowns if all the X's react, as expected, to his O's.

For Fuller, whose man-to-man defense is geared to stuff the run, Houston has been the ultimate frustration. Everything he tried against the Cougars' pinball-productive run-and-shoot offense last year failed.

Before the 1990 season, there had been whispers even in the Texas athletic department that maybe Fuller had lost it, that maybe his revered 4–3 scheme had become outdated. It couldn't cope with Cougar High, as detractors call Houston, a commuter school that once held some night classes in a Houston high school.

Houston helped carve out its reputation with athletics, including its Phi Slama Jama basketball team and its football squad. The Cougars are number three in the nation in the Associated Press poll, despite being the only unbeaten title contender. Skeptical voters bring up Houston's probation status, received for illicit payments to players by previous Cougars head coach Bill Yeoman.

But for Houston, it's not hard to be humble; it's downright impossible. Athletic director Rudy Davalos says his only regret is that he doesn't have enough money to hire private detectives to tail all the "Simon pure voters" to check into *their* backgrounds. Nevertheless, Houston is on probation and ineligible to appear in a bowl game. Texas is Houston's de facto bowl game. If the Cougars can beat the Longhorns the way they have the past few years, Houston just might get its first national championship in football.

The run-and-shoot offense looks like X's and O's gone deranged, backyard football on AstroTurf. "It's organized recess, basketball on the turf," says former Texas A&M football coach Jackie Sherrill, who shows up at a Texas practice in midweek to do a piece for a Houston television station.

Sherrill knows that's a colorful oversimplification. Otherwise, Klingler wouldn't need to pore over the 370 pages of plays and alignments in the quarterback playbook.

The run-and-shoot begins with John Jenkins, Houston's thirty-eight-year-old offensive whiz kid who routinely runs up the score and shoots off his mouth about how his precious offense is unstoppable. Jenkins is a favorite of the press, but has few friends in the Southwest Conference coaching fraternity, some of whom talk privately about how they'd love to rub it in his boyish face.

But, who can blame Jenkins for his every-day-is-Christmas exuberance? His offense, which he honed as offensive coordinator of the Houston Gamblers under Jack Pardee, is the wishbone of the '90s. This season his Cougars have overcome every foreseeable defensive scheme from Texas A&M's bring-the-house blitz to Rice's three-man front, give-and-contain plan.

Jenkins is so engrossed in his tinkering that he is up by 4:15 to see what new plays he and Julian, the Houston custodian and only company he has for two hours, can come up with before sunrise. He keeps his files in his garage, which is wired with an alarm system.

"I bet I've thrown away more football than John Jenkins knows," Fuller scoffs. Pam Fuller, that is. Every scouting report her husband has ever drawn up, he has kept in boxes in the attic. When Leon is asked if he still has his high school game plans from Nederland, he sheepishly answers, "Yes, but I haven't looked for them lately."

Jenkins is even more obsessive. "Hey, if the third World War broke out in two-a-days, I wouldn't hear about it for two weeks," Jenkins, a Civil War history buff, says proudly.

This time around, Fuller is going to war with a different strategy. Texas will line up in a nickel package. Fuller will use regular strong safety Lance Gunn at free safety to roam the field and put free safety Stanley Richard on Manny Hazard. Cornerback Grady Cavness will shadow Tracy Good. The Longhorns will blitz early to rattle Klingler. The defensive line would then be counted on to wreak havoc, Fuller explains.

"Coach Fuller doesn't have to yell," Cavness says. "He can say it in a calm voice and it's stern."

Texas defensive backs, so often maligned a year ago, know it's their biggest test of the season. Klingler has thrown for 34 touchdowns with only 13 interceptions in 463 attempts. The Texas defensive backs come to Ted Gray, the new Longhorn equipment manager. They're looking for ways to discard equipment like out-of-fuel pilots ejecting cargo.

"The DBs wanted everything as light as we could possibly have because they figured they were going to be running all day," Gray says. "They wanted the little back thigh pads and knee pads and hip pads. We've got some real, real small ones, foam rubber knee pads and thigh pads."

Most of them want to wear the light Nike shoe called the Field General, the short, nubby-cleated ones that Texas's running backs wear on game day. Nike gives Texas 325 pairs of shoes at the beginning of the year, but had quit making the Field General in 1987. Gray scrounges around and comes up with as many pairs as he can.

Stanley Richard, the speedy Texas free safety, however, is more concerned about what he's going to wear on his chest. He raises eyebrows when he tells Al Carter of the *Houston Post* how he found a toy badge in his dorm room earlier in the season. Rarely at a loss for words, or tackles, the 6-2, 198-pound senior crowns himself "The Sheriff" and says he will restore law and order against the Houston Cougars. Jenkins makes a note at his Tuesday press luncheon and jokingly suggests that Houston will come in and try to gun down the sheriff.

"The more people talk shit about us," Texas offensive tackle Chuck Johnson says, "the more I enjoy beating the shit out of them."

When Texas game captains Johnny Walker, Oscar Giles, Kerry Cash, and Stanley Richard walk onto the field for the opening coin toss, the crowd is already roaring louder than a jet engine.

On Houston's opening possession, the Cougars' game plan is obvious. Throw deep. Texas's intentions are just as transparent. Fuller blitzes with one linebacker and sometimes two. Klingler's first pass on first down is a bomb, but it's too long. After a draw to Weatherspoon, Klingler fades back and unleashes another bomb down the opposite sideline, but cornerback Mark Berry is there for the interception. Unfortunately, he separates a shoulder on the play.

On Texas's opening series, quarterback Peter Gardere drills a pass to Jerry Parks, which the Houston cornerback catches and returns for 22 yards. When the Cougars take over, the Longhorns come with the blitz again. Houston moves to the Texas 8, but Klingler fumbles.

When Gardere loses the ball on a keeper the very next series for the game's fourth consecutive turnover, it's clear both teams are tighter than piano wire. Houston, though, clicks first. Klingler finds Hazard breaking free from Richard for a 23-yard touchdown pass. The Sheriff has been shot.

"That was a rocket," McWilliams says. "I was impressed. We use an all-out blitz, and he's throwing off his back foot, almost lying down, and he gets the ball down there with enough zip on it."

Texas backs off the blitz. Fuller turns the pass rush over to his front four: Giles, the senior defensive end with the 30-inch vertical leap. Shane Dronett, the sophomore at the other end who used to hunt alligators. The two junior tackles, Tommy Jeter, who blocked a field goal against Penn State, and James Patton. Patton is a 6-foot-3, 272-pounder who outgrew defensive end. Strength coach Dana LeDuc boasts that Patton can bench press 480 pounds and squat 585. "He's as strong as anyone we've ever had here," LeDuc says. "He's up there with Steve McMichael and Gene Chilton."

Behind the line's steady pressure on Klingler, Texas's defense stymies the Cougars. After the touchdown pass to Hazard, Houston loses the ball again when Jeter recovers a fumble.

Now, Texas's offense is at full throttle. Butch Hadnot, fast becoming the workhorse in Amedee's one-back attack, almost walks in from the 5 to score the tying touchdown. On the sideline, Amedee gets Gardere on the headset and chews him out. Gardere nods and says, "Yes, sir," before Amedee lets on he's only joking.

One series later, Adrian Walker dives over from the 2 to put Texas ahead 14–7.

After a Lance Gunn interception, the Longhorns are on the move again. Gardere finds Keith Cash for 42 yards to the Houston 38. Hadnot again finishes off the drive, scoring from a yard out for a 21–7 lead. The Cougars answer with a field goal, after Gardere's string of 10 straight completions is snapped.

He starts on another string. He rolls out of the pocket to the right and finds Keith Cash running free behind Jamie Mouton. Cash has to wait on the ball, but the play is good for 62 yards to the 4. Adrian Walker takes a pitch and tightropes the sideline for a touchdown and a 28–10 lead. The stadium explodes with noise.

At intermission, the Texas players scream at one another in an adrenaline rush. They're not just beating the nation's third-ranked team, they're kicking their butts.

McWilliams and his staff can't relax. They know how fast Houston—and Klingler—can strike. And Klingler's scrambling ability has amazed them.

"He really shocked me," McWilliams says. "A couple of times we had guys chasing him and couldn't catch him. I mean secondary guys. I was really surprised that they got away from all the dinky stuff underneath. If there's one thing we do well, it's stop the deep stuff."

Jenkins had hoped to hit Texas deep early to demoralize the Longhorns. Now, trailing by 18, he feels he *has* to go long.

Before he has the chance, Texas drives 71 yards for an 8-yard touchdown run by Hadnot, who almost knocks Houston cornerback Jerry Parks into the cheap seats.

"I was pumped," Hadnot says. "I was like a wild dog just let out of a cage. I hate to run around people. I like to punish people. I like to give licks, not take them."

The Cougars, meanwhile, are licking their wounds. Three possessions, three punts. They can't even make a first down in the third quarter. Chris Samuels scores from the 1, and then Pollak adds a field goal to open the fourth period and make it 45–10.

During a television time-out, Texas middle linebacker Brian Jones turns to Richard and says, "This is the reason you come to college. This is what I dreamed about, eighty thousand people cheering."

"I was telling everybody all week they were overrated," Johnny Walker says. "Watching them on film, I knew their defense was very, very weak. I think we could have put sixty points on the board."

"We beat them bad," Jones says. "I just wish we got eighty."

The Longhorns are pushing sixty late in the game when Gardere, attempting to sneak in from the 1, loses a fumble after a quick snap.

"I wanted that last touchdown," McWilliams says after a still sweet 45–24 win. "I won't lie. I wanted that fifty."

Why, he was asked.

"It was just a Houston thing," says McWilliams, who obviously has no regrets about running up the score on the Cougars. "Against them, you can never have enough points."

The crowd obviously couldn't get enough either. Thousands ring the field in the closing seconds as the fans in the north end build up like a storm cloud. Rick Hayes, a sportscaster for the local NBC affiliate, is jostled during his live newscast from the end zone and can't finish. One crazed fan leads a charge on the goalpost in the north end zone, only to have public-address announcer Wally Pryor say, "Will someone get that idiot down?"

Strength coach Dana LeDuc charges out to meet the crowd of two thousand, which is threatening goalposts that have never, ever been torn down at staid Memorial Stadium. McWilliams looks over and wonders, "What's Dana doing?"

Kicker Michael Pollak asks a few of his teammates if they're going to stick around on the field and sing "The Eyes of Texas."

"Fuck no, we're getting out of here," they reply.

With 24 seconds to play, hundreds of win-starved Texas fans race onto the field. Finally, when the clock runs out, Graylin Johnson and a teammate grab McWilliams and thrust him on their shoulders.

McWilliams can only wave to John Jenkins. Once down, McWilliams races for the locker room, jumping over one of the chairs set up in the south end zone to accommodate the overflow crowd.

"You couldn't walk, you had to kind of slide," Pollak says. "I was sandwiched, I had no control over where I was going to go; it was like being at a rock concert."

The Texas defensive backs had planned to sprint across the field and bow before Jenkins. But in the mob scene, only Grady Cavness and Van Malone make it over to do the honors.

Brian Jones mugs for the local TV cameras and yells, "Get your tickets. We're going to the Cotton Bowl."

Texas offensive tackle Stan Thomas shouts, "Klingler, I despise the guy. His Heisman hopes are gone. Good-bye, Klingler. We mashed them every play. I wanted to brawl when the game was over. I still wanted to hit somebody."

Richard, after "holding" Hazard to seven catches and two touchdowns, sidles up to McWilliams and says, "Coach, they didn't shoot the Sheriff. They got me in the leg, Coach, but they didn't get me."

In his private box, athletic director DeLoss Dodds smiles and vows to give up the pipe he's been lighting constantly since 1960. He was going to quit after the football season, but why put it off?

"I just decided," he says. "I feel so damn good I'm going to quit." And he does.

McWilliams has never felt so good. At his press conference, he hesitates to say how high he plans to vote his team in the coaches' United Press International poll, but says Notre Dame will get his top billing.

And, speaking of Notre Dame, would the Irish have beaten Texas the way the Longhorns had played against Houston that night? Would the big, bad Miami Hurricanes? Would Colorado? Would anybody?

"No, I really don't think so," says McWilliams, who never boasts. "Not tonight. We were clicking on everything."

He adds, "Maybe Fuller went to his garage and dusted off some old stuff."

Morning comes early to Leon Fuller's house on Sunday, where the huge victory brings everything but sleep.

Fuller turns to wife Pam and says, "Geez, am I going to have to be a genius again this week?"

16

"Just a Release"

The Texas fans have just cheered, screamed, and shouted the Houston Cougars right out of a possible national championship in the loudest, rowdiest game in the history of Memorial Stadium. The fans are back; the Texas bandwagon is rolling again.

Some of the Texas fans, however, never went away.

Scott Wilson's home on the north end of Austin could pass for an auction house of Texas sports memorabilia. Tacked to the ceiling of the garage there's a red banner he ripped down in Fayetteville the weekend of the Big Shootout with Arkansas in 1969. The sign pissed Wilson off because it urged the Hogs to beat the Irish, as if they'd already won the Big Shootout. It was Texas that triumphed 15–14 and won the right to face Notre Dame in the Cotton Bowl, and Wilson who left Fayetteville with yet another unusual trophy.

Not far from the banner, there's a long stick of wood with the white paint just about bleached off it. It doesn't look like much, but it's the baseball foul pole from Texas's old Clark Field, and it meant enough to Wilson that he held on to it with one arm draped out of his car while he steered and shifted gears in his Austin-Healey with his free arm.

In his bedroom, the thirty-nine-year-old lawyer has 1,100 baseball caps hanging from the walls, ceiling, dressers, and just about everything else that's not moving. His living room, kitchen, and bathroom are plastered with banners, clippings, and pictures from various sporting events. If Texas plays it, Wilson has seen it.

"They say Texas fans are fickle," he says, "but just about everyone is fickle compared to me." Although he's best known as the leader of Texas baseball's bleacher bums, the Wild Bunch, he's also a football fanatic. "I've attended a hundred and sixty straight football games," he says. "People will tell me they've been to more than that, and I'll say, 'Funny, I didn't see you at the Freedom Bowl in 1984.' We pulled up to the stadium two hours before the game to tailgate like we usually do. We asked the policeman where to park, and he motions to the lot and says, 'It's all yours, guys.' Two hours before the game, we were the only ones in the lot."

The Freedom Bowl, played before a crowd generously listed at 24,093 on a gray, drizzly December 26 night in Anaheim, California, was the acid test for followers of Texas football. Even the team didn't want to be there playing Hayden Fry's Iowa squad that day.

"We voted as a team that we did not want to go," recalls 1984 Lombardi Award winner Tony Degrate. "One walk-on raised his hand, and he pulled it down real quick 'cause everybody looked at him.

"Fred told the seniors we should especially want to go out as winners. We said, 'Well, Coach, we'd just like to end the season now.' It didn't end on a good note. Some of the guys felt like our practices were punishment. We had some lousy practices."

The embarrassing end result was a 55–17 loss to an Iowa team quarterbacked by Chuck Long.

"I told people we were in our Highway Patrol Defense," Scott Wilson says. "We kept 'em from going over fifty-five."

Two years later, he was shown on TV wearing an anti-Akers button pinned to his white cap. "I kind of became the poster boy for the Fire Fred movement," says Wilson, who was quoted in *Sports Illustrated* on that topic.

Wilson gets to Texas sporting events all over the country, but acknowledges, "There's a lot of competition from the pro teams for fans. This isn't Arkansas, where you get in the darn Winnebago and drive a couple of states over to go to the game. They don't have pro sports. How many pro teams do they have in Tennessee?

"I guess some of the fans were sort of spoiled by the Darrell Royal years. In the 1960s, it was considered a setback if you lost a game. In 1961, they lost to TCU; that screwed up that year. In 1962 they tied one and then lost to Lynn Amedee and LSU in the Cotton Bowl. In 1964, they lost one and messed up that year."

Texas won Associated Press national championships with undefeated teams in 1963 and 1969 and could have won a lot more. From

1961 to 1983 the Longhorns had nine one-loss seasons. Fans grew to expect—and demand—that kind of success.

Jones Ramsey worked as a sports information director at Texas A&M when Bear Bryant was there and at Texas in the Darrell Royal years. He noticed that the two coaching legends had a lot in common, but that the fans at the two schools were decidedly different.

"The Aggies tithe and the Longhorns tip," he says as he leans back in an easy chair. "Any ordinary Aggie is going to give ten percent. They'll do that and be happy to sit in the end zone. Texas fans think they ought to have a fifty-yard-line ticket and a parking pass for ten dollars a year.

"The Aggies are ten times more patient than Longhorns and ten times more loyal. They'll put up with a team losing more and longer than Texas fans will. Aggies fans will contribute more."

Ramsey says Texas fans may be like that, in part, because of the Permanent University Fund, that gusher of West Texas oil money from land set aside by the legislature for the university when no one thought the vast acreage was good for much of anything. It still isn't, really. It's the West Texas crude lying under it that's been the boon for Texas.

Texas fans look around at what the oil money has wrought and see no earthly reason to lose to lesser schools. Memorial Stadium has a listed capacity of 77,809, but 83,053 were squeezed in for a 1978 game with Houston and 82,457 showed up to shout the Cougars down in 1990. It may not be the biggest stadium in the country, but there aren't many larger or nicer.

There aren't any stands in the south end zone, but there is a world-class weight facility, the Neuhaus-Royal complex, that's got an AstroTurf practice field on top that's fifty yards wide by seventy yards long.

Austin, with its varied nightlife and nearby lakes, is widely considered the nicest place to spend four years in Texas, and it certainly beats the hell out of some place like Norman, Oklahoma. Texas, not Oklahoma, is known for its high school football. The campus is The University of Texas—with a capitalized *The*—to the school's publicists, who treat it as the flagship of a very proud state.

Texas fans don't see any reason not to win national championships, which the Longhorns routinely do in several sports a year.

Since the Longhorns last won a national championship in football, they've copped them in baseball, swimming, golf, and women's basketball, volleyball, swimming, indoor and outdoor track, and cross-country.

Nothing, however, jacks up Austin, gets it rocking and rolling like a late-night jam session on Sixth Street, than when the football team gets on a run. When the Longhorns are trampling opponents, fans can forget about the real estate slump that has plagued Austin for the last half decade, or the recession that's still lingering in Texas. When the bandwagon starts rolling, everybody jumps on it.

When the program bogs down, however, a lot of fans jump off. "That used to really bother me because after we'd lose a game, people would talk about how bad we were," says Texas offensive tackle Stan Thomas. "Then once you win a game, everybody wants to buy you a drink. I think the Texas fans are too wishy-washy. They don't really back you most of the time unless you're winning. I'd rather be playing at Texas than SMU, though. If you ain't got no fans . . . something is better than nothing."

Texas may be the heart of football country, but, unless they're winning, the Longhorns don't have sellouts for all their games, the way Ohio State, Michigan, Tennessee, and some other traditional powers do.

Win and 80,000 will show up in support. Start losing four games a year and attendance can fall by 20,000 a game. When Darrell Royal and Arkansas's Frank Broyles stepped down in 1976 on one of the most momentous days in college football, only 49,341 fans were on hand for that game in Austin. Texas, after all, had lost five games by then.

"The mentality of the Texas fans is if we don't go to a major bowl, we shouldn't go to a bowl," said one high-ranking school official. "Some Texas fans maintain that posture.

"If I could change one thing, I'd change the attitude and mentality of the Texas fans. They have no earthly idea of how to support a program. We've got forty thousand exes in Houston, but the coach's show is not sold in Houston. The Texas football-basketball network was not sold two weeks before the season. If you asked fourteen guys to donate a thousand dollars, not a one would do it. Texas exes don't go into business. They don't own the companies that advertise. They're journalists, bankers, doctors, engineers, scientists, lawyers. The Aggies are the businessmen."

Texas has its diehard fans like Wilson that you'll find at other major college powers around the country. The only difference is that they show more orange, like Newt Hasson, a forty-year-old orthopedic surgeon in Westlake, a suburb of Austin.

Hasson, who played football at Duke from 1968 to 1971, is 6-foot-3. Make that 6-foot-4 when he's operating in his cowboy boots. "I'm not an eccentric fan," he says. "It's just a release from the pressures of work."

One wall of his operating room at the South Austin Medical Center is painted orange. There's a Longhorn logo stenciled on another wall. "They couldn't put a Longhorn rack on the wall because they couldn't sterilize the real thing," says his wife, Pam.

Hasson did his residency work at Stanford, but Pam says, "We wanted to live where football was really big. In California you just have the game; you don't have all the trappings you do at Texas. He liked Texas's winning teams and he liked Darrell Royal. Besides, it wasn't an outlaw school."

"My years playing at Duke coincided with the greatest years in Texas history," explains Hasson, who has a Tibetan terrier named Bevo and was negotiating to name his third child Bo, for burnt orange, until Pam gave birth to Meredith instead. "The Longhorns were the college team of that time. To me, Texas football is college football."

Hasson was impressed at the first home game he attended. "There were eighty thousand fans singing 'The Eyes of Texas,' " he says. "That was really chilling."

Their seats have improved since, although Pam Hasson recalls, "We sat behind Frank Denius once. I told [UT] 'Never ever put our seats behind him again. Never put us twenty rows behind him.' The man stands up practically the whole game."

"Some of my friends say sitting near me is like drawing the black bean," admits Denius, a sixty-five-year-old lawyer and former president of Southern Union Gas. "They say I should be down on the sidelines so I don't distract the other fans."

Denius, who says he has missed only eleven Texas football games since World War II, has been on the sidelines for a lot of them. He was also with Darrell Royal when he went up to Cleburne to recruit a blue-chip high school center named David McWilliams. When Royal had dinner at the Nighthawk with a high school coach that he would hire as an assistant, Fred Akers, Denius was on hand.

Before the NCAA outlawed such assistance, Denius says he helped recruit on weekends and gave free legal advice to players. He's a fixture at Longhorn practices and says, "I like watching the defense to see how the kids are progressing, what they're learning." He's seen it all since Bobby Layne was quarterbacking at Texas and says, "I think we could have beaten anybody in the country that night we played Houston."

Not all Texas fans, however, are as relentlessly upbeat as Denius,

Wilson, and Hasson. Some start keeping score in recruiting the min-ute the regular season is over. They phone any time Houston-based recruiting expert Max Emfinger is on a radio call-in show. They want to know where that blue chip from Baytown is headed. If he hasn't committed, they'll ask which way he's leaning, how his visit at Okla-homa went, or where his girlfriend is going to school. Some will even know which assistant coach is supposed to be recruiting him—and that coach's track record in the past.

"I think there are two different kinds of fans," Texas athletic director DeLoss Dodds says. "The majority of them love the university, and they want to see us do it the right way. Of course, they want us to win, but if we don't, they're not going to jump off a bridge or some-thing. Then there's the group, the call-in show people. If you win, they almost go out and take over the world. If you lose, they are just in a complete depression."

Only at Texas could you find a man trying to make a living from a newsletter that doesn't just tout the school's athletic program; it seeks to change it with some of the strongest language you'll see in print.

In a lot of ways Robert Heard's small, independent publication, *Inside Texas*, is ground zero for fan dissatisfaction. When Texas isn't number one, Heard wants to know why. To a few, himself included, Heard is Frank Erwin with a Macintosh.

"Erwin and I never got along," he says, "but he was the same way. He lived night and day to make this the greatest university, and I feel the same way. He was extremely conservative and I'm a liberal, but I loved him for his love of the university. I champion public education, and I champion the main public university of my state."

To university administrators, Heard is just a loose cannon lobbing shots at Bellmont Hall, the home of Texas's athletic department. Heard took over a glossy publication with four hundred subscribers, *Longhorn Sports*, in the mid-1980s. At the time, the publication was paying a hundred dollars a year to use the name Longhorns. Admin-istrators decided that wasn't enough to have Heard's name even remotely associated with their program. Forbidden to use the old name, he switched to *Inside Texas*, which debuted on January 1, 1986.

In one issue he likened former Texas basketball coach Bob Weltlich to a rattlesnake.

In a following issue he apologized. To rattlesnakes.

"My influence in his firing was slight and indirect," Heard says. "But I'll tell you, it was fun."

When Weltlich was "reassigned" after the 1988 season, Heard concentrated more of his shots at DeLoss Dodds. To Heard, Dodds is DeLOSS or DeLo$$, a bureaucrat concerned mainly with the bottom line.

When all the conference realignment talk in 1990 resulted in only the defection of Arkansas from the SWC and a denial by Dodds that anything had been officially offered to Texas from the Pac-10, Heard was outraged. He wrote in his August 27, 1990, issue, "Presidents and chancellors of the Pac-10 reached a no-expansion consensus in a conference call August 21, leaving DeLoss Dodds standing on the corner with a tin cup. Dodds pushed the Pac-10 so hard and so awkwardly it became public. How often do you suppose all 10 of the CEOs of the Left Coast league hold a conference call? Maybe once a decade. A heavy-handed yahoo from Kansas forced them to take that emergency step. . . . Lying may be more acceptable at Kansas (I doubt it) but for sure it's the quickest way to anger a Texan. This is the single most revulsive characteristic in Dodds's makeup, one that infuriates people of their word."

On the same page, Heard quotes a Kansas State insider who calls Dodds, "the biggest turd in college athletics."

Dodds keeps trying to ignore the criticism. Heard keeps dishing it out.

Heard is a former Associated Press correspondent and says, "I used to grouse like crazy about the AP and some of its old, conservative ways and things they wouldn't cover and the way they'd butcher my copy, but I loved being a reporter. Still do."

Heard cranks out his acerbic newsletter in the den of a modest home in Austin's Travis Heights, which is shaded by several huge and ancient live oak trees that twist skyward. His study is crammed with bare metal filing cabinets dripping books on history and sports. He sits at a small table where, taped to a wall, there's a newspaper headline that proclaims DETERMINED TO BE HEARD. A large man, he dwarfs the tiny 512E Macintosh computer.

"I probably put in sixty to seventy hours a week on the newsletter, and I work twenty hours on Sunday," he says. "I work right up until eight P.M. when I put it to bed Monday. If I've got five more minutes to work on it, I'll use those minutes. I'll keep honing. I don't let go until they take it away from me.

"I've got about fifteen hundred subscribers and they're coming on now because of the recent football successes," he says of the newsletter, for which subscribers pay thirty-six dollars for twenty issues.

"It won't begin to pay me for the effort that I make, the talent that I bring, and the time that I spend until it hits twenty-five hundred or three thousand. It's all tied to the football program. This is a football state; my success is tied to their success. The numbers won't come until the football team wins and wins big. My talent will be irrelevant then. When you get to the national championship level, the top five, that's when they're selling toilet seats at the co-op and helmet phones and glasses and that kind of stuff. People want to be part of the action."

Oddly enough, Heard, who now spends so much time catering to the most demanding and critical of Longhorn fans, never went to school at Texas. "I'm the youngest of four boys," he relates. "My daddy was a Baptist preacher. He went to Baylor. My mother went to Baylor. I went to Baylor at seventeen and I went to law school there, but I wasn't a Baylor kind of guy. I would have been much better suited to Texas. I was the baby, the radical of the family. I was still pulling for Baylor, though, until the Texas A&M-Baylor game of 1966."

Baylor lost 17–13 and Heard recalls, "I'm walking out of the stadium, and there's an older Baylor couple walking in front of me. The woman made some remark about the loss. He said, 'Well, that's Baylor.' And I thought, 'Well, it may be Baylor, but, by God, it's not me.' I remembered that attitude from when I was a student. There just wasn't that need to win, at whatever they were doing. They were great on moral victories. Boy, we gave them a tough time, didn't we? To hell with that. When he said, 'Well, that's Baylor,' that was the watershed. I thought, 'That's all.' "

Heard, who has also written several books on Texas sports, says of his newsletter, "I'm kind of a steam valve. If people have a grievance, they can talk to me off the record and tell me about things that need to be corrected. I enjoy tweaking the nose of people who are hypocritical—coaches like Barry Switzer and Jackie Sherrill—I enjoy ferreting out that kind of stuff and doing the very best, most skillful job I can of ridiculing them. I have a talent for that."

At Bellmont Hall, the frequent target of Heard's barbs, they like to joke, "It's just a shame Charles Whitman wasn't a better shot."

They're talking about Charles Whitman, the sniper who killed sixteen, wounded thirty-two, and pinned down an entire campus during a day-long shooting spree from the observation deck of the Texas Tower before he was shot to death. Heard was one of the wounded.

"People made me out to be a hero," Heard recalls of that infamous day on August 1, 1966. "Hell, I wasn't a hero, I just forgot my Marine training to zig and zag. Others said I was lucky. If I was lucky, he would have missed."

When the call came that someone was shooting from the Texas Tower, Heard rushed out of the AP office where he had begun working only seven months before, drove to campus, and entered from the northeast side.

"There were some police there and more were coming," he says. "The guards warned us about it. We pulled up two blocks north of the Tower behind a highway patrol car that had just stopped, and two highway patrolmen got out and started putting together shotguns. I thought, 'You're crazy, a shotgun is not going to do you any good at this range.' Of course, what they were planning on doing was going up there in the Tower and killing the guy, not shooting him from below. They started toward the Tower and we followed them.

"We were out of the sight of the Tower, behind some buildings. I didn't know that there was an observation deck on the Tower. The only thing I knew about the university was Gregory Gym and Memorial Stadium. I'd never even been on the campus, except for sporting events. I thought that somebody—or somebodies—was shooting out the window of one of the top floors of the building. I determined I was going to follow these highway patrolmen, I mean, they're going there and that's where the story is."

They trotted across the street toward the Tower. "I'm behind the home economics building at that point," Heard recalls. "I looked a couple of times and pulled my head back, and I thought, 'Well, he can tattoo me in the eyeball.' I'm going to count to five to throw him off. Then, I'm not going to trot, I'm going to run.

"I'd had a knee operation and I wasn't a hundred percent, but I did run as fast as I could. I just forgot my Marine training to zigzag. It was such a short area—I went back later and stepped it off. It was only twenty-six yards. I thought I could blow across it. He hit me with a six-millimeter Remington with a telescopic sight. I was only about a hundred and seventy yards from him, and he barely got me before I went out of his sight.

"The bullet he used makes a small hole going in and a big hole coming out. It was a deer rifle, and it was designed to kill. It's not like an M1 rifle or an AKA for that matter. They're designed to wound. In war, you want to wound because it will take two other people to take care of that guy. Hunting deer, you want to kill. You don't want them to run off somewhere where you have to track them."

Three yards from safety, Heard was struck. "The shot hit me like a brick and knocked me a quarter-turn around," he says. "I'm going full speed and my arm is flapping out, so I reach over and grab the wrist as I'm falling. I went about three more yards, which is what I needed. I was out of his line of vision. I hit the sidewalk and it was hot; it was a blazing, hundred-degree day. I sat up and the blood just fell over like a Niagara on my white shirt. I yelled out, 'Help, I'm hit.' Some people in the biological sciences building—I never did find out who they were—dragged me under the trunk of a Studebaker. They were brave people because they didn't know that he couldn't see me. In fact, he tried to see me.

"The highway patrolmen, who went around by the side of the biological sciences building, looked up and saw him. It was so early in the thing that he wasn't yet ducking behind the wall and shooting through the rainspouts. He was looking down trying to find me, looking where he had shot me. Nobody was shooting back at him at this point."

Heard was loaded into one of the first ambulances to arrive on campus. That was around noon.

"Three more inches and I would have been dead. The bullet would have hit my heart and lungs," he says. "I had a severe wound, but it wasn't nearly as bad as some of the others, so they didn't get to me until six P.M."

Heard remembers being left in the hall for a while at Brackenridge Hospital, which was so bloody that doctors and nurses slipped on the floor as they hurried by.

"They had operating rooms going full blast," he says. "They put me in a room up on the third floor. They had a pressure bandage on my arm but it wasn't working. My GP, Otto Brandt, probably saved my life. He'd come to the hospital to see if any of his patients were there. He'd been in World War II and said he hadn't seen wounds like that since then. He discovered that my pressure bandage had loosened and I was literally bleeding to death. I'd lost five pints of blood, and I can remember him reaching inside my shoulder with his fingertips and holding the artery while he yelled out the door into the hallway for someone to bring another bandage. I'm kind of foggy through this period. I was in shock, in and out of consciousness."

Heard, however, had a story to file, and told it to another AP reporter.

"Garth Jones got up there and he took notes," Heard remembers. "He wrote a story under my name which went all over the world. Boy, I got clippings from India and Asia. It would say 'By Robert

Heard' and it would be in another language. It was just a short piece, about eight to ten inches, but it was a first-person deal. Terry Young of the UPI said his office was mad they didn't have a matcher."

Whitman, who'd carried a small arsenal and several days' worth of supplies up to the Tower, was gunned down and killed in the most gruesome day in Austin's history.

Heard still carries the scars from that day. There's a sunken cavity where the left deltoid and upper biceps muscle should be. The bone in his left arm was shattered. Scores of little pieces of bone eventually worked their way through the skin, and eight of the larger fragments were shishkebabed together by doctors with a metal rod as thick as a pencil.

"I've got fifty percent disability," he says. "If I was a weight lifter, it would bother me, but I can still type."

That he can.

"How Sweet It Is!" his newsletter exults after the 45–24 Houston win. "This victory ranks among the most satisfying in UT history because of who they beat and by how much and how they did it."

After Houston, Heard has just three games to go in the regular season, the most hectic, stressful time of his year. Maybe when the season's over, the chest pains he started experiencing in September will go away and let him fully enjoy Texas's success.

17

Cash and Kerry

Almost three decades ago, Darrell Royal riled half of Fort Worth by likening the TCU football team to a bunch of cockroaches. That was after his 1961 team suffered its only loss of a 10–1 season to a TCU squad that was on its way to an undistinguished 3–5–2 record.

"Really, what I said was pretty appropriate," Royal recalls as he settles into a soft red couch in a hallway lounge on the second floor of the Barton Creek Country Club in Austin.

"I said it's like a cockroach; it ain't so much what he eats and totes off, it's what he falls into and messes up. Their team wasn't one that was eating anything. They weren't after a conference title or a national title or any kind of a title. They were just falling into it and messing up stuff other people were trying to do."

On a Saturday that dawns drab and still, a 7–1 Texas team ranked number seven in the nation is trying for the 1991 Cotton Bowl and maybe the national title the school hasn't won since Royal left.

TCU, which is sinking fast with three straight losses after a heady 5–1 start, is just hoping to fall into some kind of miracle. That's what Saturday's *Fort Worth Star-Telegram* proclaims it will take for the banged-up Horned Frogs to beat Texas.

Jim Wacker's team can't tote off anything big, like the Cotton Bowl bid the players were dreaming about earlier in the season. With their new offense, they're just Triple Shooting for an upset—or at least a passable performance on a national TV game. Wacker's Horned Frogs, who routinely get run over by Texas A&M and Texas at the tail end of their season, need an effort that won't drive away any more recruits from a school that was once living a souped-up Cinderella story straight out of a Dan Jenkins novel.

In *Life Its Ownself*, Jenkins, a former *Sports Illustrated* writer and ex-TCU golfer, concocted the wildest of fictions. His little alma mater, with its 7,000 students, is set on the wrong side of the tracks from glittery sister city Dallas. For decades, the best TCU could hope for was to fall into some football wins. Jenkins, however, imagined the Horned Frogs winning big-time.

In 1984 life was imitating *Life Its Ownself*. The Horned Frogs had suddenly discovered purple pride under coach Jim Wacker. The son of a Lutheran minister, Wacker's aw-shucks, golly-gee enthusiasm was just the kind of rah-rah that had been missing from football in the cynical, cold-as-cash SWC. The Horned Frogs went a stunning 8–3 before losing in the Bluebonnet Bowl to West Virginia, 31–14.

In 1985, when the NCAA was once again coming hard after SMU in Dallas, Wacker preached a fiery sermon to his players about how TCU was winning the right way.

Great delivery, wrong topic. Shortly after the speech, star running back Kenneth Davis revealed he had been paid thirty thousand dollars to give it the old college try lugging the ball for TCU. That night, at 11 P.M., players were summoned to the coliseum for a team meeting that was more like a funeral. Players wept openly. By the time the confessions and the hasty investigations had stopped, TCU's football team had lost seven players. The Horned Frogs were headed for a 3–8 year, and NCAA probation.

Since that day Wacker's program, which once attracted blue-chippers, was in a blue funk. Every season was a losing one, every rumor had Wacker on his way out.

The rumors subsided in the first part of the 1990 season, when Wacker looked as though he was back with an offense that was radically different from his beloved veer. He'd used that run-oriented option offense while rapidly climbing the coaching rungs at Texas Lutheran, North Dakota State, and Southwest Texas State.

In 1990, Wacker's team is airing it out with a run-and-shoot offshoot dubbed the Triple Shoot. The offense started out attempting to balance the run and pass. That didn't last long. As the Horned Frogs kept falling behind early, they just had to keep throwing the ball downfield to a group of talented receivers headed by tight end Kelly Blackwell, Stephen Shipley, and Richard Woodley. The Triple Shoot even includes a no-back offense where the only person behind the quarterback is an official.

When sensational starting quarterback Leon Clay was knocked out with an injury, the Horned Frogs just started airing it out more. Matt Vogler, a 6-foot-2 transfer from Auburn, flabbergasted everyone by throwing for an NCAA-record 690 yards against Houston. Hell, that was more yards than Bobby Layne passed for in his first year as a Texas quarterback. The next week, in a loss to Texas Tech, Vogler put the ball in the air 72 times, even though his left shoulder was separated.

As the week progressed it looked as though Wacker's nephew, 6-foot-5 Illinois high school product Tim Schade, would be forced into quarterbacking action. Wacker had been planning on redshirting his nephew, who hadn't taken a single snap in college football. Wacker wasn't excited about wasting a year of Schade's eligibility, but this wasn't some game that would just slip by unnoticed.

This was Texas. And CBS, which was providing a rare national TV game for little old TCU.

Vogler is slated to start against Texas. But how long can he last? The Texas front four has just finished bloodying Houston quarterback David Klingler and killing his Heisman Trophy hopes.

Bearing down on Vogler from right end will be Oscar Giles, 246 pounds of pumped-up muscle. Waiting to wrap him up at left end is Shane Dronett, the 6-foot-6, slightly spacy sophomore prodigy who's become the team's sack leader. Up the middle there's junior Tommy Jeter, one of the bluest of chips when he was at Deer Park High School. He's flanked by James Patton, a junior who's already developed into one of the strongest Longhorns ever to test his bench press in the weight room.

Vogler has to face that group before lunch. The kickoff has been squeezed up to 11:08 A.M. on a charcoal-gray morning where the temperature is hovering in the 50s and the 3 mile an hour breeze is barely enough to ripple a flag.

Texas players meet before the game. Tight end Stephen Clark urges everyone not to take TCU lightly and to get off to a quick start.

Easier said than done. TCU is one school that Texas isn't looking to pay back. The Longhorns don't owe the Horned Frogs anything except a big thanks. TCU is one team that couldn't take advantage of the darkest period in Texas football since before World War II. It was way back in 1967 that TCU last beat Texas.

Many Longhorns are actually looking forward more to playing on national TV than playing the Horned Frogs. Since 1985, Texas hasn't played anyone other than Oklahoma in a national telecast on one of the big three networks.

Then, there are some individual battles to decide. Kelly Blackwell, a 6-foot-3, 238-pound junior, is leading the nation's tight ends with 59 receptions. Texas offensive coordinator Lynn Amedee, however, will tell anyone who calls up his Monday night radio talk show that he'd rather have 6-foot-4 Kerry Cash—even if Cash enters with just 21 receptions for 278 yards. That total could have been more except that Texas quarterback Peter Gardere was judged to have been a step over the line on a pass that would have been a 76-yard touchdown to Kerry Cash against Houston. That pass also would have given Gardere a school record of 398 yards instead of the second-best total of 322 yards.

That reception also would have kept Kerry closer to identical twin Keith. With his 5 catches for 154 yards against Houston, Keith is becoming the surprise star of the 1990 season.

Both Cashes and Johnny Walker came to Texas from San Antonio Holmes. "We all had more than fifty catches in our senior year and we spent a lot of time on the sidelines in the second half, after we already had games won," Walker says. Each also had at least 11 touchdown catches in his senior year.

Walker, a two-sport star, was the best prospect. "It's easier to name the All-America teams I *didn't* make," he says. It's also easier to name the balls he's dropped at Texas rather than all the difficult ones he's caught. While Walker maintains he runs a 4.5-second 40-yard dash, some pro scouts question his speed. Nobody, however, has any doubts about his hands.

"He'd be a first-round pick if he was featured at some place like Miami," Baltimore-based NFL draft expert Mel Kiper says.

After two years of feeling lost in the Texas offense, Walker blossomed in his junior year under the new offensive scheme of Lynn Amedee. While double-covered star Tony Jones felt frozen out of the offense running sideline routes that Gardere couldn't hit, Walker made the tough catches over the middle. He piled up 55 receptions and 785 yards.

Kerry Cash, who'd beefed up to tight end, also came into his own with 28 catches for 391 yards. Identical twin Keith, meanwhile, languished as a second-team flanker behind Jones. His only claim to fame was the alley-oop route his brother also ran. Of the 23 passes he'd caught coming into his senior year, 7 were for touchdowns.

The Cashes had always been close. They'd worn the same clothes, played ten years of competitive football together, and even grown identical Fu Manchu mustaches at Texas, where they roomed together.

The word at the beginning of the season, though, was that Kerry was about to leave his brother behind, just as he did in the weight room. Kerry was working himself into an NFL-style, 235-pound tight end. In the pros his 4.6-second speed for the 40 would be an asset at that spot.

At wideout, where Keith remained at 215 pounds, it would be a liability in a sport looking for run-and-shoot Smurfs who could break 4.4 seconds at the same distance.

In his senior year, however, Keith is benefiting from the attention that his brother and Walker are receiving from defenses. If there's anyone who's going to be single-covered in the trio, it's going to be Keith. It's the ninth game of the season, and Walker still doesn't have a touchdown.

As the early kickoff approaches, fans slowly file into Amon Carter Stadium, which looks like a medieval fortress set up on a bluff that towers over the parking lot. The stadium shows every one of its sixty years. Only some streaks of purple paint on the ramps brighten an otherwise drab mass of concrete.

Almost one-half of the 39,007 fans who fill the stadium are Texas fans, not purple-clad TCU Wacker Backers. Even the strong showing of Texas's Metroplex exes, however, isn't enough to spark Texas. For the first time in the season, the team doesn't run onto the field pumped up and ready to play.

Texas expects to win this one because it's Texas. TCU's last home victory against the Longhorns came in the Eisenhower era, 1958.

Against the lowly Horned Frogs, the Cashes figure to get a couple of alley-oop touchdowns each. Butch Hadnot should run for about two hundred yards . . . except that the offensive line, which has been so stable for the 1990 season, is in turmoil.

Starting left tackle Chuck Johnson watched from the sidelines during the week. "I want to play . . ." he said as he laboriously made his way on crutches to his car Thursday before the game.

But this is TCU, not Baylor, a better team that is coming up in a week. So Johnson, a professorial-looking junior, was giving way to backup Shay Shafie.

On Thursday, the mother of offensive line coach Clovis Hale had died. Hale's job had reportedly been on the line during the off-season. In 1990, however, he's cajoled, cursed, and hands-on coached his unit into the biggest surprise on the team. Hale misses the game to attend his mother's funeral in Colorado City.

"Coach Hale is the one who would always fire us up," offensive right tackle Stan Thomas explains. "In the warm-ups I could tell we were flat. In the first half, everyone looked dead. I tried to fire some people up, do some talking, but it didn't work."

Texas wins the toss and elects to receive. Adrian Walker muffs a knuckleball for a few anxious moments and then returns it to the Texas 30. Hadnot is coming off his first-ever 100-yard game in college. Against Houston he rumbled all over Jerry Parks and the rest of the Cougar defenders for 134 bone-jarring yards.

Hadnot is Lynn Amedee's favorite, the big back he needed for his offense. Amedee comes out showing reverse, but instead the ball goes to Hadnot for 4 yards. On second down the 215-pounder is swarmed under after a yard gain by a TCU defense that's geared to stopping Big Butch. On third-and-five Texas quarterback Peter Gardere starts off in his typically wobbly fashion. He throws incomplete to Chris Samuels in the left flat.

In their first series on national TV in more than two years the Longhorns have gone nowhere and impressed no one. They settle for an ugly-looking Alex Waits punt that travels 45 yards before Anthony Hickman returns it 6 yards to the TCU 26.

Vogler, sore left shoulder and all, comes out to lead the Horned Frogs. On the third play from scrimmage he hits Shipley, a tall Cris Collingsworth, who one-hands the ball for a 31-yard gain down to Texas's 39.

Four plays later TCU is on the Texas 9. On first down Vogler hits Cedric Jackson right where he laces his shoulder pads, and a sure touchdown bounces off his chest. TCU settles for a 26-yard field goal.

Texas gets the ball back, but Gardere is still scatter-arming balls all over the lot. On third-and-eight from the Texas 11, Gardere sprays one over the middle that Johnny Walker dives at and snares for a drive-saving 17-yard gain. Eight plays later, from the TCU 43, Gardere heaves a prayer in the vicinity of two TCU defenders and Keith Cash. Amedee screams in disgust. It's another Hail-Kerry pass from Gardere, except it's for Keith.

It's two-on-one. TCU's two—Anthony Hickman and Tony Rand— fall to the AstroTurf when the 6-foot-4 Keith Cash outjumps them. Cash ends up cruising into the end zone with a 43-yard touchdown.

In the second quarter TCU moves to the Texas 31. On fourth-and-seven at the 31, however, the Horned Frogs can't figure out what to do. The indecision and imprecision that has marked Jim Wacker's career at TCU strikes again. TCU calls a time-out to, to, well, punt.

Kevin Cordesman pops one up that goes all of 4 yards. Unbeleeevable, as Wacker likes to say at better times.

Texas can't go anywhere. TCU is stunting, blitzing, and confusing the Texas offensive linemen, who don't have Hale's help on the sidelines. The Texas attack is looking so bad that Lynn Amedee, who's being mentioned as a longshot for the head coaching job at his alma mater of LSU, inserts Jimmy Saxton at quarterback.

Saxton is the son of James Saxton, a former All-American Longhorn scatback. He's an alumni favorite, and Texas coaches have been ready to turn to him and the option game several times when Gardere has struggled.

On third-and-fourteen from the Texas 31, Saxton has to scramble. He sticks the ball out halfway to Dallas. He fumbles. TCU recovers, but a 47-yard field goal try falls short. Not, however, as short as Saxton's chance to mount a challenge to Gardere.

Peter the Late returns, but the Longhorns still don't go anywhere behind an offensive line that has no punch. Thomas, touted as an NFL first-rounder, looks like the drive-killing Thomas of last year. He's drawn three flags in the first half.

With 43 seconds left, Texas starts on its own 40. Gardere—while not hot—gets lukewarm. With 24 seconds left, he throws in the vicinity of a diving Keith Cash, who gets a 23-yard gain to the TCU 7.

Time is ticking away when TCU—not Texas—stops the clock with a time-out. The Horned Frogs try to regroup, but the strategy backfires when Gardere hits Kerry Cash for a 7-yard touchdown. Texas heads into the locker room with a 14–3 lead.

It's not a happy place. The Longhorns have rushed 17 times for a piddling 19 yards.

Amedee can't snap the Longhorns out of their lethargy. With little more than four minutes left in the third quarter, right end Roosevelt Collins comes crashing in and crunches Gardere, who coughs up the ball. Left tackle Kenneth Walton gathers it in at the 9, and suddenly TCU, down 17–3, has life. Three plays later TCU has advanced only to the 6. The field goal team comes in to the moans of TCU fans.

The noise quickly turns to cheers, though, on a perfectly executed fake when holder Mike Noack flips a little shuttle pass to Cedric Jackson, who dances into the end zone. After the conversion, it's Texas 17, TCU 10. With another touchdown and a two-point conversion, TCU could "cockroach" the game.

At the end of the third quarter and the start of the fourth, Texas puts together a 12-play, 91-yard drive that ends when Gardere throws a 5-yard pass to Keith Cash. Actually, it was intended for brother Kerry. Keith cuts in. "I was getting ready to spike it," Kerry says. A

187

Texas fan had actually told Kerry he would name his future son after him if Kerry caught two touchdowns. So much for immortality.

From there, the rout is on. Butter-fingered speedster Mike Davis successfully juggles a 55-yard bomb for a touchdown. Bubba Jacques blocks a punt and Van Malone returns it 21 yards for another TD. That's it for the scoring, Texas 38, TCU 10.

TCU's Vogler is sacked only twice and manages to finish the game. Vogler, however, is harried into completing just 20 of his 51 passes. Gardere, after his shaky start, puts up impressive stats in yet another game.

On his Monday night radio show Amedee sums up, "Two hundred and sixty-nine yards, four touchdowns on an awful afternoon. What a great game."

Especially for the other Cash, Keith. While Kerry's only catch is his 7-yard touchdown, Keith grabs two scores and finishes with four catches for 87 yards. He's becoming the team's money player.

18

Trying to Do the Right Thing

Mourners are filing into the Pilgrim Rest Baptist Church, which is nestled next to a cornfield in Simmesport, Louisiana. They talk in hushed and saddened tones as they settle into the hardback pews and wait for the Reverend C. A. Harris to deliver the eulogy for former Texas linebacker June James.

Four days earlier, on May 8, 1990, James's car had swerved off U.S. Highway 61, slammed into a guardrail, and tumbled over and over, killing James instantly. Life in what had been the fast lane of football stardom had abruptly come to an end.

The mourners, including Eric Jeffries, Richard Peavy, and former Texas All-Americans Mossy Cade, Tony Degrate, and Jerry Gray, remember James as a street-smart but not street-hardened product of Kansas City's south side. James, who played from 1981 to 1984, came to Texas with dreams of a pro career, a dream the fast, physical linebacker lived for a brief time after starring at Texas.

The mourners glance to see who has come to represent the university and find that about the only white face in the crowded church belongs to James Blackwood, Texas's recruiting coordinator.

"Somebody had called UT and asked who they were sending," said one of June's closest friends. "They said they weren't sending anyone. He told them, 'June touched a lot of people's lives. If you don't send someone, it could cause a lot of problems.'

"So they sent Blackwood, who had nothing to do with June. I don't even think June knew who he was. That just rubbed me the wrong way. I'd like to think my position coach would come to my funeral if

189

I died. I thought maybe they'd wear a patch this season in his honor but . . ."

The expectations of black players at Texas often have to be readjusted, frequently downward. There are 203 athletes in the Texas Hall of Honor. Their pictures line the walls on the second floor of Bellmont Hall. Only four blacks are so honored. The first, two-time All-SWC fullback Roosevelt Leaks, was inducted in 1985, thirty-three years after Texas began recognizing its most illustrious stars.

Texas has tried to make up for lost time. It's said all the right things, put out all the right feelers, showed up in all the right black homes. Some black parents send their kids to Austin with the hope that times have changed the state's largest university. Other blacks refer to the university as Mr. Man, a generic title that reflects little warmth and even less compassion.

"I know, as a whole, black people are disturbed by how few black kids there are at UT, by how few black kids are being recruited and graduated," says Lawrence Sampleton, a tight end who was an All-SWC player at Texas before playing four seasons with the Philadelphia Eagles and Miami Dolphins. "Socially, things are just not geared toward blacks at all. A lot of the classes, I was the only black in them. But I think Texas is trying to do the right thing."

There are twenty-seven predominantly white fraternities at Texas and only four black ones. Of the seventeen sororities, two are black. The team picture on page 122 of the 1990 Texas football media guide provides the most glaring example of a school often linked to white superiority. There is the shot of the 1970 UPI national champion team. The lone black face in the sea of ninety-two white players belongs to Julius Whittier, the first black letterman on a Texas football team.

"I didn't have any situations that were overtly racial or placed me in a no-win situation," says Whittier, a forty-year-old lawyer in Dallas. "Teammates, their tongues would slip. Most of the times it happened, they felt bad that they let it slip. I really can't say any of the situations I found myself in were unpleasant.

"I had some guys calling me names, but that's football tactics so I'll be thinking about something other than blocking their ass. I even had a black guy from UCLA call me an Uncle Tom.

"When I was there, I was involved in all kinds of circles, from hippies to cowboys to academicians, and I had a great time. I made some friendships that endure to this day. It's a top-notch university. I wouldn't have wanted to have been anywhere else. I felt I was on the pulse of America."

Many black athletes who came to UT feel that the walls of racism remain in place. The steps to knock them down have been incremental. In the fall of 1990, only 3.7 percent of a student body of 49,617 claim an Afro-American heritage. That's in a state whose population is 12 percent black. Of 2,339 faculty members, only 42—just 1.8 percent—are black. That's barely up from 34 a decade ago. Whittier never sat in a classroom taught by a black professor.

About half of the 1990 football team is black, but there is only one black assistant coach. Aside from two black academic counselors hired this year, there are no black administrators, no black trainers, no black managers, and few black faces altogether.

"I don't think there are enough black anybodies," says Donna Lopiano, the progressive-minded athletic director of the Texas women. "We have a real credibility gap. It's going to take four or five years to reestablish the trust and strong relationship with the black community, but I think the university is committed to doing it. I think there is systemic racism in any large institution in the South, but there's a difference between systemic racism and intentional racism. I believe people are trying real hard to make sure this place is not racist. But bureaucracies are huge dinosaurs."

Texas's reputation as antiblack seems to persist, however.

"I didn't realize that UT is not that strong with the black community," says former Texas defensive tackle Tony Degrate, the Lombardi Award winner in 1984. "They're very vocal about it. The way they envision Texas is being this white, superior school and the only blacks accepted there are the ones that excel at sports.

"When we used to play Oklahoma U, my relatives would holler for OU, but say, 'We want you to play good.' Because their perception of Texas is . . . well, I'm going to be quite frank. They said the blacks that went to Texas were Uncle Toms."

Heisman Trophy winner Earl Campbell, the most famous black athlete in the school's history, now serves as a special assistant to the university vice president for student affairs and is a staunch UT flag waver. Still, he penned a column assailing the athletic program for having too few blacks in administration.

Others also note a need for black secretaries, a black assistant athletic director, and more than the one token black assistant coach.

Most of the leaders and stars of this 1990 football team are black. Linebacker Brian Jones. Free safety Stanley Richard. Receivers Johnny Walker and the Cash twins. Defensive end Oscar Giles. Big Stan Thomas.

"It's definitely a black team," Thomas says.

"A lot of the players who are active in community service are black," says Madelon Highsmith, president of the Texas Angels, a group that helps in recruiting. "Of course, a lot of the white players are linemen. Give me a break. All they do is eat and play football."

Highsmith says that she's seen race relations on the team improve dramatically during the time she's been with the Angels. She adds, "At Texas you might find somebody with green hair in your class, but that's a strength. It forces you to be tolerant."

"We wouldn't be winning if we didn't get along," star running back Butch Hadnot says.

Yet the white players, and even some of the blacks, refer to the third floor in Jester Center, where most of the blacks live, as "Little Africa."

When he was playing, Campbell noticed how most of his white teammates had a different pair of slacks every day or wore jeans and starched white shirts.

"I didn't have none of that," says Campbell, who still remembers being so poor that he once walked to First City Bank to ask for a ten-dollar loan. "I was just pissed off at the whole world. It wasn't the world's fault, it wasn't my fault, it wasn't my mother's fault, it was just the way it was."

He never got his ten bucks, and he remembers driving around campus in a green '68 Oldsmobile. Nevertheless, the way he remembers it, he and his white teammates were pretty tight.

In 1990, however, integration hasn't caught on in the dining hall.

"We eat on different sides of the room," says a white starter on this year's team. "That's just the way it is, I don't know why. You can eat anywhere you want, but it seems strange. We'd be sitting at a whole table, and there'd be room, and a black guy would be over there sitting by himself. There are a lot of problems. It's been that way since I've been there."

When Texas was losing in the late '80s, alumni often complained that Texas had too many blacks who had not been weaned on Longhorn tradition, too many blacks who were more loyal to their own NFL ambitions than they were to the orange and white.

In 1990, fourteen of the twenty-two starters are black. Two of the starting linebackers are black. So are two of the offensive linemen, a rarity for Texas. All of the secondary is black. The receivers and the running backs are black.

The quarterback is not black. Except for Donnie Little's three years from 1978 to 1980, that's always been the case.

"Texas is not going to play a black quarterback," says former Texas A&M coach Jackie Sherrill. "They're just not. Florida State is not going to play a black quarterback. Penn State's not going to play one. Ole Miss is not going to play one. I think it's pretty well understood if you're black, there are certain coaches you go play for. I think I have a history of being fair to them."

Sometimes even a black tailback doesn't get a fair shake at Texas. The star of the 1988 Texas team was Eric Metcalf, the stop-on-a-dime running back now with the Cleveland Browns. At the awards banquet that year not one black, not even Metcalf, received an honor.

"I think it's kind of strange that Metcalf didn't receive one award his senior year," Degrate says. "The people identified the Texas program back then as Eric Metcalf. It's just kind of strange a guy of his caliber doesn't receive any awards. You can't justify it. It doesn't make sense. . . . That doesn't look good. What would you think if you're a black recruit and you're sitting up there going, 'Whoa? What's going on here?' "

Until Heman Sweatt, a postman from Houston, fought and finally won a five-year battle to be admitted to the Texas Law School with eventual Supreme Court Justice Thurgood Marshall as his lawyer in 1950, Texas was white to the bone.

Sweatt chose Texas "instead of Texas A&M or wherever," Darrell Royal says, "because this is the spot. It's the one I'd choose if I was going to knock down some doors. I'd get right in the eye of the storm."

That same year W. Astor Kirk was granted permission to enroll in the University of Texas graduate school but was told to take his classes individually at the YMCA across from the Drag. Former Texas history professor Joe B. Frantz wrote in *The Forty Acre Follies*, "Not caring to get into another court case, the university then permitted Kirk to come onto campus and into class, but seated him at the back of the classroom with a metal ring around his desk-chair so that his blackness wouldn't rub off on the white students. Kirk was abased, the other students were embarrassed, and eventually the barrier came down."

Washington State's Duke Washington became the first black to play in Memorial Stadium in 1954. His appearance actually was in violation of university rules since the Board of Regents didn't drop the color barrier at the stadium until Texas hosted the 1957 NCAA track meet.

It wasn't until 1963 that the Regents allowed blacks on Texas teams and sprinter James Means became the SWC's first black lettermen when he entered UT in 1963. Darrell Royal, however, didn't manage to recruit a black to his football team until six years later.

About the same time that a 193-pound offensive tackle from San Antonio Highlands named Julius Whittier showed up in 1969, Royal was trying to recruit the first black basketball player to Texas. If not for his desire to remain in the Washington, D.C., area, James Brown, a skinny, 6-foot-5 forward nicknamed "Rails" from DeMatha Catholic High School in Hyattsville, Maryland, could have been a black pioneer in Austin, Texas.

"Darrell Royal was about to make a trip up to Washington to recruit me about a hundred and fifty years ago when I was in high school in 1969," says Brown, who instead became Harvard's third-leading all-time scorer and is now a CBS sportscaster. "They were looking to bring in their first black basketball player. Royal was like the governor. I was very candid and said I probably wanted to stay close to home somewhere up East.

"Football was king in Texas. I sensed, but didn't really have any form of appreciation at the time, of how far we had come as a society. Clearly things were separate at that time, and I guess there was a degree of discomfort I would have had going in and being the first."

Roosevelt Leaks felt that discomfort even though he enjoyed an immensely successful career at Texas during its glory years in the early '70s. The bruising fullback ran for 2,923 yards in three seasons but was subjected to racial harassment even from his own teammates until a few of his white teammates like lineman Jerry Sisemore stood up for him.

Racism, Royal says, is anywhere you want to look for it.

"You'll always have prejudice," Royal says. "That's at any school. Blacks are prejudiced, Hispanics are prejudiced, Anglos are prejudiced. Scratch anybody and it'll show. Some people, you just have to scratch further than others before it comes out."

Before Earl Campbell ever set foot on campus in 1974, he heard talk that Royal was a racist. He was convinced otherwise.

"I just remember people saying, 'Darrell Royal hates blacks. It's a prejudiced school. You're not going to make it,'" Campbell says. "I felt the one person I was going to have most of my dealings with was Darrell Royal. I made up my mind when I was eighteen years old, that if he's prejudiced, he's going to have to respect me because I'm going to respect him. Today, we're the best of friends.

"If people like you and me let our children mind their own business and we didn't teach them [racism], they wouldn't learn it. Some people don't want it to die. We keep putting fire on the furnace. I think the black side has come a long way at the University of Texas.

I think the white side has come a long way, but at some point, both sides have to bury the old hatchets and get on with 1991. Are we going to be going at it in 2000 like this?"

While Campbell is Texas's most visible former black star, Leaks's success at Texas was instrumental in luring Campbell, Raymond Clayborn, and other talented blacks to Texas.

"Roosevelt Leaks was the first superstar," Royal says. "He did more to kick down doors and break barriers than anyone. Earl knew he could be at Texas and be a star, which blacks didn't know until Rosey came."

When Clayborn came to Austin from Fort Worth in 1973, he says there were only six blacks on the varsity.

"I always liked Texas. When it was all white, I still pulled for Texas to win," says Clayborn, a defensive back who has spent most of his fourteen NFL seasons with the New England Patriots. "When I was younger, though, I always favored Oklahoma because they had all the blacks."

Finally, Royal began getting them. By the time he retired, he had as many black players as the next coach. But he never had a black quarterback. Fred Akers, in his ten years, played one. David McWilliams has played one sparingly. While Arkansas, TCU, Baylor, and Texas Tech all have played black quarterbacks in 1990, Texas didn't have one on its roster, although it wasn't alone in the SWC.

The first one in the school's history almost didn't come. In fact, he was told not to come to Texas by nearly every school that recruited him.

Donnie Little was the best player in the state in 1977, a gifted athlete who quarterbacked Dickinson to the state title, beating Brownwood in Texas's Memorial Stadium in the final. He had offers to go everywhere but picked Texas. He got no letters from Texas fans telling him not to become a Longhorn. At least not beforehand.

"If I'd got 'em then, I probably wouldn't have come," Little says. "When did the letters start? When I took a snap. When they said, 'This shit is really happening.' "

Little will never forget the first game he played in as a freshman. He and A. J. "Jam" Jones, a fluid running back from Youngstown, Ohio, came out of the locker room at Rice Stadium and onto the field.

"When we came back out, it was like, *boom*," Little says. "I was like, 'Wow.' And Jam was like, '*Wooooow*' because he was from an all-black school. He said, '*Look at all these white people.*' And he was serious. He goes, 'Man, if we have a riot, we're going to get *killed.*

Wow.' He was serious as shit. We're running out and he's going, 'Wow. This is some wild shit.'

"When I got into the game, the PA announcer said, 'UT is about to make history. This will be the first black quarterback to officially take a snap.' I was waiting for the play to come in. I hear this in the huddle. I was like, what? It didn't dawn on me. I thought, 'Man, this is weird.' It didn't sink in."

When he scrambled for a first down, Texas fans applauded progress. He didn't always run for first downs, however. He'd throw an interception, and the boos would come crashing down from the heights of Memorial Stadium. The hate mail followed.

"Some of them, they didn't want a black leading their prestigious, fine white university," Little says. " 'We've never had 'em before, and we can win without you. And black people should stay at running back and receiver.' "

A friend of Little's tells of one of the first times his mother, Margaret Little, came to a Texas game.

"Donnie threw an incomplete pass or something," he says. "Some fan yelled, 'Get that nigger out of there.' Donnie's mother stood up and said, 'That's my boy.' Then Donnie never let his mother come to another game because it upset her so much."

Little helped Texas to a 35–12–1 record from 1978 to 1981 but ended his career at wide receiver, in part, he says, to enhance his pro chances.

He was the final cut from the Atlanta Falcons in 1982. After four years with Ottawa in the Canadian Football League, he returned to Austin. He landed a job at St. Stephen's, a predominantly white private Episcopalian school west of Austin. There the 31-year-old Little pulls down about $25,000.

Little holds no animosity toward any of those who criticized him during his career and says straight out, "I love the school." Yet, it bothers him that, in almost a decade since he left, Texas has had but one other black quarterback.

Donovan Forbes came highly touted out of Baytown Sterling in 1986. Big at 6-foot-2. Strong arm, much stronger than Little's. A tough runner. By the time he had left in 1989, he had started one game—the final game of his career against A&M because regular starter Peter Gardere was hurt.

"I think he got shafted, I think he got a bad deal," Little says. "I've heard this guy had all the physical attributes. I heard he had a great arm. He had the knowledge to read. He had the scrambling ability, yet he didn't play. One time I was told he didn't play because he couldn't get a snap in practice. I said the guy has all these other qualifications, don't you think we can work that out if we got to do overtime getting the snap from center?"

The failure to play Forbes—who others say ate himself out of an opportunity by ballooning up to 230 pounds after knee surgery before his final season—cost Texas a chance to entice other black quarterbacks, Little says.

"I was a little bit upset for recruiting reasons," Little says. "Those were the years we were getting the shit beat out of us. National TV exposure. Against Oklahoma, two or three quarterbacks threw five or six interceptions. For recruiting purposes, why don't we get him in the game? He can't do any worse. Houston, sixty–forty. He's from the Houston area. Why don't we get him in the game? He can't do any worse. Aw, man, they had so many opportunities that were feasible to give him a chance."

Offensive tackle Stan Thomas adds, "If they had given him a chance when he was supposed to start, that guy would have been another Andre Ware or Kevin Murray. They screwed him over bad, I mean real bad. He was a great athlete, had a helluva arm."

Thomas, however, doesn't blame offensive coordinator Lynn Amedee, who groomed Murray while he was at Texas A&M.

"Amedee wants the best players out there. I think the alumni really pressure the head coach. They don't want a black quarterback. Period. Will we see another black quarterback? Not in the future. No time soon. Isn't that bullshit? It's alumni, all alumni. A lot of them are racists."

Thomas adds that black athletes, even black quarterbacks, have a better deal at Texas than the average student.

"The regular black student is treated like shit," Thomas says. "He can't go to fraternity parties, where if I wanted to go, hell, everything's on the house for me. If a black student walked in, they'd probably do something to him. You don't have a social life.

"I won't say the whole institution's racist, but a lot of people, a lot of students that go to Texas have never even been exposed to black people. They come from rich families; they come up here and it's like culture shock for them. They need to recruit more blacks. They need more black teachers. They need more black coaches, the whole thing."

The often subtle racism that exists at many universities became more overt on the Austin campus in the spring of 1990 during the school's annual Round-Up celebration, when many alumni return. It spilled over into the headlines when the Phi Gamma Delta fraternity, the Fijis, handed out T-shirts bearing the face of a "Sambo" atop the body of basketball superstar Michael Jordan. Another fraternity, Delta Tau Delta, smashed a junk car painted with racial slurs. The black community was incensed.

"I think the blacks should have just gone and kicked ass, called 'em out and not blamed the whole university. It would have been over with," says John Butler, a black sociology professor at Texas since 1974. He serves on the men's Athletics Council and was on the search committee that recommended the hiring of McWilliams. "It would have been tensed up for about two months, but it would have been over with. But I'm a child of the sixties.

"What are you going to do, run tell a big, white man? 'My gosh, they're wearing some sweatshirts.' What kind of shit is that? You go over to the frat house, you call 'em out, and say 'If you're bad enough to make a T-shirt, let's see if you can back it up.' You got the whole black student body out there; they're going to back down. The point is this: you can't stop and teach people to be decent.

"When I was at LSU, we didn't run to the president and say, 'My oh my, somebody called me a nigger.' We took care of that shit right there. We just whipped their ass. You don't worry about it. You defend yourself. Do like the Vietnamese. Do like the Jews. Do like the Japanese. They kick your ass in the classroom."

During Round-Up, McWilliams canceled one day of spring practice to let his players march on the campus's West Mall in protest of the incident.

"You don't go and put a Sambo head on Michael Jordan's body and stick it on a T-shirt and expect people not to get pissed," says offensive tackle Chuck Johnson. "You don't spray all kinds of racist epithets on a car and beat it to hell with sledgehammers and expect people not to get upset. It's hard to make me mad, but it can be done, and that kind of stuff is totally unnecessary."

Johnson and his black teammates marched to the state Capitol and then to the Fiji house. The leaders of the march spoke to the crowd. Some people sang.

"None of them were willing to come out and face us for what they'd done," Johnson says. "Or own up to it, man to man. I'm not talking about fighting or anything, just come out and answer to what you'd done. And explain why, like a man."

After heated protests from black students and demands that the fraternities be kicked off campus—they were later suspended—school president Bill Cunningham scrambled to resolve the crisis. Cunningham, a sincere, caring man, usually gets high marks from blacks.

Not this time. His office called Dodds with an unusual request: Cunningham needs some black athletes to appear with him at a speech. Betty Corley, Dodds's secretary, mustered only three blacks, defensive back Willie Mack Garza and basketball players Courtney Jeans and Panama Myers.

The catch is that no one told the athletes why their presence had been requested. They felt like dupes when he was shouted down by an angry crowd of four hundred on the West Mall. The demonstrators wanted dialogue, not rhetoric and a six-page speech. Cunningham stalked off and students chanted "No more lies, no more lies." Campus police locked the doors to the administration building as angry students clamored to be admitted.

Roy Vaughan, executive director of the Ex-Students' Association at Texas for the last 27 years, was with Cunningham that day and recalls seeing one demonstrator waving a sign urging, KILL RICH, WHITE BIGOTS.

"I find incredible irony in that," Vaughan says. "That's about as racist a sign as you could ever see."

The powderkeg situation depressed Vaughan, who has been on campus during the tenure of nine presidents and calls the tireless Cunningham "maybe the brightest jewel we have on this campus."

He adds, "That was the saddest time in my twenty-seven years here, when freedom of speech was denied the president of the University of Texas. Bill Cunningham walked into an absolute trap. It was a set deal. He was doing what John F. Kennedy did: he was declaring war on racism."

Cunningham issued an apology to the athletes, but it was vague, bureaucratic, and, if anything, just reinforced the aloof image the university has been trying to shake for decades.

"My father didn't like Texas at all," says split end Johnny Walker. "He told me Texas had a reputation as a racist institution. He was very upset when I announced I was going to Texas."

Walker picked Texas as much for the school's powerhouse baseball program as its football tradition. He played hardball well enough his junior season to become a fourth-round draft pick of the Atlanta Braves.

The raw-talent outfielder, who could blossom into the next Bo

Jackson or Deion Sanders, signed for a $172,000 bonus, which could have swelled to $300,000 if he had passed up his senior season in football. Charlie Smith, the Braves scout who recommended Walker, predicts he'll be in a major-league uniform in three years. "A lot of people talk about him as a Willie McGee with power," Smith says. "He's been compared to a Bake McBride, but Johnny's got a lot more power."

It's been in baseball that Walker has run into the most racism, from teammates used to all-white playgrounds. He says he got into fights and shoving matches with white teammates in the Texas locker room after he was subjected to racial slurs.

"I can't call Coach [Cliff] Gustafson a racist," Walker says. "I was called nigger by players on the Texas baseball team, but not by the coaches. I never really had any problems with the coaches. They sympathized with me."

Very few black athletes at Texas have racial problems with coaches. They just wish there were more black coaches.

The excuse at Texas is always time. It takes time. But how much time? How long, Lord?

Cunningham points out that while not enough strides have been made, more than $4 million has been spent in financial aid to minorities.

"I think Cunningham's great. He's a personal friend, too," Butler says. "He brought this university to a mega-university. Texas broke away from the Southern pack by hiring good professors and emphasizing research and writing.

"Cunningham built the business school from zippo to I don't know how many endowments. It grew like wild when he was dean of the business school. He was a good professor. He single-handedly increased the number of black MBAs when he was dean, and they have an endowment program from corporations to black students."

"I think we need to do better," Dodds says. "I think we're making strides, but we need to continue to get better."

They could do better, some think, if UT would put in a general studies program, a degree plan for students who simply want a liberal arts major without specializing. Others see that as a license to recruit athletes who have little intention of a serious education and are ill-equipped to handle the demands of college. Many other schools with Top 20 football programs have such general studies programs. Longhorn backers scoff at the recreation, industrial education, and poultry science majors around the conference.

"The Aggies created a premajor called General Studies—read teeth-brushing," *Inside Texas* publisher Robert Heard writes. "And they have other places to hide them after they are ready to settle on a 'real' major . . . recreation, parks, and tourism sciences. Sciences! Give me a break."

Texas's last attempt to adopt what it called an interdisciplinary program died in 1989. It was kicked around two faculty committees before finally being killed because the faculty reasoned that athletes would gravitate toward that plan and stigmatize it as the glorified basket weaving found at other football factories.

Jim Vick, chairman of the Texas Athletics Council and a Louisiana State grad, says, "If you give me a catalogue for any major athletic program and give me an hour, I can tell you where the easiest programs are. I think general studies programs are widespread. Michigan has one. It has a very unstructured sports studies program. I feel our academic standards are as high as anybody's."

Arizona assistant AD Gayle Hopkins, president of the National Association of Academic Advisors, says some schools call their general studies programs by many names but "I'd say ninety-eight percent of all Division I programs have them, outside private schools. The negative connotation is what kills it. But general studies is a comprehensive college experience."

"Notre Dame is an easy place to get an education," a high-ranking official at one Southwest Conference school says. "I've been up there and we've talked to people that have been there. They're taking kids no different from the kids we're taking. And they're graduating, however many they say, ninety percent? Or is it two hundred percent?"

DeLoss Dodds says, "We're in there with the toughest. The difference between Stanford and here is if you get in there, you're going to make it. Stanford doesn't flunk people out. I'm not even sure Stanford gives F's. I know at Stanford you can drop a class with an F, take it over, and that F is gone. Can't do that here. You get an F here, that baby is tattooed on your butt for the rest of your life. There's some places, you can go right up to finals week and drop, but not here."

"It's tough," Butler says of Texas. "The reason is there is no place to hide here. There are no special programs. You have to make it like every other student here. Heck, the regular student has it tough. They're taking only the top twenty-five percent of the senior classes or an 1130 on the SAT. Michigan has a complete program for athletes, but it was put in twenty, thirty, forty years ago. You don't find people majoring in general education at UT. Darrell (Royal) mentions the need for one every time he sees me."

Butler doesn't think Texas will ever have a general studies program.

"The NCAA and the news media would be right on it like hot on water. They should have put it in forty years ago. To put it in now, when all the stress is on academic performance, I'm not sure if the university could take it. If you do put one in, it's on the front page of *Time*. But other schools have them.

"The faculty is against it. I don't know what the percentage would be, but it's high. The faculty here is against anything that lowers standards."

The black faculty members, in particular, Butler says, don't want such a program.

"People will think the only way [blacks] were able to get into Texas was because of this program," Butler says he was told at a faculty party. " 'If you're an athlete and you finished at UT, you must have gone through that program.' Whites have a tendency to lump all blacks together. These parents said, if UT considers that, we'll send our kids to A&M. And they did. They may have that program at A&M, but it was put in forty years ago."

What Texas has put in instead is one of the most expensive, comprehensive academic support systems in the country for its athletes. Texas athletes have their pick of qualified tutors and the run of a new $750,000 study center lined with Macintosh computers. Texas's own sports information people sneak down the hall at Bellmont to the center to work on releases because the athletes have access to better hardware and software than they do.

Texas uses its academic support system as a blue-chip sales tool, but at Texas it's always been assumed that *who* you'll know is more important than *what* you'll know.

Come to Texas, they told Donnie Little, and you can write your own ticket. Texas has CEOs in every board room in the state and all over the world. You'll never have to worry about a job. Little says he bought it, hook, line, and sucker.

"We've got young men who've given their blood, guts, and all, who have degrees and can't find a job," Little says. "Or if they find a job, they're a manager at HEB. It's not bad, but one of the tools they use in recruiting is, 'Look, you come to Texas, you play there, you finish and get your degree. We have some of the most successful businessmen in the world who are Texas alums.'

"To me, that was, like, wow, that's a plus. Maybe I do want to stay in Texas. Why don't I go to Texas? I get a great degree from a great school, and then I'll meet some of the most fascinating and rich and powerful and successful people in the world. But that hasn't happened. I've seen kids come out with degrees, and I'll say, 'You got a job?' And they'll say, 'Nah, man.' It's like they didn't go to school. They got a shovel in their hands.

"Maybe it's not so much that they owe us something, but maybe the school or the athletic department should feel a little responsible. I'm not saying it hasn't been done, but there's not enough of it happening. I say, 'Let's set up a network. Come to UT. Play for four years. You want a professional career? Great. If you don't, here's what we'd like to offer you.'"

Dodds says the school is doing just that.

"What's happening now," Dodds says, "is we've got organizations in every major city in Texas. And if somebody comes to us and wants a job, we can't get them a job, but we can point them toward people who will help them get interviews and that sort of thing."

Bill Bethea, Texas's career counselor and academic advisor, has been on the ground floor of setting up just such a network. In his first year in the position, since September 1989, his office has helped place 15 players—four of them minorities—in jobs and assisted with countless other job interviews.

"We're doing a lot of the right things," says Bethea, who sets up career days and seminars, "but I don't think we can be an employment agency. It's not designed for that. We're in the counseling and referral business. We help them prepare resumes and teach them how to do interviews.

"The problem is most athletes have tunnel vision. They're tunneled into professional athletics, and they think their education is something to fall back on. It should be just the opposite."

One of the eighth graders at the Episcopal school where Little coaches is John Cunningham. Little and six other black former Longhorn football players paid a visit on John's father in August 1990, just before the football season started.

Bill Cunningham served them chicken fajitas and black beans and heard them out. Several white former athletes were invited, but none showed.

The blacks who did spoke candidly. They discussed the need for better job placement for former Texas lettermen. They wondered aloud why Texas was recruiting sons of powerful donors rather than more talented football players.

Degrate says, "There's been some guys on the field that shouldn't have been on the field. People would ask me why does this guy start and this guy doesn't? Is he a better player? Is it because his parents donate more money?"

The ex-players pointed out the lack of blacks in visible positions in the athletic department. They lamented the shabby treatment of former players, including the allotment of poor seats at home football games.

Cunningham listened.

Texas is good at listening.

"Every football player that came out of there had the greatest respect for Bill Cunningham," Little says. "A lot of them didn't know the man. He has this certain charisma about him. He's honest, and he's up front. He had our respect."

Those seven players, however, wanted something in return. Not for themselves, but for the university. After playing for it, sweating for it, bleeding for it, winning for it, they wanted to be part of it.

Little sighs when asked how many Texas exes have offered him jobs in the last four years. "They haven't knocked my door down," he tries to joke. "I was also turned down a lot when I didn't have my degree. We're stereotyped. We're jocks. If you don't have your degree, it shows all you went to school for was to play sports. They didn't know that while I was in school, all they wanted from me was to play sports."

Eric Jeffries heard the same message other blacks did when he was preparing to graduate from LBJ, an Austin high school. Although he makes a middle-class salary as an insurance salesman in Austin, the message he now delivers to athletes at his old high school isn't as bright as the one he heard from Texas recruiters.

In 1989, LBJ had two of the best players in the state. Both linebacker Kenneth Alexander and defensive back Greg Lane had strong academic backgrounds. Alexander went to Florida State, Lane to Notre Dame.

"I really believe Texas is going to have a problem recruiting people out of LBJ because of past graduates and the experience that they've had," says Jeffries, a defensive back from 1983 to 1986. "I go back to LBJ, and they ask, 'What did Texas do for you for those four years?' I have a choice of either lying to them or telling them the truth. And the truth is, I paid my own way. Education was given. That's something I'll be grateful for always. But as far as anything else, it wasn't there.

"Some universities have a great network set up so when players come out of college, they don't have to worry about jobs. I'd say Oklahoma has that. I'd even go so far as to say A&M. Texas has the capabilities of doing it if they want to, and that's what hurts so bad."

William Graham, a black, thirty-one-year-old former Longhorn safety, disagrees.

"You got to find a way to get in," say Graham, who now sells luxury cars in Austin. "I think the opportunities are there, but sometimes you've got to push the door. You can't just knock on it. The idea that a lot of people have is that because I went to Texas, I'm supposed to have an office building and be a CEO of some company or be a vice-president. My parents owned a company. I started off sweeping the floors in their nightclub before I could work the cash register. Most guys want to walk in with no experience and be given a plush, fifty-thousand-dollar-a-year job. I don't think it works like that. I've helped a lot of guys get jobs. I tell guys 'If there's something you want, you've got to go get it. But you've got to be resourceful.' "

Graham, who proudly wears his T sweater to games, adds, "Black kids felt isolated at Texas, and a lot of them would leave. With the athletes, we had a network so we could deal with it a lot better. I had never seen foreign cars, BMWs, the nice cars the white kids were driving. Kids with checkbooks in their pockets. Girls, once they got to know you were ball players, kind of took a liking to you once they found out you weren't bad and weren't going to attack them. A lot of them would say they never went to school with a black before."

Earl Campbell worries about the after-effects of 1990 Round-Up, with good reason. Minority enrollment in September 1990 rose for every group except blacks. After three straight years of increases, the number of blacks enrolled dipped from 1,866 to 1,830. Whittier remains upbeat.

"I believe Bill Cunningham has his heart in the right place as did Darrell Royal," Whittier says. "The incidents at the University of Texas are no different than things you'll see at universities around the country. There are some universities that have held their fingers in crossed positions and said, 'Thank God it wasn't us.' "

Whittier worked in Boston for two years in the mayor's office dealing with labor relations and says he experienced more racism there than he ever has in Texas.

"It's a cesspool up there," he says. "I would rather deal with rednecks that I know how and why they feel the way they feel than deal with somebody who's reputed to be open-minded and American in their feelings about race. I would say that about the entire Northeast.

I got called a nigger by a white boy for the first time on the streets, and I didn't do anything about it. You can raise an angry crowd of racists of about two hundred people in Boston in less than three minutes. You get out and fight with them, and you got a whole neighborhood on your ass."

Campbell is more concerned about how rival recruiters will use the racism exposed during Round-Up.

"They'll pull out all the stuff that happened on campus involving Dr. Cunningham and that fraternity," he says. "When Coach McWilliams goes to recruit kids, all those coaches will have all that stuff that was written on the black issue laminated. I tell you one thing, there's going to be some good kids who run away because of what went on. I'm not saying it was Cunningham's fault or Mc-Williams's fault, but that incident is not going to help us."

Vaughan agrees that Round-Up will be used against Texas for years to come.

He says, "I think that incident set us back immeasurably in our ability to make progress. There are so many people like me who absolutely have our jaws set that we're going to solve this problem. It's not going to go unsolved. There is no doubt there's some racism on the campus. And there doesn't have to be much of it."

Jeffries faults the university for the false promise of great jobs after playing careers end.

"Everything they say is true, but it's never put into action," he says. "They've got CEOs of so many companies, but as far as those doors being opened to you and you being aware of those people out there, it's just not there. I'd have to say it's worse for blacks.

"The end result is what you do with those players after they have served their purpose for you. They need to open up the doors for them. If they're not doing that, that player is being used by the system. That's just the bottom line of what's happening.

"The sad thing is something could be done. All Texas would have to do is gather up a consensus of these players and see exactly what they're dealing with. There are some ex-players who are struggling and don't know where their next paycheck is coming from. From the ex-players, they can learn what to do with the players that are coming in the future. Sad to say, a majority of the black players gone now don't want to have anything to do with Texas."

During the August meeting at Cunningham's home, Dodds told the ex-players of the new program headed by former assistant baseball coach Bill Bethea that's designed to help ex-players find jobs.

"I have not heard of a lot of people getting jobs out of it," Jeffries says. "What's the use of having a system set up that's so good and so great if you're not reaching out to people? They didn't even know how to get into contact with most of the people. The ones they've got on the list are done pretty much by word of mouth. It's probably a year old, maybe a year and a half."

Jeffries says he doesn't know of a minority athlete who has landed a job because of the program.

Jeffries adds, "They genuinely wanted to do something, but they hadn't been used to blacks graduating, first of all. They don't know what to do with them. They weren't prepared for a great number of black players getting degrees. If I call a guy and say you should do it, most of what they're going to say is, 'Man, it ain't nothing but talk. It's the same old stuff.' They don't have much enthusiasm about it because they've heard it all before. Having an excellent program set up doesn't do any good if you're not reaching the people and it's not reaching them."

Not all of those former players are black. One prominent white player, linebacker Jeff Leiding, knocked around Austin for sixteen months after his pro career ended and says he got little assistance from anyone other than dining hall director Tom Pate.

"I would say they're attempting to become the Chase Manhattan or the Citibank of college football," Leiding says of Texas. "Bottom line. Did anybody help me? Are you kidding me?"

Leiding, who blames himself for leaving UT with only 78 hours toward a degree, returned to Austin in 1989 with a wife and child.

"Most of the athletes are coming from an environment where they've been well protected," says Leiding, now in the meat business in Kansas City. "You bring them into an environment where they're still partially coddled. You've only got forty-eight months or sixty to figure out what in the hell you're going to do for the rest of your life. One-half of one percent of you are going to go on and play in the NFL, and they need to be told that. Was I? Oh, no. I was always told I was going to make it, even by the scouts.

"I gave up on worrying what my grades were. I knew what I had to do to pass, to keep my GPA to a certain point where I could go line up on Saturdays, and that's all I did. I blame myself all the way. You're accountable for your actions, always.

"I hated to see the program go in the direction it did—on the field and the way people treated people. It became more of a feedlot operation like what I'm in now. Here we have all these young yearling calves. I bring them into a feedlot and we beef them up. We make them perform. And in the end they take them to the slaughterhouse and cut their heads off. Does that steer know he's going to get shot in the head when he walks in that chute? Nope. It just happens to him."

19

Back in High Cotton

Texas kicker Michael Pollak trots onto the new electric-green All-Pro Turf at Floyd Casey Stadium in Waco for pregame warm-ups and immediately notices the wind. It's gusting up to 25 miles an hour and swirling worse than the breeze at the end of the Oklahoma game, which was stiff enough to shove aside R. D. Lashar's late field goal attempt.

Pollak lines up for a 30-yard gimme. He aims dead center between the uprights. In mild shock, he watches as his kick starts off true and then banana hooks so far wide to the left that it almost bounds into an ambulance parked twenty yards from the goalposts in the south end zone.

He aims a little farther to the right and tries again. Another miss. And another.

Offensive coordinator Lynn Amedee, a former quarterback and field goal kicker at Louisiana State, strides over and tells Pollak to aim to miss, to kick outside the right goalpost and let the wind push the ball through.

The strategy works. In pregame, anyway. It had better hold up in the real thing, because Texas figures to need Pollak's bare foot and every other edge it can find against Baylor, a team that humiliated it 50–7 right in Memorial Stadium in 1989.

The sixth-ranked Longhorns have been good in the 1990 season, but they've also been shock-the-nation lucky. When left tackle Chuck Johnson missed the Texas Christian game with a leg injury, it was the first time all year that Texas had lost a starter. When Texas needed an opponent's field goal to blow wide, it did on the last play against Oklahoma.

The hard-luck, hardscrabble Baylor Bears, meanwhile, have overcome a nightmare season to keep Cotton Bowl dreams alive at a school that, with 12,000 students, is the world's largest Baptist university.

In the spring of 1990, Baylor's coach of nineteen years, gravel-voiced Grant Teaff, switched from his successful, pass-oriented attack to the ground-bound option offense that even veer fanatic Jim Wacker had junked at TCU. Teaff made the radical move despite having a senior quarterback, Brad Goebel, with a chance to break many of the school's all-time passing records.

Goebel never got a chance to adjust to the new offense. Before the season-opener against Nebraska, he broke his hand, becoming one of eighteen Baylor starters or costarters who will miss a total of sixty games. Steve Needham, a third-year sophomore, threw the first passes of his college career against the Cornhuskers. Needham had plenty of help from the Baylor defense, even though the Bears are without departed All-Americans James Francis and Robert Blackmon. It's Nebraska, though, that pitched a 13–0 shutout.

Arizona State beat Baylor 34–13 the next week. The following Thursday, 275-pound redshirt freshman guard John Karkoska suddenly collapsed on the practice field. He was quickly iced down and rushed to the hospital as his body temperature soared to over 105 degrees.

Baylor players and coaches made repeated pilgrimages to Hillcrest Baptist Medical Center, where doctors struggled vainly to find out exactly what caused Karkoska's kidneys and liver to shut down. Though it seemed a classic case of heatstroke, it hadn't been all that hot or humid on the Thursday when Karkoska was felled.

On Saturday, September 22, the Bears planned a pregame prayer for Karkoska's recovery, but that was abruptly shelved. After a 13–9 comeback win over Sam Houston State, Teaff—who learned of Karkoska's death ten minutes before kickoff—sadly gave his team a forty-minute eulogy instead of a victory speech.

Baylor did its mourning privately. No black arm bands, no impassioned "Win one for John" speeches.

"We didn't want to throw his name around and make a big public spectacle of it," says senior free safety Michael Welch. "It's been a tough year, but they say pain has no memory."

"It's been about ten years rolled into one," Baylor offensive guard John Turnpaugh adds. "Win or lose, after this season, we'll all be numb."

The Bears, however, not only survived, but prospered. After a dispirited start they have rallied to a 6–3–1 record, heading into their showdown with the Longhorns. They're even in line for a bowl bid —if they'll just lose to Texas.

Due to the vagaries of the bowl system, the Poulan Weed-Eater Independence Bowl in Shreveport, Louisiana, will take them right away if they play themselves out of the Cotton Bowl picture with a loss to Texas. The Independence Bowl, however, also wants the Bears to guarantee a school sale of 15,000 tickets to the December 15 game.

Teaff, who became a locker room legend by successfully swallowing a worm to inspire his team to beat Texas in 1978, torches that bridge. He gambles that his team can get to Dallas by edging the Longhorns and then watching Texas A&M beat the hell out of Texas on Thanksgiving Day.

"I'm almost livid," Teaff says. "It's ridiculous. We could well end up tied for second or no lower than third and be sitting at home. That's not fair. That's not right.

"I tell you the bowls are hurting themselves. There are going to be a lot of people more aggressive than I am about that, that are going to get after them over some form of a national championship."

While Teaff's team has its back to the cotton, Texas doesn't really need any extra motivation for this game. "We owe Baylor," Pollak says.

A year ago Baylor pinned a 50–7 beating on Texas in Memorial Stadium for the Bears' most lopsided win in a series that began in 1916. Teaff was a team captain of his Snyder High School football team in 1951 when Baylor had last won in Austin.

Texas fans count that debacle as one of the worst football games in the school's history. Texas athletic director DeLoss Dodds considers it one of his lowest lows in ten years on a very demanding job.

"People in my business want the best organization they can have, and they want the best effort they can have," Dodds says. "In that game, none of that was there. It was the first time I saw a Texas team not put out the effort. It just wasn't there."

The Bears gained a mere 252 yards on offense in that 1989 rout, but they had three scoring drives that totaled 17 yards.

"I thought they quit in the third quarter," says Santana Dotson, Baylor's outstanding junior defensive end. "Basically they're the same team that we beat last year in Austin."

Even Texas had a hard time defending its effort. Says one offensive starter, "It didn't seem right out there. It just didn't seem like we tried to win that game."

Peter Gardere, Sr., watched the 1989 game from the stands and tried not to get physically sick. His son, the starting quarterback, had a bum shoulder but convinced the coaches he could contribute. He did—two interceptions.

"The doctor said there's no way in the world he can throw without excruciating pain," Gardere's dad recalls. "He had no zip on the ball at all. He was throwing against the wind with nothing on it and had two quick interceptions. That's demoralizing."

Baylor led 43–0 before Texas showed up on the scoreboard. Welch, the Bears' hard-hitting safety, says, "You could see in their eyes they didn't want to play."

With the Cotton Bowl on the line, Texas might be too ready to play. Texas coach David McWilliams wants his team loose. He jokes that he plans to burn the team buses so they won't have any way to get home if they lose.

Teaff, meanwhile, is oozing confidence. Why not? Baylor has won seven of the last eight meetings in Waco, or the Bermuda Triangle, as McWilliams labels the Waco-Bruceville-Eddy microplex. Texas football teams mysteriously, but routinely, disappear at Floyd Casey Stadium.

The Texas game has always been a high point of Baylor's season, and none was higher than the Bears' 34–24 upset in 1974 that deprived the Longhorns of a seventh consecutive Cotton Bowl.

That was the cornerstone game, the one that gave Baylor its first SWC championship in fifty years and signaled a turnaround for the modestly sized private school. Baylor was so delighted with the win that the score was left on the brightly lit scoreboard throughout the night.

"When Baylor beat us once, the door was kicked in," says John Butler, a member of the Texas Athletics Council. "Used to be, when teams walked into Memorial Stadium, they were already down twelve, fourteen points. There was fear in their eyes."

"I always thought of the Texas program as class," says Teaff, the dean of SWC coaches. "They represented the finest, the best. They were thought of as *the* university by the citizens of this state. I've always respected them, but I've never feared them. I always felt that when we step on the field with them, we ought to be able to give the best we have."

That was often enough, particularly in Waco, where the most renowned upset of Texas is forever known as the "Worm Game."

In 1978, before his 2–8 team took the field against ninth-ranked Texas, Teaff spun a rather bizarre tale about two Eskimo fishermen.

The younger one was having no luck catching fish, and he was curious because the older man was fishing in the same spot and using the same equipment and the same bait and catching fish like crazy. Finally, the young man asked his older friend's secret.

"You have to keep your worms warm," the old man said as he opened his mouth to reveal a wad of live worms.

Some Baylor players were on the edge of their benches. Others were thinking, "No wonder we're two and eight."

Then, Teaff took out a live nightcrawler he had bought at a bait store before the game and said, "Today, men, I'm going to keep the worms warm!" He dropped it into his mouth, the story goes, and swallowed it. "Actually I only chomped on it twice and spit it out," Teaff says now. "They're as bland as they can be. But you can eat a bucket of those things. They're nothing but protein."

Baylor's players bit on Teaff's speech and thrashed the Longhorns 38–14.

Up to that point, Teaff's Bears were a lackluster 32–42–3 in almost seven complete seasons. Afterward, his Baylor teams are an impressive 80–54–3, which allows Teaff to quip, "I haven't had to eat a worm in almost eleven years."

Teaff's strength this season is his stingy defense, which might have been even better if he could have signed safety Stanley Richard and end Oscar Giles, two Texas players he recruited hard.

Giles worked for a Baylor alum for five years, stacking groceries. Teaff tried to sell the Palacios star on Baylor's smaller campus and a student body that's one-fourth the size of Texas's.

Teaff came closer to landing Richard, a superfast prospect from Hawkins, the same town that sent Texas the strapping running back named Edwin Simmons who never quite became the next Earl Campbell that he was touted as. After Richard initially put Texas on hold during recruiting, then head coach Fred Akers returned the favor, even though Richard was listed by at least one scouting service as one of the top 100 players in the country. Secondary coach Dean Campbell then had to beg Akers to offer Richard a scholarship.

"A few days before signing date, Texas told me they didn't have any openings," says Richard, who was also a state champion hurdler. "The following day they lost somebody and offered me. I thought I was gone to Baylor. I wanted to play with the best, and Baylor was leading the conference in interceptions nearly every year."

Instead, the Sheriff, as he's now known, is getting set to lead his Texas defense against Baylor.

Before the Bears leave the locker room for the kickoff, Teaff notes how far this Baylor team has come and how little was expected of it. The Bears had been picked to finish no higher than sixth in the SWC, and that was before the avalanche of adversity.

Teaff has one last comment for those who doubted his bad-news Bears. He points to a clump of mistletoe he has taped to his butt and says all the critics can "kiss my ass."

The Baylor players react as if Teaff has just kept a worm warm.

Out on the field it's clear, sunny, and 73 degrees, perfect football weather even if the wind is gusting and swirling. About 10,000 cotton-craving Texas fans are in the stadium, many of whom are Austinites who've made the hundred-mile trip north to Waco. Some travelers take a full hour just to navigate the two-mile, four-lane stretch on Valley Mills Road from I-35 to the stadium. Bevo, the Texas Longhorn mascot, gets caught in the gridlock and doesn't arrive at the game until midway through the first quarter.

Baylor gets the ball first and comes out passing. The shock value quickly wears off, and Teaff settles in for a war in the trenches.

Teaff switched to the veer for a reason. He has a budding star in Robert Strait, a 6-foot-1, 230-pound fullback who tied a national high school record at Cuero with 127 career touchdowns while piling up a whopping 8,404 rushing yards, the third highest career total in national schoolboy history. Texas had recruited Strait hard. Word leaked out that to get him, Texas would consider unretiring Earl Campbell's number 20 jersey so Strait could wear it.

Texas's only Heisman Trophy winner was not amused by that idea. Athletic director DeLoss Dodds swiftly said that was just a rumor that would never become a reality.

Strait, however, didn't become a Longhorn. With Strait in their backfield, the Bears attack Texas right up the gut, just as Colorado and Oklahoma did with such great success.

On the first series, Strait grabs a handoff, blasts off right guard, breaks a couple of tackles, and rumbles for a 15-yard touchdown.

After Santana Dotson devours Gardere for a sack and forces a Texas punt, the Bears go on the move again. The drive stalls at the Texas 1, and Jeff Ireland boots an 18-yard chip shot for a 10–0 Baylor lead.

Texas hasn't been this flat all year. Maybe there is a jinx in Waco.

In the second quarter, Dotson sacks Gardere again. Gardere then misreads a defense and is picked off by Michael Welch at the goal line when split end Johnny Walker breaks outside and Gardere throws inside.

When the Longhorns get the ball back but can't move, Baylor is poised to deliver a game breaker. Texas punter Alex Waits stands inside his own 10-yard line, awaiting the snap. Baylor cornerback Charles Bell lines up on Waits's far left. Waits, a left-footed punter, knows Texas doesn't plan to block Bell because Lance Gunn is supposed to pick up the inside rusher.

"That was the scheme going into it because we didn't think he was going to rush," Waits says. "But when he's down there in the starter's blocks digging in, you can tell he's going to come after it. I wasn't going to punt the ball if he was even close."

Waits was born in Scotland, and his grandfather was a professional soccer player who represented his country in international play. Waits has always been a heady player and a good athlete.

In junior high school he was a big left-hander with a controlled 80-mile-an-hour fastball and big-league dreams when he blew out his arm. He did the same to his left leg at Texas, feeling the hamstring pop in a running drill last year. When it didn't look as though he'd be able to come all the way back as a punter, Waits went to David McWilliams and volunteered to be a kamikaze special teamer, anything to help the team.

The hamstring has healed, however, and Waits's running punt helped save the day against Oklahoma.

As Bell flies in, Waits pulls the ball down, sidesteps him, and punts the ball underneath another charging Baylor player. Sixty-six yards later, the ball rolls dead at the Baylor 15. Disaster is averted. Instead of a blocked kick and a 17–0 deficit, Texas now has Baylor in something of a hole.

The Bears can't go anywhere, and Texas regains possession at the Baylor 44. Butch Hadnot picks up 5 yards, but two Carders passes fall incomplete.

McWilliams turns to Pollak for a 56-yard field goal try. It is 9 yards farther than he's ever kicked in his life, a yard more than the 55-yarder he has set as a goal for the season. He does, however, have the wind at his back. It's not blowing in his face the way it was when he warmed up at the other end.

"I've been waiting for that all season long," Pollak says. "I thought I was going to get my chance in the SMU game."

Pollak's 56-yarder, the longest by a Longhorn in five seasons, cuts the deficit to 10–3. Texas still trails, but with 59 yards total offense in the first half—a minus 6 on the ground—the Longhorns are lucky the score isn't a lot worse.

"They were running straight up the gut," Giles says. "We played these passing teams the last four weeks, and it seemed like we weren't ready to play the run. At halftime, we got together and said it would be terrible to go out like this. What we said is 'Nothing's going to be easy.'"

"They were blowing us off the ball," adds B.J., Texas linebacker Brian Jones. "They were killing us up front."

Big play B.J. begins the second half by ripping the football from Strait on the first play. Baylor recovers, but the Longhorns serve notice that this isn't 1989.

On Texas's first series, Chris Samuels breaks for 28 yards on a draw play to the Baylor 32. Two plays later Amedee calls for a deep fly pattern to Keith Cash. Gardere drops back and turns, only to see Baylor linebacker Daniel Morgan and end Robin Jones crashing in from the right side. Right guard Scott Gooch cuts down both of them with a body block. Gardere stops to avoid the pileup, straightens, and fires a 31-yard dart to Cash over a sprawling Charles Bell for the tying touchdown.

When Baylor is forced to punt again, Samuels turns in another big play, returning it 20 yards to the Bears' 36. Now it's time for Hadnot to out-Strait Strait. Baylor is talking trash to him. "They said, 'You run like my grandma.' I just ignored it," Hadnot says. "Didn't nobody scare me. I'm kind of hard to intimidate."

Hadnot picks up 11 up the middle. Behind blocks from Johnny Walker and Samuels, he skirts left end for a 19-yard touchdown. Samuels carries the ball only six times all game but is having an excellent game, blocking for Hadnot and returning punts. Even so, Gardere has had to set him straight in the huddle.

"Chris kept yelling to check out of a play because Baylor was overplaying, but I told him 'Don't worry about it.' He said it a couple more times, so I said, 'Shut up and don't worry about it.' I yelled at him pretty good," says Gardere, who rarely gets to do his Amedee impersonation.

Pollak adds the extra point for a 17–10 lead, but Texas offensive tackle Stan Thomas is ejected for fighting with Baylor linebacker Lee Bruderer, who admits later he did punch Thomas once.

"It was one of those SMU punches," says Thomas, who in 1989 incited SMU's Kenny "Sugar" Rea into a short one-punch bout that got the Mustang ejected and left Thomas writhing in pain after a low blow.

Thomas says of Baylor's Bruderer, "Every time we kicked a field goal or an extra point, he was hitting me in the groin. I grabbed his facemask and punched him. Then I saw the flag and thought, 'This can't be on me.' I guess his goal for the whole week was to get me thrown out of the game."

Shay Shafie comes in for Thomas. Injured Chuck Johnson had unselfishly taken himself out in the first half, telling line coach Clovis Hale he couldn't handle Santana Dotson at less than full speed. That brought in Charles Seafous. Offensive guard Duane Miller, slowed by an ankle injury, has played little, allowing junior Scott Gooch his finest hour.

Three reserves are in for the stretch run. Shades of Colorado?

The two teams trade field goals, and Texas finds itself leading 20–13 with less than one quarter between it and the Cotton Bowl.

"We call ourselves the Regulators," Gooch said, speaking for his fellow subs. They have a newspaper article about their roundly criticized series in the Colorado game tacked on the Neuhaus-Royal bulletin board as a constant reminder. "The coaches always tell us there's not going to be a warning when our bell is going to ring, and we have to always be ready to fight."

Texas, facing the wind, starts The Drive from its 20 with 12:16 left in the game. Seventeen plays and almost eight minutes off the clock later, Pollak lines up a 38-yard field goal into that same stiff breeze that was toying with him in pregame warm-ups. If good, the field goal will break Jeff Ward's Texas season record of 19 field goals. Far more importantly, it will break Baylor's back and put Texas in the Cotton Bowl after a seven-year exile.

Aim just outside the right goalpost, Amedee had told him. Pollak can't quite bring himself to do it. He targets a millimeter inside the right goalpost and   it's good!

As one last futile Baylor drive dies to assure Texas's 23–13 conference-clinching win, the Texas partisans in the crowd sing, "Nah nah nah nah, hey hey hey, good-bye."

But it's hello to Dallas. Texas recruiting coordinator James Blackwood is so elated he slaps a big bear hug on a surprised Robert Heard, the publisher of *Inside Texas* who has castigated Blackwood in a few of his newsletters.

Cotton Bowl president John Stuart, a Longhorn alumnus and former Athletics Council member, had tried to wish those final seconds off the clock.

Stuart had phoned Texas earlier in the week to ask how many Cotton Bowl hats to bring to hand out to players in the winning locker room.

None, he was told. *None?* McWilliams didn't want his team forgetting about the upcoming Aggies. He also said he wanted no photographs of a Longhorn player wearing a Cotton Bowl hat until after the regular season.

"David's really tense," Stuart says on the sidelines, "for a laid-back kind of guy."

Just as Gardere is about to down the ball on the game's final play, a Texas trainer breaks open a bag of store-bought cotton balls. The Texas players look at them curiously—they haven't gone through this celebration before. Then they reach in and clutch handfuls of the soft balls and fling them into the cool November air.

Wide receiver Graylin Johnson sticks two swabs on each eyeball and prances around the field, chanting, "Cotton-eyed Joe, cotton-eyed Joe." Stan Thomas sticks a wad of cotton in his mouth and mugs for the TV cameras.

Keith Cash jumps into the arms of offensive tackle Shay Shafie and then hugs receiver coach Clarence James, screaming, "Finally, finally!"

Texas fans spill out of the stands and swarm the field in a delirious celebration.

In the locker room, Brian Jones manages to find a Cotton Bowl cap. It belongs to trainer Eric Day, who bought it at the State Fairgrounds in Dallas after the Oklahoma game. Jones playfully swipes the hat.

Other players are talking conference championship rings.

"I'll have to get it on my right hand," Richard says as he extends a left hand with a swollen ring finger. "Look at that. I've been here a long time, and the most excitement I've seen is a Bluebonnet Bowl. We're in condition to go four quarters, even five quarters.

"We're on a shock-the-nation tour. We did a lot of things that a lot of people said we wouldn't be able to do. Not only did we have to deal with the media, we've had to deal with a lot of people because we did not have a lot of supporters at the beginning of the season. The only thing we had was our team, our coaches, and our athletes. As we began to win, week by week, a lot of people started getting behind us. . . . A lot of people said we wouldn't be able to do it; now here we are at the top of the hill, pushing people down."

The seven-year dry hole for one of college football's premier programs has turned into a gusher.

In a madhouse locker room, school president Bill Cunningham presents McWilliams with a new five-year contract. The previously embattled McWilliams had just one year remaining under his old contract. The players shout their approval and McWilliams jokes, "I noticed a couple of the players didn't clap. I got their names."

Blackwood, Texas's hyperactive recruiting coordinator, skips up the second-floor metal stairs to the visitors' locker room and overlooks Baylor defensive coordinator Pete Fredenburg.

"Take that, Pete," Blackwood taunts, shoving a pair of Hook 'Em Horns in his direction.

A puzzled Fredenburg asks, "What are you doing, James?"

When Blackwood persists, Fredenburg becomes livid. "Well, kiss my ass," Fredenburg yells. A few Texas players, noticing the ugly scene, add to the spectacle and spit toward Fredenburg.

Out in the parking lot, defensive coordinator Leon Fuller shares a shot of Wild Turkey with wife Pam and friends.

Teaff is magnanimous in defeat and is exhorting Texas to beat Miami, which is accepting its Cotton Bowl invitation the same day.

"They had no choice but to make that drive," Teaff says of Texas. "That was a real, real key to the championship. That's what you have to do. They could be national champions if things fell right. They may not be that good, but who in the heck in the country is that good? This is one of those years that you don't have to be that good to be national champion. Just be in the right spot and win a couple more football games. 'Course they might give it to Notre Dame if they beat Colorado. But if they beat Colorado, I think Texas has a legitimate chance. But they've got to get by the Aggies first."

Oh, yes, the Aggies. They can wait at least a day. Now it's time to party since McWilliams hasn't burned the buses.

Earlier in the season about a dozen players—all of them white—started meeting after games at Nasty's, a funky, kind of grungy, rugby hangout northwest of campus. They didn't know or much care where their black teammates went to celebrate.

A few of the players and Texas Angels, who assist in recruiting, have decided it's time for a change. Fliers are passed out. There's a party at Toulouse on Sixth Street. Everyone who is of age is invited.

About thirty players, blacks and whites, attend.

They're finally together. On the field and off. They end up drifting down to Ivory Kats, a piano bar, and singing together.

They're going to the Cotton Bowl at last.

"At one point last year we were in this position, right after we beat Arkansas," Richard says. "Everyone started saying Cotton Bowl. Cotton Bowl. Cotton Bowl. We were looking down the street, looking for the Cotton, and Tech came in and kind of cut our feet out from under us. So we realized we could not let that happen again this year. We started concentrating on the next game. And the next game. You do that, it's just a little hike to the Cotton Bowl."

20

Love-Bombs Away

Tena Bradley has a dream. It's a very positive dream. In it, she sees herself working with the players of her favorite college football team and helping the coach get through some very troubled times.

Unfortunately, a heavily stressed Barry Switzer, rocked by scandal after scandal, leaves Oklahoma in June of 1989 before she has a chance to talk with him.

In the summer of 1990, Bradley, a perky, vivacious thirty-two-year-old blonde who attended Oklahoma for a couple of semesters in the late 1970s, is living in Austin. She decides to approach the local team. The Dallas Cowboys, that is.

In the new era of coach Jimmy Johnson and owner Jerry Jones, they have left Thousand Oaks, the California hideaway favored by Tom Landry and Tex Schramm. They're now training in the 100-degree summer swelter of Austin, where droves of fans will risk heatstroke just to watch the Cowboys they've worshipped so long from afar do things like walk through pass patterns and take water breaks.

At the Cowboys' new training facility on the St. Edward's University campus on the south end of town, Bradley approaches Jones with her idea. The Cowboys' talkative, hands-on owner says, let's do lunch. A quick one.

"It was mostly out of courtesy," he says.

Jones and his 1–15 Cowboys don't have much to lose. He listens to a short presentation from Bradley.

"A lot of the things she talked about were already incorporated into our program," says Jones, one of the country's most upbeat businessmen. "I think her line was, 'Would you give me a blank check if I promised you could go to the Super Bowl?' "

Jones would not. Bradley is 0-for-2. So she shops for another team. She is obviously thinking positive.

Bradley convinces Texas coaching legend Darrell Royal to breakfast with her at Barton Creek Country Club. Royal refers her to Earl Campbell. "You're just what we need," an enthusiastic Campbell says. "There's not much camaraderie over there."

Paydirt.

Campbell tells her to see David McWilliams, who is coming off two straight losing seasons.

McWilliams can't do lunch. He's way too busy trying to resurrect the Texas football program. Finally, he promises her an hour on a Sunday to make her pitch. Three and one-half hours later, Bradley is in business.

She's hired out of pocket for approximately $4,000 a month at a bureaucracy-clogged school where many longtime degreed employees are making far less. At Texas, a state school, by law most jobs have to be posted. Many draw hundreds of applicants. Most jobs, however, don't involve a football team that desperately needs to win.

Soon, Bradley is at Texas practices. She's in McWilliams's office for weekly sessions that sometimes last as long as two hours. She's meeting with players, being everything from a big sister to a confidante. She works up homemade posters with the words *Cotton Bowl-bound* on them for the weight room, which some players swipe to hang in their dorm rooms. Bradley, to use the phrase coined by her Sylvester Stallone look-alike associate Ron Brown, is "love bombing" the program with her own brand of outgoing, positive motivation.

"I think Coach McWilliams was looking for some kind of catalyst," says Michael Pollak, Texas's walk-on kicker who used some positive thinking himself to break the school's single-season record with 20 field goals. "She's good at getting you to set goals and then find ways to meet them."

Bradley's company business card for Inner Prizes Inc. urges, "Changing your life, by changing your mind!" She's had bleeding ulcers and recurring bouts with psoriasis. Yet Brown, a vice-president of the company, says, "She's the most positive person I've ever been around. She's up almost all the time and it's not a put-on or a show. She truly loves people."

Brown likes to tell the story about the time Bradley was trading up cars from a Honda to a Lincoln and wanted to get her cellular phone out and put it in her new car.

"She parks it out back at the car shop," Brown recalls. "We go out to dinner, and when we come back, there's a note on the car. 'Sorry we backed into your car.' They've dented the hood and there's twelve hundred dollars' worth of damage. She has to get a couple of estimates, and then she has to get it fixed. But she baked cookies for the guys who hit her car—and she makes a mean chocolate chip cookie."

Bradley works individually with about two dozen of the Longhorns, including quarterback Peter Gardere.

She has not gained the complete confidence of all the players, however. One starter says, "I felt like I could trust her. But I felt also Coach Mac probably knew a lot of the things I was telling her. I'm careful what I say around her because I knew she was talking to the coaches. At the same time, if I wanted something to be said, I could talk to her and be pretty sure it would get back to the coaches."

Pollak adds, "It's not like she turned my life around; she fine-tuned a couple of things. A lot of what she talked about was pretty obvious, but it's stuff people don't do, like writing out your goals. I read mine at the beginning of the day and at the end."

Among his goals for the season were to hit on 20 of 25 field goal attempts and to nail one from 55 yards. Heading into the Texas A&M game he's made 20 of 24. The 20th, against Baylor, was good from 56 yards.

Mark Berry is really smitten with Bradley's "love bombing" and goal setting. The week of the Houston game, he writes down "four interceptions" as his goal, even though he doesn't have one all year. On the third play of the game against the Cougars, the Texas cornerback picks off a David Klingler bomb. Unfortunately, he separates his shoulder and can't return.

One of the teaching aids Bradley uses is a book by Og Mandino, *The Greatest Salesman in the World.* The mix of positive thinking and religious figures in the self-help book upsets some of the team's Christian players, who start talking about just what kind of message she is spreading.

"They all wanted us to go to this seminar," one Longhorn regular says of Bradley and some of his teammates. "Some players came up to me and said we got a problem. They were saying, 'I don't think Coach Mac knows what he's getting us into.' I was kidding, saying 'Hell, he probably sold his soul to the devil for a winning season.'

That wasn't true, of course. Just another thing we had to overcome. She was in conflict with Fellowship of Christian Athletes and Athletes in Action. She was upset people were talking behind her back. It got straightened out, though."

McWilliams also likes to bring in different speakers to address the entire team, such as A. C. Green, the Los Angeles Laker forward who's also a minister. The religious message of a couple of speakers rubbed some players the wrong way. "We had some guy say you had to live your life for Jesus; that was a little overboard," says Pollak, who's Jewish. "It would have been all right if the meeting was optional, but the problem is he wanted everybody to be there. I didn't enjoy listening to that guy tell me I was going to hell because I didn't believe in Jesus, but I didn't want to make any waves. I think Coach Mac's intentions were good. He was so happy that things were going well and he thought this was helping."

McWilliams also brought in a Vietnam veteran who lost an arm and an eye when he jumped on a grenade to save his buddies. He had thirty-two operations, was once given up for dead—and he now gives one hell of a talk.

So does Lewis Timberlake, a Texas-based former insurance executive who speaks to everybody from IBM to the National Dentist Association for $2,500 a pop. McWilliams likes to bring him in before the biggest games. "I told David most everybody who is successful has failed first," Timberlake says. "It's a test of character. Lincoln was beaten eight times before getting elected President. J. C. Penny lost forty million dollars."

Bradley and Timberlake are the latest in a widely varied line of motivational approaches at Texas.

Royal's style was simple, straightforward. "The way he motivated you was by expecting you to do it," says James Street, the quarterback who led Texas to a national championship in 1969. "It was before I was there, but I heard the story about him going to the blackboard in the Texas-Texas A&M game and writing the score up on it at the half."

The Longhorns, who'd lost four of their last five games in the 1965 season, were down 17–0. "Coach Royal told us he could put all kinds of diagrams on the blackboard, but that it would not help us a bit," quarterback Marvin Kristynik later related. "He said it was just a matter of whether we wanted to win bad enough. Then, just before we went on the field, he wrote on the blackboard, twenty-one to seventeen. Then he said, 'That's what you can do.' "

Two quarters later, Texas was celebrating a 21–17 victory.

"He was just so matter-of-fact about that stuff," Street says. "Even before the Big Shootout he was very businesslike. He expected you to do good when you went out there. Most of his talks were when he would get really upset. He got mad in the Oklahoma game my sophomore year. His motivational talk at half was simply, 'I will take everybody off the field if we go back out and play like we did the first half. I'll take everybody off. I mean you. And you. And you.' He started pointing at people—players and coaches. He was talking to everybody. He said, 'I will not be associated with a game like this. There's a helluva fight going on out there and we're not in it. I mean we are not a part of it.'

"I think we were behind seven to zero," Street recalls.

Texas won that game in 1967 as well, pulling it out 9–7.

Royal, a child of the Depression, recognized that hard work wasn't always enough. He wanted his players to think they were going to get lucky. He liked to say, "If you fall into a mud hole, check your back pocket—you might have caught a fish."

When Fred Akers arrived from Wyoming after Royal's hard-luck 5–5–1 season in 1976, motivational talks became more controlled, more elaborate, and more sophisticated.

"We were the first college football team in the country to use deep relaxation sessions to improve, to concentrate," says Akers.

Akers believed in positive thinking, visualization, mental imaging, and winning. He was the only one in a family of nine children to attend college. As a young student, he once won a national essay contest on the role of the automobile in society, and his family didn't even own one. As sharp as he was, athletics had been his ticket up and out. Winning was very much a part of the image he liked to cultivate and project.

"I only played in four losing ball games from the time I was in the fourth grade to the time I went to Arkansas," he says. "We won. We didn't do anything but win."

Akers liked to bring in Lou Tice of the Pacific Institute of Seattle during the summers to talk to his team, even if some of the players were so exhausted by the heat and the practices that they all but nodded off during Tice's talks.

"I'd known Lou since the year before I went to Wyoming," Akers recalls of the former successful high school coach. "I met him while I was out recruiting. He'd done motivational work for individuals, businesses, a few sports organizations, and even for entire towns. A

225

town up in Montana, their primary economy—mining—closed down. People didn't feel they had much hope. Their self-esteem had been shot. He met with the leaders of that town and worked with them. He got credit for restoring the community. Gave 'em hope. Without hope you don't get much action, and all you see are the bad things."

Usually Tice would come in during two-a-days to lay the foundation. Akers took it from there. The coach some players called "Little Napoleon" handled the pregame preparation. In the spring before his third season in 1979, Akers brought out T-shirts for the players to wear to reinforce his team-first philosophy. In big, bold orange letters was the word *team.* Underneath in smaller print was the word *Me.* His Purdue team in 1990 wore them as well.

"He was so competitive, he seemed to be at his best in the big games," says Robert Brewer, a quarterback under Akers who is now a fund-raiser for Texas. "Except for bowl games, his record backed that up. He owned Oklahoma like nobody has before or since. He would bring out the competitive instincts in the team before the game. You could see his intensity. I think that exuded to the team."

At least, to most of the team. Brewer still remembers a strong Akers lecture during a 7–5 year in 1980 when the team started out 5–0.

"He chewed us out because we were falling apart," Brewer says. "He got on us because we weren't taking care of business over at the dorm or in the classroom. He gave us about a fifteen-minute tongue-lashing, the biggest tongue-lashing I ever heard. It was right after practice before the A&M game.

"Fred said, 'Now are there any questions?' Jitter Fields, who at the time was a walk-on special teams guy, stuck his hand up and said, 'Yeah, Coach, do you think next year we can get our names on the backs of our uniforms?' It got deathly silent. Then the whole room burst out laughing, and even Coach Akers started laughing. But you know what, the next year we had our names on our uniforms, and we went to the Cotton Bowl."

Akers wanted his teams calm, controlled, and performing comfortably on a higher plane.

"If you're going to be at your best, you're going to do that when you're most relaxed," Akers explains. "Why do you think you take a big, deep breath before you shoot a free throw? You're relaxing so you can concentrate. When it's third-and-one, I want our guys taking a good deep breath, knowing they're relaxed. You can be the most emotional by being relaxed, because you can concentrate harder.

"It's amazing how much energy you waste in the dressing room.

That's what we try to avoid. You want your emotion and excitement out on the field. You don't want to waste it by being so tight and tense and beating up the locker room and breaking chairs. Britt Hager was always very tense.

"You can't hit 'em till you're out on the field. It's like Muhammad Ali. You watch any of his fights. The guy over there that he's fighting is holding on to the ropes, dancing and jumping up and down, working his mouthpiece over. His jaws are tight. Muhammad Ali is laying on the ropes waving to the crowd. He knows the guy can't hit him until he's out there. The energy you waste before the ball game might not be there in the fourth quarter when you need it. You'd turn the lights down, have them close their eyes, and talk 'em through it."

"Imagine yourself at a place where you can relax," his deep voice would resonate before every game. "There's a billboard with the word *relax* printed on it."

"I imagined myself out on a lake because that's where I'm most comfortable," says former Texas quarterback Bret Stafford. "I've got to give Fred credit. If it worked for one person, it was worth it. He made you think constantly how to relax, that you've got to relax to perform. The best analogy he ever used is, when you're playing on a skyscraper, you've got a plank. You're used to walking on that level. You take Joe Blow off the streets, and he tries to walk across that plank, he's not going to make it. That was usually said in the bigger games. I think the maturity level had a lot to do with how much you got out of it. I'm sure it didn't hurt me. There were several times on the field when I'd take a deep breath and tell myself I've got to relax. I did that before throwing the touchdown pass on the last play of the game to beat Arkansas."

"Fred would turn the lights down low," recalls William Graham, who played safety for Akers from 1979 to 1981. "It would be total relaxation, total control of every muscle, every fiber. My freshman year, I can remember sitting there thinking, 'Whoa, this is really deep.'

"He'd start at the toes. Take a deep breath and relax. He'd move up to the ankles, calves, knees, and thighs. Then it was up to your stomach, back, chest, arms, and head. By the time he was done with all this, you were so totally relaxed it was unreal.

"He'd say, 'Now you're in control. We're prepared. We're going to take 'em up one hundred stories and play on the top of a building. Nobody can play with us at a hundred stories. Whoever gets knocked off and is the last man standing is going to win the game. We're going out there and kick behind and take another victory.' "

"He went from your toes, up to your neck, right up to your eyeballs," adds punter Alex Waits, who was in Akers's last recruiting class in 1986. "We'd just turn the lights off and we'd lay down on the ground. He'd work his way through the body tightening and loosening, relaxing muscles. He had it all—he thought he had it all—figured out.

"It was kind of strange the first time I ever went through it. It was like, What is this guy doing? I was used to my high school coach. He was a big man, about six-foot-five, and wide. He had these bloodshot eyes. He used to just scream at us right before we went out on the field. We were so scared of him, we just wanted to get out there and kill the other team.

"Then, I come to Texas and here's this little man, maybe five-foot-ten, and he's got us down on the floor with the lights off telling us to relax. There's a big difference."

Not everyone was a fan of Akers's newfangled techniques and the processes like mental imaging that were coming into vogue in the once hidebound world of sports.

"They thought it was boring. I did, too," said former Texas place-kicker Raul Allegre, who spent part of 1990 with the Super Bowl champion New York Giants. "People hated it. They are too young then. But I've gone to a sports psychologist since, and it helped me a great deal."

Even some inside the Texas camp poked fun at the technique of visualization.

"Abe Lemons had the classic line on that," says one longtime Texas official. "He asked a football player what he thought he was doing. The player says, 'I imagine myself running with the football, and then I imagine myself scoring a touchdown.'

"Abe says, 'What about that guy on the other team who's imaging himself tackling your ass?' "

Former Texas middle linebacker Jeff Leiding always marched to the beat of a different drummer, saxophonist, or whoever was playing in the band past curfew.

"Fred was never a motivator. We just flat out wanted to win," Leiding says. "I didn't pay attention to all that relax your eyeballs and your hamstrings and all that other garbage. It was thirty minutes of fine-tuning. You funneled all your thoughts and got focused. As far as the wiggly toes and pinkies, I never really paid any attention.

"Well, when I was impressionable as a freshman, I did. That's what led to me nearly killing myself in the Arkansas game."

That was in 1980 when Akers delivered his pregame message before a nationally televised game on Labor Day night against Arkansas. "You have to visualize what's going to happen." Leiding visualized himself making a bone-crunching tackle on the kickoff. The first three Texas kicks, however, sailed into the end zone and weren't returned. On the fourth, Arkansas returner Thomas Brown hauled it in and headed upfield.

"I could see that wall," Leiding recalls. "There was no way to go around it. So why not go over it? It was one of those freaky things that comes over you where you just say, 'Bonzai!' "

Leiding launched himself over the wedge and slammed into Brown with such force that the hit became an instant Longhorn legend, even if Leiding did end up suffering a pinched nerve on the play.

Other players, however, say they never could get sky-high with Akers's method.

Graham says, "I was on the kickoff team, and I'm looking at the man I'm supposed to block. I still don't feel that adrenaline the way it's been pumping all my life. I proceed on my blocking assignment, and the guy knocks me flat on my butt. I'm going, 'Wow, what happened?'

"It continued that way for the whole game. I'll never forget the next day, when we were reviewing the special teams film. The coaches couldn't help but point out, 'Son, what's wrong? You were getting knocked around like a dummy all day.'

"I had no excuse. I wasn't going to blame it on the fact that I was too relaxed and couldn't get up. From that point on, I said I wasn't going to listen to that crap anymore.

"The next week, Fred goes into his thing. I grab the opportunity to take a nap. Then, I played fantastic. I'm going, 'All right, the heck with this crap.' The rest of my career, it was nap time. Some of the positive visualization was good, but not this relaxation stuff. You can't switch it on."

When Akers was removed in 1986 after a 5–6 season, his only losing year at Texas, players tried the exact opposite approach, dwelling on the negative while trying to get way up for games.

Waits recalls, "The seniors would get up and give little motivational speeches about how sick they were of losing to this particular team every year. If I hadn't known the history of Texas, I'd have thought we'd never won a conference game.

"We had talent back then, but we just didn't have the attitude. It was kind of like we were beat before we even played the game. They would dwell so much on losing the year before. Or, they'd say these guys have got so much talent. I wasn't used to that. I was always, 'These guys are human, we can beat 'em, we've got to play a good game, let's go beat 'em.' "

In his playing days one of the most emotional Longhorns was the star middle linebacker with the Fu Manchu mustache, Britt Hager, who's now with the Philadelphia Eagles.

"Britt probably was the craziest," Waits says. "He would get so worked up sometimes I was afraid he was going to pass out because he would get so red in the face. He would slam his fist into things and just start screaming. He had a wide variety of terms, but I guess 'motherfuckers' was his favorite. He exerted so much energy in the locker room, I was surprised he could go out and play, but he did it."

Waits was once amazed by that behavior. In the 1990 season he sometimes feels like imitating it. "This is the most relaxed team I've ever been associated with," he says. "It's confident; we just go out there and play. But, sometimes, when we have a bad first half, I just want to start screaming at some guys, 'Wake up, let's get going.' We're not going to be able to afford to do that against Miami. We're going to have to come out from the get-go like we did in the Houston game. If we don't do that, then it's going to be a long day for us."

In the 1990 season, many of the seniors have taken it upon themselves to motivate the team. Stanley Richard, Texas's star safety, likes to tell teammates how many tackles or interceptions he's going to make. Then he goes out and backs it up.

The defense plays confidently, knowing Richard, the last line of defense, is playing like an All-American.

Although it's the defense that's winning most of the games for Texas, it's the offense that gets talked up on Lynn Amedee's weekly radio show. There is, however, little of the intrasquad animosity that scarred some of Akers's teams.

Waits says, "When Fred was around, the defense would be out on the field the whole damn time. They'd come off and they were tired. They were angry, and they'd start cursing at the offense, 'You're not doing your job, and we're having to be out there too long.' That's no way for a team to act. This year, if one area isn't doing its job, the other areas will pick up, either the special teams or the defense.

"Before, something bad would happen and it would fall apart. It would look like a thousand leaks sprung in the dike. There'd be people scrambling around and getting on each other. The offense would get on the defense and the defense would get on the offense.

"This year, it's hard to explain. It's just that inner confidence we have in each other. There's no reason to worry about the guy who's playing next to you. You know he's going to do his job. I think a lot has to do with the seniors on this year's team. We've pretty much been losers the whole time we've been here. In the past, that was the big concern, we'd always dwell on the shortcomings of our team. We finally decided to get off that subject and start thinking more positively. It has worked."

The Texas seniors are not only football talents, but extroverts. Talkers. Leaders.

"This is the classiest bunch of kids I've seen in years," Lewis Timberlake says.

In some past years, the Longhorns have had trouble finding stars who could also go to functions and create the right kind of image. Now they're loaded with players, many of them black, who enjoy speaking before groups. Big defensive end Oscar Giles also likes getting involved in community projects.

The biggest project, however, remains the team. The seniors want their last team to be something special, and they take responsibility for it. Graduate assistant Bill Bobbora, who played at Nebraska, suggests something the Cornhuskers used with success.

"That's Inner Circle," senior tight end Stephen Clark says. "It started out being just twenty-five leaders getting together on Monday in a lounge at the dorm, but we opened it up so that anybody could attend. We wanted to be free to talk about some things without the coaches. We talked about what players thought about games, about practices. If there were any quarrels, we wanted them all out in the open. If we thought somebody wasn't pulling his weight on the team, we'd tell him."

The team even has its own slogans, starting with "Whatever It Takes." It's printed on their T-shirts. The players shout it any time a videocam gets in sight.

Timberlake says, "I told them they needed to have a theme. Whatever It Takes became their philosophy."

That was followed by the "Shock the Nation Tour," as the players called it. That one started in the summer when Brian Jones, a big Muhammad Ali fan, was watching a tape with Ali saying he was going to shock the world. The players are talking about their football season as though it's a touring rock show.

Whatever, it's working. The Longhorns are 9–1 and headed to the Cotton Bowl. Maybe Jerry Jones is taking notice.

21

And It's Good-bye
to Texas A&M

It's ten o'clock on Sunday night at Memorial Stadium, and Lyndon Tilson is getting a hero's welcome. A long, twisting line of students camping out for their tickets to the Texas vs. Texas A&M game cheers as the sophomore from Austin and four of his buddies wheel a 15.5-gallon keg of Coors Light up, up, up the ramps all the way to a landing between the seventh and eighth floors.

"We brought up bags of ice, too," Tilson explains later. "There was a shitload of TVs and Nintendos and a lot of baseball games. . . . I saw only one tent, though."

The madness begins one day after Texas's comeback win over Baylor. Word spreads Sunday evening that some students are starting to line up at the stadium for the tickets that are scheduled to be distributed there at 9 A.M. Monday. Although every Texas student who pays a fee for athletic events is theoretically entitled to a ticket—and maybe a chance to get one for a date—students have to claim them every week. That way, Texas officials have the best idea of how many students are going to show for games and can try to sell the rest of the student allotment.

First come isn't necessarily best served. The student tickets are chosen with a random lottery so that the first student in line has the same chance for the better seats as does the last student. Of course, if the tickets are all gone . . .

Panic hits. This is Texas vs. Texas A&M. As Texas's rising defensive star, Shane Dronett, says, "This is what college football is all about, two teams that hate each other."

Texas A&M, with its super-straight military background, serves as the butt of so many recycled Polack jokes for Texas students and exes. Even Texas's women's basketball coach, Jody Conradt, likes to spice up the Lady Longhorns newsletter with an Aggie joke.

Texas used to beat Texas A&M regularly in football, even when the Aggies had Bear Bryant as a coach. Heading into the 1990 game, the series record stands at 63–28–5 in favor of Texas. After six straight A&M wins over Texas, however, the joke is on the Longhorns.

How many Texas students does it take to stand in line for tickets to an Aggie game?

Four thousand, maybe more. A full thirty decks. The students fill eleven decks of one stadium ramp, eleven of another, and eight of a third at the other end of the stadium.

The line keeps twisting and twisting, seeming to stretch endlessly through the bowels of the stadium. While the rest of Austin sleeps, Memorial Stadium is turning into a refugee camp for students.

They bring blankets to protect themselves against the bone-chilling cold of the concrete ramps. A few lug in folding cots. One group brings a couch.

At 5 A.M., Tilson and a friend sneak out into the stands of Memorial Stadium's upper deck. There, seats are traditionally turned down to spell out a message to passing motorists on nearby I-35, which cuts through the heart of town as it rolls north–south from Dallas to San Antonio.

Seats are folded down to spell out "UT." It takes Tilson and his friend two hours to alter the message to something that seemed more appropriate, less bland for the occasion. They spell out "Fuck A&M." Detected, they hide in a rain gutter, but are still caught by a female university cop. "She was cool," he says. "She made us change the seats back to blank, but we left our initials."

By morning, there's a full-fledged mess on the ramps. Newspapers. Beer cups. Food scraps. "Everyone stunk so bad, it was like a pig farm up there," Tilson says.

Some of the students have jumped ramps to better their place in line by a half-dozen ramps or so. It doesn't look that dangerous. A leap of, what, eighteen inches? But when you're up nine floors . . .

No ramp jumpers are hurt, but when the ticket office opens in the morning, it looks as if a soccer riot could break out at any second. Students, a lot of them pasty-faced from the all-nighter they've just pulled, are squished up against barricades that have been placed at the bottom. Students above keep pressing down, clamoring for tickets.

In groups, students are led into the ticket office. They put hands on shoulders and elephant-walk to the office, so that no one can cut in.

Most students wait and wait and wait. They work crossword puzzles in corridors where discarded papers now blow around with the latest whim of the circling wind. They try to study. They miss class and order pizza from the Domino's man who stops by.

"I'm surprised there hasn't been fistfights and bloodshed," one student says.

"There's no order. Every now and then you'll see a Tie. They come out looking like undercover cops," he said of the students hired to help keep order. "They're the only ones out here wearing ties. They'll look around to make sure everything is going all right, but then they'll go to class and you'll see a new Tie, and he won't know who's supposed to be where in line."

Senior history major Rebecca Noel is just about at the end of the line Monday morning. "We were thinking of coming over last night, but we decided not to. This morning, I knew we were in trouble when we saw the sleeping bags."

Junior Tim Engler adds, "We weren't expecting this crowd. It was a snap to get Houston tickets. We're skipping classes, but that's nothing unusual."

Almost everything else about Texas vs. Texas A&M week is, however.

Texas players begin concentrating on the Aggies at a Sunday night barbecue in the T room, a lounge inside the stadium complex reserved for lettermen and current athletes.

Last year, after the Longhorns had been humiliated 50–7 by Baylor, the mood was downbeat. "It was like a morgue," says Gary Johnson of Bert's Bar-B-Q, which catered the dinner. "Peter Gardere remarked on that going through the line. People just wanted to eat and get out of there."

This time, players are loose and still celebrating their latest comeback win. "There was about a hundred and fifty of them, but they eat like three hundred," says Johnson. The Longhorns graze on eighty pounds of sliced beef, eighty pounds of ribs, six gallons of beans, and six gallons of potato salad, and wash it all down with thirty-five gallons of iced tea. Even Johnson is amazed that they still have room to go through ten gallons of banana pudding.

They also get a treat from Captain Video, as they call film and computer specialist Mike Arias. He has pulled his typical all-nighter fueled by caffeine and high-powered protein drinks, to break down game films. He has, however, also put together tapes of former Long-horn stars talking about how much it means to beat the Aggies.

Earlier that morning, Arias drove halfway to College Station to swap game films with his Texas A&M counterpart, Bob Matey, at the Blue Moon Quick Stop, which is fifty-two miles from College Station, and forty-eight from Austin. The Blue Moon has cement floors, cin-der-block walls whose white paint stops halfway to the floor, barbecue sandwiches selling for $2.50, pecans for 80 cents a pound, and worms in the freezer going for $2.19 a dozen.

Over still more coffee, Arias and Matey swap a few war stories. Their schools use a lot of the same methods when it comes to studying football, and neither worries too much about the expense.

"Texas A&M has spent one-point-eight million dollars just on video equipment," says Jackie Sherrill, former Texas A&M football coach and athletic director. "They're so far advanced over anybody else, it's phenomenal. Just like Texas. Texas bought two pieces of equipment to analyze itself that cost thirty-two thousand dollars apiece."

They even use the same computer software developed by Daniel Ginzel, a 5-foot-9 part-Czech, part-Cherokee computer whiz from College Station. The twenty-three-year-old Ginzel has never been closer to action on a football field than when he was playing the flute for his A&M Consolidated High School band, but he knows enough about computers to design slick software for both A&M and Texas.

Neither school has the edge, right? Aggie coach R. C. Slocum says, "I get nervous every time he goes to Austin."

But the Aggies and Longhorns don't cooperate on everything. The 21–10 Aggie win in College Station in 1989 began with a free-for-all. At the coin toss, the entire Aggie team marched out toward the Longhorn side, supposedly so that they could turn to the crowd and sing their alma mater as they do before every home game.

The Texas players, led by offensive tackle Ed Cunningham, took exception. They thought the Aggies were trying to get in their face and intimidate them. Matt McCall, A&M's mammoth offensive tackle, stuck a finger in Cunningham's face. Cunningham swatted it down, and Dronett put a body slam on McCall. It quickly escalated into a wild melee. Aggie linebacker Aaron Wallace had grabbed Texas line-backer Brian Jones by the facemask. Texas fullback Jason Burleson sat on some Aggie's chest.

"It was like that movie *Slapshot*," Texas center Todd Smith says. "They have the big fight before the referees get there. The good thing is, in football, nobody gets hurt because everybody has pads on."

This year, the verbal war starts early in the week and heats up fast. "I'd rather beat A&M than Miami," offensive tackle Stan Thomas says. "I'd like to play them right now, today."

Later, Thomas is asked what he expects to be doing late in the game. "I think in the fourth quarter, I'll be sitting on the sidelines with my shoulder pads off, eating hot dogs," he says.

Dronett adds more bulletin board material for the Aggies. As a freshman in the 1989 game, Dronett was matched up against McCall. "I took him to school," Dronett boasts. "I don't care if he remembers me or not. He'll remember me on Sunday."

Although he's walking around on crutches because of a torn groin muscle, Texas A&M junior linebacker Anthony Williams shows he can still get off some good shots.

"They're overrated," he says of the fifth-ranked Longhorns. "They talk a good game, but I haven't seen them dominate a game. Their offense hasn't shown me anything. If they would happen to beat us, they'd be so broken up against Miami they might forfeit.

"Peter Gardere is an average quarterback. No composure. He's a throw-it-up-in-the-air type quarterback. Johnny Walker and the Cash brothers have bailed him out all year. Texas is a big-time organization, but he's not a big-time quarterback."

Of Texas's middle linebacker he adds, "Brian Jones is a great athlete, but if we ran a 4–3, he'd be over there with the Twelfth Man towel. Why couldn't he play for us? Heart."

Jones arrived from UCLA as one of the biggest talkers ever to hit Texas. In his senior year, however, he's toned down. He refuses to get into the name-calling and turns almost sullen.

"Brian looks mad," Thomas says. "He's been quiet, not like his usual self. I think he's in for a good game. It was an insult to him and he's holding it all inside."

Thomas, perhaps the world's biggest kid, isn't about to do that. Even though he's been warned by McWilliams to put a lid on it, he blurts out, "I want six or seven pancakes this game. We're going to mash them right off the ball. Williams, he ain't going to play, not with a groin. If he does, I'm going to smash him on every play."

Playing at home, with its best team in seven years, Texas has to win this game or spend the off-season wondering how it's ever going to beat A&M again. As for the 8–2–1 and somehow unranked Aggies, the game is a chance to salvage what's been a disappointing year. They'd been picked to get back to the Cotton Bowl behind a strong Heisman Trophy candidate, tailback Darren Lewis, and Robert Wilson, the best fullback playing college football.

The season, however, soured in the fourth game when Lewis was kicked out of the LSU game for throwing an elbow in a second-quarter sideline altercation. A&M lost 17–8. Although Texas has the Cotton Bowl bid sealed, there's still a lot on the line.

"It's wild. The state is dominated by, run by, the alumni of these two schools," says Jim Helms, a former Texas running back and 1990 running back coach at Texas A&M. "The rivalry just grows and grows and grows. There's not anyone who sits on the fence and says, 'I don't have a favorite.' "

The same can be said for A&M's traditional Texas-size bonfire. You either think it's the greatest tradition in the world, or that it's the Bonfire of Insanity.

Kelly Harper, president of the two-year-old Aggies Against Bonfire, votes for the latter. She's a junior at A&M majoring in wildlife and fishery science and plans to go into the Peace Corps. She'd like to someday help save a rain forest. She notes, however, "In Brazil they're burning forests to earn a living. We're doing it for a party."

Harper is trying to think globally, act locally. Not all the locals are amused. When she turns on her answering machine, she gets half a dozen obnoxious calls. Physical harm, death; they promise it all.

She doesn't back off. "I think the main concern is that the university condones the bonfire," she says. "Everyone is being taught that it's okay to be wasteful."

Her group contacts the Texas Air Control Board, which will monitor the proceedings. "No one had ever complained before," she says. "Every year the fire marshal sends out a flier. It has a map that has this big gray area, a couple of miles. If you're in there, they tell you to hose down your roof, mow your yard, put flammable materials someplace safe, have a hose connected to an outdoor faucet, and clean out your gutters. Every year they have some people get holes burned in their roofs."

At 4:30 P.M. on Thursday, the Aggies Against Bonfire have a short seminar on nonviolence at the Front Porch Cafe. Then they pile into some pickups and head for the big blaze at Duncan Field.

"How will history judge Bonfire?" they chant. They sing "America the Beautiful" and do TV interviews, all before the towering stack of lumber becomes an inferno.

"The students tied a yellow ribbon on the top layer of the bonfire for the troops in the Mideast," Harper says. "That was kind of ironic because they used four hundred gallons of jet fuel to light the fire. Some of the trees were a hundred years old."

BONFIRE: LOVE IT OR FUCK OFF, reads the helmet of one student scrambling around a stack of lumber so impossibly huge that it's supported by four stakes that look like telephone poles because that's what they are. A third of the workers are shirtless, having doffed the top half of their "grodes," as the work clothes that they never wash are called. Chain saws buzz. One group lifts small logs, sounding off in military-style cadence, "One, two, fuck TU."

Much of the tall timber comes from land being strip-mined by the Texas Municipal Power Agency. There's 7,000 logs in the resulting stack, and "logs" is a euphemism. When an Aggie says that, think full-blown trees that have to be swung into place by a crane.

It took nine cuts to get the lumber, and a "cut" means working from 6 A.M. through 9 P.M. on Saturdays and Sundays. Aggies started doing that the first weekend in October outside Carlos, thirty minutes southeast of College Station. It takes two and a half weeks just to stack a small rain forest worth of Texas trees.

"UT's getting to be a jungle," says Stephen Knight, an Aggie sophomore from Corpus Christi. "No school other than A&M could get together and do this. People come out to the bonfire for weeks and weeks afterward and toast marshmallows."

Kenton Heinze, a junior from Westlake, outside Austin, adds, "I never liked the University of Texas, the liberalism. I didn't like the Drag. I came to the bonfire when I was a senior in high school. I figured it'd be some little pep rally, a little stack of wood. The bonfire's one of the main things that brought me here."

Heinze is wearing a pot, or helmet, that dates back to 1968. The fiberglass pots are passed down to underclassmen after each bonfire. There are sixteen different kinds, including Red Pots, Center Pole Pots, Brown Pots, Senior Leader Pots, and even Pink Pots for the students working the concessions. The eight Senior Red Pots are in charge. Eight Junior Red Pots are next in the chain of command. At least one Red Pot guards the stack twenty-four hours a day. The bonfire and the pots are a big deal at A&M.

Trent Kelley, a Texas A&M junior from Conroe, says, "There's supposedly an endowment [at Texas] that if anyone can steal a pot, they'll get ten thousand dollars. Two years ago, there was one theft attempt. The guy grabbed a pot off someone's head and jumped into a car. They put an axe handle through the windshield. They got the pot back."

Junior Mike Flatten, from San Antonio, adds, "There used to be big competition to start the bonfire early, but 1978 was the last serious attempt. A Texas fraternity paid someone to pour gas on the bonfire.

Six guys ran him down in the backyard of someone's house and pounded him."

An outhouse with a sign, T.U. FRATHOUSE, always adorns the top of the bonfire. And, tradition has it, if the bonfire burns past midnight without collapsing, the Aggies will beat Texas. It's been caving in early for years, however, and that hasn't hurt the Aggie football team one bit. Thursday's bonfire collapses almost twenty minutes after it's lit. No matter. The 40,000 or so who show up know who's had the best team. William Thomas, the Aggies' star linebacker, says, "We're going to beat 'em seven, eight, ten times."

The streak started during Jackie Sherrill's tenure at Aggieland. In 1982 Sherrill was hired away from Pittsburgh at the then-obscene salary of $267,000 for one reason. The Aggies wanted to beat Texas in football.

Sherrill succeeded. As Fred Akers found his fans and recruits drifting away, Sherrill's forces pulled in more and more of the top players in Texas. Rumors swirled throughout the state on just how that was done. The NCAA slapped A&M with a two-year probation in 1988 substantiating some of the rumors.

"Quite frankly, the NCAA was investigating A&M since 1972," Sherrill says. "The NCAA kept A&M from winning a national championship because of the negative press. It kept the one, two, three, four, or five good players a year from coming in there, and they could have won it. It's really unjust."

While some questioned Sherrill's method, few argued the fact that he built a machine. A&M established a new tradition, being the most thorough, hardworking school in the SWC when it came to recruiting.

Sherrill's hasty departure in December of 1988 slowed the Aggies for one recruiting season, but not permanently. In his debut against Texas, former Aggie defensive coordinator R. C. Slocum came away with a 21–10 win that just cranked up Texas's need to win another notch.

Even Slocum realizes nothing lasts forever, winning streaks over archrivals among them. He's been fishing with McWilliams before, and he knows what they both face in alumni that never want to lose, never think their team should lose.

"Some schools like USC, Penn State, Georgia, Alabama, and Ohio State were pretty dominant every year, but it's not going to be that way again," Slocum says. "It's hard for fans to accept that. They have a hard time accepting the reality of parity. Fans can create a lot of turmoil. Your own fans can cause your program problems because they can be such a negative thing."

But rivalries like Auburn-Alabama, Michigan-Ohio State, USC-UCLA, and, yes, A&M-Texas, never change.

"I was taught to hate the Aggies," says Stanley Richard as he's leaving practice late in the week. The Sheriff, as he's now known, has his tin badge pinned to a rather gaudy shirt. "How can you not hate them? This week the coaches play their fight song in our locker room and they keep playing it louder and louder as the week goes on. I hate it. I'm tired of it, but it motivates you. It gets so you don't want to hear it again, you don't want them to have the opportunity to play it.

"We're going to beat down the Aggies, but we're going to make sure none of them get hurt," he says. "They've got to beat Brigham Young for us."

BYU is ranked fourth in the AP poll, while Texas is in the national title picture at number five behind top-ranked Colorado, Georgia Tech, and Miami. Notre Dame is ranked seventh.

Saturday, Texas officials expect a possible stadium record crowd to help the Longhorns win. Some 2,800 folding chairs have been set up in the south end zone, which is the reason Texas uses to ban the Aggies' French-75 howitzer cannon as a safety precaution. Texas's own 10-gauge cannon, "Smokey," naturally, will still be on hand at the other end of the stadium to fire after every Texas score.

"They say theirs doesn't make as much noise as ours," says Lt. Col. Don Johnson, an assistant commandant of the 2,053-member Corps of Cadets. "Of course, ours has been firing more lately than theirs. Maybe it's six years of frustration. I don't know."

Texas officials also slap a five-cadet limit on how many handlers the Aggies can bring for their collie mascot, Reveille. "Two years ago they came over here with twenty-two people and we let them in," says Al Lundstedt, Texas events manager. "If we can handle a fifteen-hundred-pound steer with five people, I would think they could handle Reveille."

Texas's crowd advantage isn't what it was for the Houston game, however, because of the early wake-up call. CBS has moved the kickoff time way up to 11:07 A.M., and few Texas fans have had a chance to fire up the way they did for the night game with the Cougars.

Worse, there's Aggies all over the north end zone. Many Texas A&M fans bought tickets for this clash earlier in the year, before Texas football became the biggest bandwagon in town. There must be 10,000 Aggies in a crowd of 82,518 that's just 535 fans short of tying the stadium record set in the 1978 game against Houston. That includes one prominent ex Aggie (rather, one prominent Aggie, because graduates of that school proudly tell you there's no such thing as an ex Aggie; it's once an Aggie, always an Aggie) in the stands. It's former A&M coach Jackie Sherrill, who got two tickets when he called the school. Texas, that is, not A&M.

One person who's not on hand is Robert Heard, publisher of *Inside Texas*. He's in Brackenridge Hospital recovering from a triple bypass. He convinces the doctors that he should be allowed to watch the Texas vs. Texas A&M game on TV. He plans to try to control his blood pressure by occasionally closing his eyes and imagining himself up in the mountains staring into the face of one of his dalmatians. He takes a slow, deep breath as the showdown starts.

A&M takes the ball to start the game and heads into a 10-mile-an-hour wind on a bright 65-degree day. Aggie quarterback Bucky Richardson enters the game as the world's most erratic 53 percent passer. With the former hurdling star, however, the Aggies don't need to pass much.

Tailback Darren Lewis has 1,541 rushing yards and a whopping average of 5.8 yards per carry. Fullback Robert Wilson may turn out to be even more of an NFL stud. The 245-pounder averages 5.8 yards per carry himself, but it's his devastating blocks that make him so feared by opponents.

The Aggies just churn upfield as if they're scrimmaging their own second-team defense. After taking over on their 20, twelve running plays take them to the Texas 17, where they're looking at second-and-ten. The Aggies run an option left. Richardson pitches to Lewis. Wilson buries the Sheriff, 108 pound Stanley Richard, with a block. Touchdown. The Longhorns have fallen behind in yet another game, as Texas A&M jumps out to a 7–0 lead.

Later, as the first quarter is winding down, Texas takes over first-and-ten at its 32. Texas quarterback Peter Gardere rolls left and has his pass for tight end Stephen Clark picked off by A&M cornerback Derrick Frazier, who returns it 5 yards to the Texas 39. Forget Texas offensive coordinator Lynn Amedee's response. Even Pete Gardere, who's sitting in the stands trying to be as inconspicuous as possible for a quarterback's father, jumps up and shouts, "Damn it to hell, Peter!"

A&M pounds down to the Texas 12, where it's second-and-seven. Here comes option left again. This time Lance Gunn takes on Wilson's lead block. It doesn't matter to Wilson, or to Lewis, who gets his second touchdown of the game.

It's 14–0 Aggies, and those are the good numbers. Texas A&M has now outgained Texas 153–8 in total yards. The Aggies have run twenty-nine offensive plays to the Longhorns' seven. Gardere has yet to complete a pass. Star running back Butch Hadnot hasn't touched the ball and won't all day because he's out with the broken finger he suffered against Baylor.

Texas has been down before, but never flat-out dominated like this. On the kickoff, though, Adrian Walker breaks free for 41 yards. Two runs later, Texas has third-and-one at the 50.

Michael Warren, former UCLA basketball and "Hill Street Blues" star, is in the stands. He's been standing for every down, even though he turned down friend Brian Jones's offer of a sideline pass for that very reason. He wanted to sit in the stands and relax the way they do out at UCLA. He didn't realize everyone would be on their feet for Texas vs. Texas A&M.

"We're going to score on this play," a fan next to Warren says.

Amedee, who worked for three Cotton Bowl years at A&M, figures that A&M will be pinching in its ends and tackles. He calls for a blast option, a play he hasn't run all season.

The Texas line blocks down, as running back Chris Samuels skies over the top. A&M defenders are still looking at the pile when Gardere, who only faked a handoff, pops through a hole on the left. Gardere's longest run from scrimmage in his Texas career is 18 yards, but he breaks this one for a 50-yard touchdown.

Leading only 14–7, the Aggies lose the ball when Lewis fumbles on the first play from scrimmage and Texas's right defensive end Oscar Giles recovers on A&M's 22, to the wild delight of the crowd. When Texas can't move, Michael Pollak comes in to try a 37-yard field goal. He knows the Aggies are good at blocking kicks, and all week he's been working at shaving 5/100ths of a second off his time. It's not enough. Frazier doesn't just tip the kick. He rejects it.

On the next Texas possession, deep snapper Chad McMillan floats the ball back to punter Alex Waits. For the third time in the season, Waits makes an incredible play to dodge a defender and kicks on the run.

Pollak and Waits huddle on the sidelines discussing their kicking woes when McMillan walks up and blithely asks, "How was the snap?"

"The punt was almost blocked," snaps Waits, who's getting tired of scrambling.

Later in the half, though, Hadnot's replacement, short-yardage specialist Patrick Wilson, breaks a couple of big gainers, and Texas scores on a 9-play, 66-yard drive punctuated by Keith Cash's 7-yard touchdown grab. After being almost knocked out in the first quarter, Texas goes into halftime tied 14–14 with A&M. The Longhorns are upbeat. They've come from behind six times to win in the 1990 season, and they sense comeback number seven.

Anthony Williams, the Texas A&M linebacker who had talked so much pregame trash about Texas, has played only sparingly. Coming out for the second half, he feels something pull at his leg. It's a five-year-old boy who has his face painted half orange and half white. He looks up wide-eyed at Williams and asks innocently, "Why did you call Peter Gardere a scrub?"

"Get off my leg," Williams answers.

Late in the third quarter Texas goes up 21–14 when senior Chris Samuels, the team's most versatile running back, drives behind left guard for a 4-yard touchdown.

On their answering drive the Aggies stall at the Texas 32. It's fourth-and-five. What to do? The Aggies go with option left, which has already produced two touchdowns. Correction, three TDs. Wilson flattens Richard and Lewis runs in for the score. There's 12:35 left in the game and it's even at 21–21.

Texas comes back with an 11-yard touchdown run by Gardere. Texas 28, A&M 21.

The Aggies, however, promptly look like the machine that was on the field in the first quarter. Forget the pass, which they've completed only four times all day for a paltry 23 yards. The option offense takes A&M to the Texas 32, where it's second-and-seven. The Aggies run left again, but this time Richardson keeps the ball, and that small variation is enough to fool Texas and get Richardson a touchdown to come within a point at 28–27.

With less than four minutes left in a season-salvaging game, the Aggies go for two. What else would they run but option left, which has resulted in four touchdowns?

The CBS mikes eavesdropping in the Aggie huddle on the sidelines pick up the A&M play. It's . . . it's option *right*!

Slocum pulls his flanker and split end for a three-tight-end alignment. Without an Aggie wideout to care about, Texas is automatically in tight formation to further squeeze the Aggie play. What's more, Wilson, the A&M fullback who's been steamrolling Texas defenders all day, isn't going to be the lead blocker. He'll be plunging into the middle.

That's also what Texas middle linebacker Brian Jones does. He blitzes, jams the middle, slams into Wilson, and forces Richardson to pitch early and deep to Lewis. Lewis heads around right end without Wilson's protection and has no option but to try to run over Texas cornerback Mark Berry at the 5. No way. Lewis is stumbling, and Berry wrestles him to the turf. Safety Lance Gunn leaps over Lewis in celebration, and Jones shoots a proud fist into the air. Texas still leads 28–27.

Texas is thinking onside kick, but Layne Talbot lines it fairly deep, and Adrian Walker fields it at the 20 and gets 10 yards.

Now the burden is on the Aggie defense, which proves no match for an aroused Texas offense that's smelling victory, Cotton Bowl, and a national championship. Texas marches all the way to the 2. Texas players want the added touchdown. So do many of the Texas fans who want Texas to cover the seven-point spread. Instead, the Longhorns run out the clock.

Fans are yelling so loudly and so shrilly it sounds like a ululating tribe. From the loudspeaker comes an announcement, "You've just seen another typical Texas-Texas A&M game. To you Aggies as you go against Brigham Young in the Holiday Bowl, we'd like to say, Gig 'Em, Aggies. To you Longhorns, Hook 'em, Horns, beat the hell out of Miami."

The crowd explodes as it spills onto the field. As the injured Butch Hadnot makes his way off, an appreciative fan yells, "We needed you today, Butch."

"No, we didn't," another says smugly.

Just before he enters the locker room, reserve linebacker Dennis McWilliams, David McWilliams's oldest son, shouts, "It's a vindication for him. All the people getting on him, all the pressures, it shows that if people will be patient with a class program, success will happen. I think this is just a great win for the whole system. Everybody was talking all year about when the letdown was going to come. I think it's a tribute to his coaching that we never had it, even after the Colorado game."

In the locker room, Texas players renew their chant for black shoes. They aren't so much joyous, however, as relieved that they've finally beaten A&M. David McWilliams is presented with a white Stetson, puts it on, and says, "I kind of feel like the Marlboro man."

Cotton Bowl president John Stuart, a Texas ex, spies athletic director DeLoss Dodds in the corner of the room and wants to pull out his Stetson as well. Dodds declines.

"Just give me mine in a box," Dodds says. "We're here to honor David, not me."

McWilliams is dissecting the crucial two-point play. "That really was the only good tackle we had on Darren Lewis all day. If we had to have one tackle in the game, that's the one I would have picked."

Defensive coordinator Leon Fuller jokes, "We fooled them. They kept expecting us to adjust and overshift. We never adjusted. We were too stupid. So they ran to the right, and we got them."

Now, just maybe, that national championship that has eluded Texas for twenty years is within reach.

"If we can beat a great Miami team, I feel we're good enough to be considered for the national championship," McWilliams says. "I think we've played in just about every situation you can play in as a team and come back and won the football game all but one time."

"All year everybody has talked about what happened last year, what happened six years ago. We never cared about that," Samuels says. "This was a new year. We got up at six A.M. last January telling ourselves that everything was going to be new. As soon as we made up our minds as a football team, all of that in the past didn't matter. It took a lot, but we did it. It's been a fun, wonderful year. Every week things got bigger and bigger. It's like, What else are they going to do? We never sell ourselves short; we always think we're going to win and pull it out in the end. It's a complete 180-degree turnaround from the past. This was the sweetest game, but in a month, I believe there will be one sweeter."

"There was a lot of pressure," Stan Thomas says. "This was a big game. At first, I was a little worried, but I knew we could do it. Whatever it takes, we do.

"If Miami talks, it really won't affect me because I do a lot of talking myself. I try to intimidate. I like it when people talk back to me; it just gets me more fired up to hit them again. They'll probably talk to the media like A&M did. That's what everybody's been doing all year. They're going to talk their game in the paper; we're going to talk our game on the field.

"Tonight, I'm going to get me a steak, probably go down and have a few drinks, relax a little bit. Let everybody jump on the bandwagon. Meet all the girls I've never met before. 'Stan, do you know me?' I'll probably be in bed about six o'clock this morning. I'm going to go out all night long, go down to Sixth Street, and see how many girls I can get."

Middle linebacker Brian Jones is caught up in all the talk as well. It's contagious.

"This is the one we've always wanted," Jones says. "We've talked about this one since last January, this and winning the conference.

This is our second goal. Our first goal was to win the conference championship, and our second goal was to beat A&M. National championship now. That's the third goal. We came in at the beginning of the season. I know none of you guys believe it, but we were actually thinking we could win a national championship, and we're right in the picture now.

"I don't care if Miami would rather be in the Orange Bowl. Nobody's begging them to come. If they feel like they're coming to a sorry bowl, we'll see. If they come in with that attitude, they can just get waxed like everyone else."

McWilliams comes over to where Jones is sitting with Michael Warren. "I'm glad nobody on the field called time out," he says of the final drive. "I think we've learned one thing this year: don't call time out or do the two-point play unless Coach Mac tells you. You'd have called that."

"You know it. I'd have called it," Jones says.

Standing near the Aggie bus, Williams says, "I thought I'd rattle a few of them. Maybe I did, maybe I didn't. But they won't beat us next year. Oh, no. But they deserved to win. I think they have a good chance against Miami."

A&M linebacker Jason Atkinson, who spent most of the day playing in Williams's place, says, "I thought even if Anthony died on the field, he'd have stayed in for two or three more plays."

In spite, or maybe because of, all the trash that's been talked, Texas players are subdued, relieved to have finally beaten the Aggies. The fans, however, aren't about to be quiet.

The Drag, the main street running along campus, turns into a parking lot with fans honking horns, holding up the Hook 'em sign, and yelling as loud as their lungs will allow.

A convertible with six screaming girls inches its way up Guadalupe Street. Tight end Kerry Cash is strolling by on the sidewalk. Suddenly he bolts in front of a car, runs another lane over, and jumps into the convertible. "Whoooo," the girls shout. "Hook 'em."

Cash leans back and flashes the Hook 'em sign and a big, contented smile. The Horns are back.

McWilliams, meanwhile, is sitting out on his deck with wife Cindy and best friend John Folmer and his wife. They're taking in the UT Tower bathed in brilliant orange lights signaling the school's first win over the Aggies since 1983.

Darrell Royal's wife, Edith, had dropped by for lunch that week and gave Cindy some fluffy cotton balls. Edith told Cindy she had a good feeling about the upcoming game and had brought them by for good luck. They'd go well with the white Christmas lights Cindy had laid out along the deck.

"It was beautiful," Cindy says. "Absolutely beautiful."

Almost as pretty as the view.

22

Briefcases, Bikinis, and Black Shoes

"I'm happier than a motherfucker," a shirtless Stan Thomas proclaims as he's just about to plug in his phone.

Thomas is relaxing in his fifth-floor Jester Dorm room, where the highlight of the painted cinder-block walls is a poster of some Bud Girls and long-legged exercise sexpot Kathy Smith, Thomas's idea of the perfect woman.

Who knows? If Thomas can move up a few more spots in the NFL draft, maybe some Kathy Smith look-alike will call on the phone that rings about a hundred times a day whenever Thomas decides to plug it in.

Agents call. Girls call. Agents with girls call.

"Hey, look at these pictures," says Thomas as he brings out a collection of a dozen shots sent to him by an agent that wants his NFL-caliber body. The shots have been making the rounds among the less fortunate Texas football players in the dorm, which is why some of the better photos have already been "lost."

"There's this agent in Florida who has a party every year on his yacht," he explains. "He picks up the tab for everything. He wants me to come down."

The color photos show girls in bikinis lounging on the yacht and hanging on a couple of NFL players who made the trip last year.

One of the girls, a blonde who's lying on the deck and has her leg curled up in a come-hither pose, makes Kathy Smith look like a prude.

"She's the one I want," says Thomas, who, at 6-foot-6 and 300 pounds, is the world's biggest kid. The son of a former minor leaguer in the Pittsburgh Pirate organization, Thomas was a late starter in football who never experienced the heavy blue-chip recruiting rush as a high schooler.

He was just some big California kid who had good size and potential and whom Fred Akers had to gamble on when his recruiting slipped. When Akers was fired, some of the Texas players were relieved. Others were downright excited to find out that easygoing David McWilliams would be the new head coach.

Thomas was stung. Akers had recruited him, and he even thought about following Akers to Purdue. When reporters swarmed around the Neuhaus-Royal complex that weekend, Thomas, one of Texas's few out-of-state players, was just about the only player on hand. A freshman, he told them something ought to be done, that Akers didn't deserve to be fired.

"I went to see him in his office, and it was kind of sad," Thomas says. "He was taking pictures down off the wall. He told me, 'I'm not the first football coach to be fired, and I won't be the last.' "

A manager on the Texas team swears that you could tell Thomas was going to be a star from his very first year. He had a lot more than size. He had quick feet and a natural ability to set up for a pass block. But, for his first three years, Thomas was noticed only when he picked up a holding penalty. Or when SMU player Kenny Rea got so mad at Thomas and his after-the-whistle blocking that he cold-cocked Big Stan with a roundhouse to the nuts that decked Thomas in the 1989 game.

In those years, Stan felt unwanted at Texas, unloved. But, before his senior year, scouts had started to notice him.

"Have you ever stood next to Stan?" 6-foot-5, 275-pound teammate Chuck Johnson says. "He's just big, I mean, really big. It's just tough to get around him."

Before the 1990 season, Thomas was better known to the pros than he was to those who followed the Southwest Conference. About midway through the season, however, word got out that Thomas could go in the first round of the NFL draft, which is like hitting the lottery, an instant entry into the millionaire's club.

Word spread fast. Everyone knew he was hot. "It's funny," Thomas says, "but I'll go out and be talking to someone and say, here's Peter Gardere, our quarterback, and people will still talk to me instead of him. People really seem to like it when I say stuff about other teams and then back it up. They can identify with that."

In his senior year, Thomas has become a star, a 300-pound sex symbol. "I used to have trouble getting girls," he says. "Now I get them for my friends. I say, 'You go with him, you go with him.' It's amazing."

"This has been the best two weeks of my life," agrees Pat Bigham, a longtime friend who's visiting Thomas from San Diego. They've just been back from a pool party in San Marcos, south of Austin, that Thomas helped turn into a wet T-shirt contest.

"Stan always had a lot of girls," another friend says. "The difference is now some of them are cute."

As for the agents, they're all persistent when they see a potential first-round meal ticket. They want to take Thomas out to dinner. If he's not there, they might ask Bigham if he wants to have dinner. Thomas's parents have to get an unlisted number. Thomas frequently unplugs his phone or gets a friend or team manager to answer it.

After Texas beats A&M, the school sets up a two-week period for agents to contact Thomas, safety Stanley Richard, and some of the less prominent Texas seniors.

Richard, a former cornerback, has seen his stock soar. "I've got him going in the second round, maybe the end of the first round," draft analyst Mel Kiper says from his Baltimore office. He adds that Thomas can go as high as the fifteenth pick in the first round.

A lot of the other Texas players have potential, like tight end Kerry Cash, who had scouts at one earlier Texas practice bugging their eyes out when he made a one-handed grab that was like the one he snared in big-game conditions against Oklahoma.

"I like Johnny Walker," Kiper adds, even though Walker has yet to catch a touchdown pass in his senior season. "He could be a first-rounder if he played in an offense like Miami's."

Kiper thinks middle linebacker Brian Jones could be a middle-round pick, which Jones scoffs at. He has some literature from scouts that shows he could be one of the five fastest linebackers in the draft. Even placekicker Michael Pollak and punter Alex Waits are talking with agents.

True, it's not as bad as it was in the wild-and-woolly days when agents were happy camping out at Texas and Akers had his most talented teams.

"You understand the talent level we had back then," Lombardi Award winner Tony Degrate says. "In Mossy Cade's senior year, there's, what, eighteen guys that went pro? That was an agent's heaven over there."

A prominent agent went so far as to set up weekly meetings in the

Embassy Suites with beer and pizza so that the Longhorns could learn about how an agent works for a client, until Fred Akers busted the weekly gatherings that were in violation of NCAA rules.

"I went there to one function because I didn't know if it was illegal," Degrate explains. "To be frank, I didn't know what all the NCAA rules were. I didn't know rule number one was I can't do this. Or I can't go accept a box of Captain Crunch. Plus, it was my senior year, so I figured, hey, this may be a good process to screen out some agents. I knew maybe it wasn't on the up-and-up, but I didn't know how bad it was. There's some things I did that were kind of borderline of whether it was legal or illegal.

"Before the Freedom Bowl I had an agent come into my room and he had twenty-one thousand dollars in a briefcase. Cash. He says if you'll sign on the dotted line, this is yours. He had this contract written out. You can get your Mercedes, you can get this piece of land. This and that. And I just looked at it.

"What they do is they call you and say, 'Listen, I'm in Austin and can we get together for dinner?' I figured that since this is going to be a big part of my career, I said well . . . I didn't always follow a straight line. If any All-American or any player says he followed a straight line and didn't accept anything, he's lying to you. There are too many temptations out there. Way too many temptations. You walk in the restaurant, the owner knows you, and he buys you a meal. We ate out a lot and never paid.

"It's a big deal to have you walk in sporting goods places. The better you do on the field, the more there is out there. It goes on anywhere, and it's always going to be like that. I mean, how many star players do you see wearing those cheap tennis shoes? You always see them in top-of-the line sweats."

Unless they're heading for the Cotton Bowl.

With the trip to Dallas come the freebies that long-suffering, bowl-deprived Texas players regard as their just reward for the years of football hell they've gone through at a university they entered expecting to play in one bowl after another.

At a seniors-only meeting the Longhorns discuss and vote on their legal Cotton Bowl booty, the first bowl reward since their Bluebonnet Bowl appearance that resulted in a win over Pittsburgh three seasons ago.

"You get a certain amount, three hundred dollars," placekicker Michael Pollak explains. "It's like 'Wheel of Fortune'—you get to go shopping. You have to get the watch, and that's a hundred and five dollars. You have to get the plaque and that's thirty-five. The seniors decide what we're going to do with the other hundred and sixty. You've got to decide among the shoes, the sweats, the T-shirts, and the cowboy hats."

The merchandise, much of it from Nike, is deeply discounted. Cowboy hats that would retail for close to $100 are only $25.

Still, the Longhorns aren't impressed. "I wasn't too pleased," Pollak admits. "I was expecting some really nice stuff. What we got at the Bluebonnet Bowl was every bit as nice, if not nicer. Everybody was disappointed. Why couldn't we go to a sporting goods store and get some really nice stuff? Chris Samuels and I were wondering why we couldn't get one thing that was really nice instead of three of four things that were just not bad."

"We didn't get some of those ugly shirts they offered us," punter Alex Waits says. "I mean there were some shirts in there that were hideous. I don't think even my grandfather would have wanted any of those."

The seniors vote to get two pairs of sweats, T-shirts, and Nike Cross Trainers. The seniors then emerged to tell the underclassmen of their decision.

"Shane Dronett asked, 'When are we getting fitted for our hats?' " Pollak says. "He wanted that cowboy hat. We voted on the stuff with a show of hands. Only a couple of guys, mostly linemen, voted for the cowboy hats."

"Shane was upset," Waits recalls. "Tommy Jeter was upset and so was Lance Wilson. "I'd have worn it if it had been given to me, but I don't see myself going out and buying a hat."

So much for the traditional Texas country-and-western image. The Longhorns, however, were going for a new look, and an old one.

Black shoes. Clunky, slow-lookin' black shoes. Not really the kind that Texas wore the last time it won an AP national championship in 1969.

No, the kind the badass teams of the late 1980s and 1990 were wearing. Like Colorado.

In the preseason, Texas coach David McWilliams had been reading off goals that the team ought to have for one of the most crucial years in Texas football history. Things like being focused, aiming high, beating Texas A&M, making the Cotton Bowl.

And getting black shoes, a player added.

Yeah, black shoes. When McWilliams was finished being taken aback by that inane comment, he allowed that the team could get some black shoes if it was playing in Dallas on New Year's Day.

When the Longhorns clinched the conference championship against Baylor, they didn't scream "Bring on A&M." They chanted, "Black shoes, black shoes!" They did the same after coming from behind to beat the Aggies.

Paint it black. That's what they're doing in the equipment room, spraying Nu-life Black 615 on rows of shoes and getting about four or five shoes out of every aerosol can.

"We ordered enough to have the first seventy kids in new shoes," says equipment manager Ted Gray, the coach who took Donnie Little and Dickinson to a state championship. "We've got enough rain shoes for about the top forty kids. And then we've been painting the remainder of the shoes. If we were wearing black, they'd be wanting white."

"Coach Mac has a contract with Nike, and we can't wear anything but Nike. That's the reason that when we paint them, we have to paint a white swoosh or whatever they call it, so everybody knows that it's Nike. Nike comped us a hundred pairs of shoes. We had to buy the rest of them, all black."

The Texas coaches were asked if they wanted black shoes, but they didn't want to get in on the trend.

They had their own concerns.

For the first time in years, the Texas staff has a truly hot product to pitch to high school stars, a 10–1 team that's in the Cotton Bowl. This year, following recommendations that were made in the preseason review of the program, Texas is trying to lure more national recruits, the way almost every other athletic program at Texas does. Instead of just driving the highways of Texas on a caffeine jag trying to keep the best players in-state, they're also flying to other states trying to skim the best of their crop.

Amedee's home state of Louisiana has a bumper crop of blue chips, and there's a couple of real promising quarterbacks in Florida, where Amedee was an offensive coordinator under Galen Hall at the University of Florida.

Amedee, however, is still miffed that he is an assistant coach at Texas instead of the man at LSU. When his alma mater went looking for a head coach in the wake of Mike Archer's bitter resignation, he was snubbed for the third time.

Again, it was Curley Hallman, a former A&M assistant alongside Amedee, who beat him out for the job just the way he had at Southern Mississippi. Amedee was ready to blow his Cajun lid.

"We had very quick contact," Amedee says of LSU. "They said, 'We can't hire you.' I was told they wanted to hire a guy with on-field head coaching experience. They didn't want another coach as an on-field trainee. I said, 'If you're hiring Bobby Bowden or Howard Schnellenberger,' I said, 'Sure. I understand. But after twenty-seven years of planning to go back to LSU, you'll not find a better guy than me.' Nothing against Curley Hallman, whom I coached with for three years, but I just don't think he is any better than I am."

The rejection bothered the former star quarterback at LSU all the more because of his close relationship with LSU athletic director Joe Dean.

"I was his son's idol," Amedee says of Joe Dean, Jr., now a coach at Central Florida. "He wore my number eleven."

To add to Amedee's indignation, Dean laid out the prerequisites for their next head coach, and it sounded made-to-order for Lynn Amedee. But Dean also said his hands were tied by the chancellor, Ed "Bud" Davis, a former football coach at Colorado. Lynn, this Bud's not for you.

"Joe Dean tells me, 'We want an LSU guy, we want someone who's going to be here ten to twelve years, and we want someone who's been around a good program,'" Amedee says. "In the next breath, he says 'I can't hire you.' Then he asks if I would be interested in being their offensive coordinator. And he wants to know why I'm bitter. Hell, he couldn't afford me."

Meanwhile, the Longhorn seniors are now thinking how much they're going to make as pros. And, they've got their own poster. The *Austin American-Statesman* rounds up the seniors, poses them in front of a wall specially spray-painted with graffiti, and they make like a rock group on a Shock-the-Nation tour.

The state press descend on campus to interview the players. Stan Thomas tells of a letter he received from a disgruntled Aggie fan from Houston after Texas's win over the Aggies.

"It said, 'Congratulations on beating A&M by one point. It'll be fun watching you get your butt whipped, you California fag from the Coast. You can't block. I'll enjoy watching you get your ass beat.'" Then Thomas ripped up the typed letter and threw it away.

Longhorn paraphernalia has become a hot item for Christmas shoppers, who are buying up everything from T-shirts to keychains with a logo of a team that has come from off the charts to on track for the national championship.

"I had them a hundred-to-one shot at the beginning of the season," says Danny Sheridan, an oddsmaker and sports analyst for the Cable News Network and *USA Today*. "Most people had them a thousand to one, but that was prejudice. They had a lot of starters coming back, and McWilliams isn't a bad coach. Texas would maul Georgia Tech."

Tech, however, has jumped over the twice-beaten Miami Hurricanes in the AP poll, in spite of the fact that Miami hasn't lost since the Notre Dame game. "The AP voters are whores," Sheridan says. "That's politics. That's not crazy, it's corrupt. Miami is the best team in the nation."

With a win over the Hurricanes, however, Texas could lay claim to a national championship if Rocket Ismail and his Notre Dame teammates could upset the number one–ranked Colorado Buffaloes, who are still stigmatized by their fifth-down win over Missouri.

What a possibility for Texas players and coaches to savor with friends and family over the Christmas holidays. On December 21, the team holds its final workout in Austin in 30-degree temperatures with a light sprinkle. The team is ready to go home.

Shane Dronett is being particularly frisky. He tapes the name *McWilliams* on the back of his practice jersey and his coach's college number 50 on the front and prances around for the local TV cameras.

McWilliams sends the Longhorns home early trying to beat an Arctic cold front that is dipping down deep into Texas, whipping up winds and icing up streets.

"Patrick Wilson has got to drive to Odessa," McWilliams says with concern about the cross-state trip. Athletic director DeLoss Dodds's secretary, Betty Corley, comes in to ask if the team can be there at the inaugural parade for new governor Ann Richards.

"I don't know if I can make it," McWilliams said.

He's thinking he'll probably be out recruiting then. As for now, he's still got a little Christmas shopping to finish. Tomorrow, son Corby will be the starting cornerback for his Westlake High School team, which will be playing for the state 4A high school state championship against Wilmer-Hutchins in Waco. The next day McWilliams and his three sons are going to a lease near Eagle Pass to go deer hunting.

After that the next stop is Dallas.

23

A Texas-Style Barbecue

Stan Thomas has polished off a small herd's worth of brisket and ribs catered by Colter's BBQ, and now he's ready for some company. He strides over to one of the prettiest women in the Longhorn Ballroom with all the confidence of a 6-foot-6 guy who figures to become an instant first-round millionaire in the NFL draft.

Big Stan asks the Miami player sitting next to the woman to move.

Forget it, comes the reply.

Miami players, sensing what could be some real action at what they consider a hokey get-together, begin to drift over.

"Who are you?" Thomas challenges. "You must not be any good 'cause I never heard of you."

Texas's huge offensive tackle is made-for-Miami cocky. He just happens to play for the Longhorns.

"He'd fit right in with our team," Miami freshman defensive end Rusty Medearis grudgingly acknowledges. "We'd probably like him if he played for us. But he doesn't. If he had done anything, there would have been a fight."

The Miami players, three-time national champions in the 1980s, are strutting their stuff.

"They were being Miami," Texas kicker Michael Pollak says. "We got a red bandanna at the door and they all put it on their heads. It looked like *Colors*, the movie. The Bloods and the Crips. I thought there was going to be a shoot-out among their own team."

"If a guy wants to wear a paper plate on his head, that's cool with me," one Texas starter says. Thomas and some other Texas players, however, have put their bandannas in their pockets.

256

Charles Pharms, the Hurricanes' strong safety and a Texan from Houston Madison, is getting down to the country music. A few of his teammates hop on stage and grab the microphone and a guitar from the band.

Game faces? Hey, this is Wednesday night. The Mobil Cotton Bowl is almost a week away.

"We were having fun," Pharms says. "I thought that's what you're supposed to do."

Miami has been a Top 10 team so long the Hurricanes think it's their birthright. They can become the first team in college football history to be ranked first or second for five straight years.

"This team doesn't know how to lose," says Medearis. "On the plane back from BYU [after a 28–21 defeat], people were laughing and giggling. It was weird. Something has to die when you lose. That didn't happen. We've won so much, we've forgotten how to act when we lose."

Thursday afternoon the frigid Dallas weather forces the Longhorns indoors from the Cotton Bowl to the Embarcadero Hall on the State Fairgrounds to talk with some of the 611 media members attending what should be a top bowl matchup. Even if Miami would rather be in, well, Miami playing in the Orange Bowl for a national title.

Third-ranked Texas versus fourth-ranked Miami. Fourth? The 'Canes are insulted. If not for Heisman winner Ty Detmer and Heisman runner-up Raghib "Rocket" Ismail, Miami would be undefeated and in the Orange Bowl, but close losses to BYU and Notre Dame ended all that.

So what's left to play for? Not much. They don't want to be in Dallas, where they're more concerned about catching frostbite than passes. They'd rather be playing Colorado than Texas. They've got no reason to care at all except that former Hurricane players are calling them a disgrace because they've already lost two games in the same season.

If they need any more incentive, Thomas is willing to give it to them.

"I walk into this barbecue," Thomas relates, "and I didn't know there would be gangsters in there. I thought I was in Huntsville State Prison. They acted like they owned the place. They all had rags on their heads."

The Hurricanes, Thomas says, were "trying to country dance like they're making fun of Texas. That's a lack of respect for us. It was like they're coming down to play us, and we're not anything."

"They kind of did look like gangsters," Texas kicker Michael Pollak

257

agrees. "They kind of acted like it. It didn't look like they were too worried. We were more quiet and reserved. I think some guys were a little intimidated by them. That's Miami's style. Texas has never been like that."

Miami president Ed Foote and coach Dennis Erickson had promised the team would behave like scholar-athletes after the Hurricanes got in a nasty fight with some Cal-Berkeley players earlier in the season. The Hurricanes were touting their graduation rate for the team's seniors, which was shaping up as damn near perfect.

A Dallas radio reporter asks if the Hurricanes are fighting a losing battle in their drive to clean up the image of the meanest, dirtiest football program in the land.

"Texas players said they perceive your players to be cocky and arrogant," Mike Rhyner says. "Do you feel that's still a problem?"

"To me," a steely Erickson says, "our players are the best human beings in the country. That's a stupid question."

Cotton Bowl honcho Hoss Brock, who *is* the Cotton Bowl, has arranged a matchup made in college football heaven, and now all PR hell is fixing to break loose.

Brock rushes in to thaw the cold snap. He's a bowling ball–round, red-cheeked Texan who calls everybody "Hoss" to avoid the embarrassment of admitting he's forgotten yet another name. He has even addressed a wife or two as "Mrs. Hoss." Boss Hoss volunteers that he attended the barbecue and says reports of animosity between the two teams have been greatly embellished.

Naturally, Friday's papers are full of Thomas's trash and Miami's reaction to it. Thomas rips 'Canes, read all about it. Uncensored film at eleven. Sorry, Hoss.

The flap is the only story of the week. After Thomas's brash remarks, the rest of the week fizzles into discussions of which team the expected bad weather will favor and how each team can win the national championship.

Texas athletic director DeLoss Dodds is sticking to his word. He still hasn't had a pipe in his mouth since the Houston game. With Texas's return to the Cotton Bowl, he's feeling better than he has in years, but he's hardly noticed.

"I've not been associated with David going to the Cotton Bowl," Dodds says. "It's not DeLoss's picture with David in the paper about Texas going to the Cotton Bowl. This is David's deal, it's the team's deal, and it's not my deal. I'm not looking for credit. I don't want credit. I want things to go well."

Miami's behavior at the first party steals all the headlines, but Texas seems bent on proving it can party with the best of them, if behind the scenes. The Horns, who are staying in the plush Loews Anatole, are getting fifty dollars per diem in meal money. Of course, that doesn't all have to be spent on meals.

The players head off in all directions, some to hangouts like Gator's in the West End, others to country bars like Borrowed Money. They may be living on borrowed time.

"We had to get up at seven to be at practice at nine out there in the cold," one Texas starter says. "My body can't handle going out and getting drunk till two, three, four in the morning. Some of those guys, I don't know how they did it, but they did. They'd practice just fine. I'm sure some of those guys were out to three, four, five in the morning. There were a lot of people having fun. We deserved it."

Another Texas starter says, "A lot of people were coming in drunk even two nights before the game. They hardly checked our rooms. First few nights, there was no curfew at all. Guys would come in whenever they wanted to. If they didn't want to come in, they didn't have to. Were starters getting drunk every night? Sure, yeah. Everybody was.

"I'm not a prude. People have to enjoy themselves. But you've got to remember we're there to play a game. Obviously the message was lost on some people."

That didn't make the Longhorns' already rugged practices any easier to get through as McWilliams tries to get across the message the game is going to be physical.

Texas offensive guard Scott Gooch had suffered sprained ligaments in a scrimmage back in Austin. Center Todd Smith bruises a leg in a scrimmage on the frozen AstroTurf at SMU's Ownby Stadium. Backup wide receiver Graylin Johnson injures an ankle. Backup defensive end Bo Robinson goes down with a hip pointer.

"I was wondering what genius drew up the practice schedule for that day," one starter says. "First defense against first offense. If you ever played at Ownby, playing on that turf is like playing on blacktop. In fact, I'd rather play on the blacktop. It was all frozen out there. Todd didn't practice again the rest of the time. He could barely walk.

"We had a scrimmage almost every day. We deviated from our norm, which was, Let's keep everybody fresh and keep our injuries down and get ready to play. We tried to play the game in practice. We got a lot of people hurt. We were basically beat up going into the game."

On Saturday night, Corby McWilliams, the coach's son, takes his friends to the Hard Rock Cafe in the family's new white Suburban. The $25,000 vehicle is quickly stolen.

By Monday, the day before the game, however, David McWilliams can't be more relaxed. Erickson seems amazingly subdued. Asked for the jillionth time about the Hurricanes' chances in weather more suitable for ice fishing, the Miami coach says it was this cold in two-a-days when he coached at Wyoming. And he can still remember when his Idaho squad faced Montana State when the wind chill was 40 below.

At a pep rally before about 4,000 orangebloods in the West End area of downtown Dallas, Stanley Richard and the Longhorns debut their latest rap tune. "Who are we, who are we, who are we? Just a bunch of Longhorns having a party."

By game day, the weather has warmed slightly. Texas fans, who make up the bulk of the 73,521, arrive uncharacteristically early in frothy anticipation. The game was sold out weeks ago, the earliest sellout for a Cotton Bowl in ten years. Where they were swilling beer out of plastic cups three months earlier on the fairgrounds before the Oklahoma game, today they are sipping hot chocolate and snuggling under blankets in 30-degree temperatures.

Inside the press box, one Texas administrator is confident, bordering on smug. He says privately that the Longhorns just might kick Miami's ass. Might not even be close.

Darrell Royal is up in a sixth-floor box with Hoss Brock at his elbow. Mike Campbell, Royal's longtime defensive coordinator who used to be so gruff during practices he was called "Bloody Mike," is with him. Bill Cunningham, the Texas president, has cut short his ski vacation to Colorado and arrives wearing a bulky coat and colorful muffler as if he just left the slopes.

Across the tunnel, the Longhorns can hear the 'Canes growling and barking like wild dogs. Erickson repeats in the locker room what he told his players two days earlier.

"Have fun," he urges the Hurricanes. "Let it all hang out."

"He became a Hurricane that day," defensive tackle Shane Curry says of the coach who'd already won a national championship at Miami. Texas is a players' team. At Miami, the players think they run the team. Their antics drove former coach Jimmy Johnson to distraction, and now Erickson has to deal with them.

It is, however, that Miami attitude that makes them more than just another 8–3 team. "We're smaller than everyone we play,"

Medearis says. "We were checking the Texas players out at the barbecue, and they were huge. We're not weight lifters, we're football players."

One on one, the Hurricanes are personable, friendly, funny. But they don't play one-on-one football. They treat it like a gang war; they always try to have more pissed-off people at the point of attack than the other guy.

New Year's Day the Miami players are woofing at the Longhorns, pointing, taunting, intimidating, even jostling them. So much for Miami Nice. And this is just in the tunnel leading to the field before the opening kickoff.

From the moment the Hurricanes streak onto the field, the Cotton Bowl seems like less and less of a home-field advantage for Texas. Only about 8,000 Miami fans are bundled up in the stands, but the temperature climbs to a tolerable 38 degrees, and there is no discernible wind. The bright sunshine burning off the moisture from the artificial surface creates a swirling steam. It looks like the atmosphere the Hurricanes are used to at home in the Orange Bowl, when they enter the field through a cloud of smoke provided by six fire extinguishers.

Defensive coordinator Sonny Lubick—Leon Fuller's old offensive coordinator at Colorado State—pulls aside Robert Bailey, Miami's assassin of a cornerback, just before kickoff. Go crazy, Lubick tells the senior. Hit someone. Make a statement. Deliver a message. Bailey nods.

Chris Samuels, the Longhorns' versatile senior, is back to field the kickoff. He's confident.

"I think some things have to fall our way definitely," he says beforehand, "but if we take care of our business, Miami might not have played a team as together as the Texas Longhorns."

Samuels fields the kickoff in his end zone and sprints up to the 14. He glances out the side of his eye just in time to see Bailey coming to blindside him from the right.

It's a technical knockout. Bailey exhorts the crowd, arms upraised like a preacher urging his congregation to its feet, and then he falls straight backward in a theatrical flop. Samuels isn't playacting. He jumps to his feet, wobbles, then drops. He has to be helped off the field.

"Hurricane football," Bailey screams as he preens and waves his arms before adoring Miami fans in the northeast corner of the stadium. "We're here. We're here. I wanted to take him out."

Stan Thomas is worried. He's been worried since Miami tried to block Texas's entrance to the field from the tunnel. Now this.

"A lot of people were real nervous," Thomas says of his teammates. "Some players weren't sure we could beat 'em. I knew before the game we were going to have some problems, because everybody wasn't fired up. Some were just scared of Miami.

"Then when they tried to block us out of the tunnel, I thought, 'Oh, man, this is going to scare the younger guys.' Miami was dancing. I like that shit. Gets me pumped up. You could look around and see after the first couple of series, some of our guys were going, 'Hey, I've had enough of this.' I tried everything I could to get everybody going.

"After Chris got hit, everybody for us had that look like 'Oh, shit, we're in for a long day.' That's what I couldn't figure out. We had never been intimidated all year long. We had all that time off. You take that time off and everybody all week had a good time . . ."

Another starter says, "I think a lot of guys didn't think we were going to be in a dogfight. Hey, we had two or three weeks off. We're the conference champs, and everybody tells you how great you are. You get to do radio shows and basically forget about what got you there.

"When that happened to Chris, I think a lot of people thought, 'Hey, we're in a dogfight.' We weren't prepared."

Miami's message never lets up. Adrian Walker picks up 3 yards as Thomas and right guard Jeff Boyd together handle Russell Maryland, Miami's Outland Trophy winner.

Butch Hadnot carries for 6. Third and one. Walker gets the call, trying to beat Miami to the left corner. He loses a yard. Another message. Thomas shoves defensive tackle Mark Caesar after the whistle and looks around for support. There's none.

Alex Waits gets off a miserable punt that carries only to the 'Canes' 49. But a pair of dead-ball penalties for a personal foul and unsportsmanlike conduct sets Miami back 30 yards to its own 19.

First-and-forty. First-and-forever. Take that, Hurricanes.

Miami shrugs. Craig Erickson, the latest in an endless line of Miami cookie-cutter NFL quarterbacks, drops back and finds Lamar Thomas over the middle for 14. He hits Wesley Carroll for 8. An offsides penalty against Texas's Shane Dronett in the neutral zone erases an incompletion, although Texas coaches never will be able to find the infraction on film. "Shane must have had his head over the line," Leon Fuller sighs.

Erickson atones for the incompletion by connecting with Darryl

Spencer for 25 yards before Stanley Richard can bring him down. Need 40? Miami gets 47. Five plays later, the drive stalls. The 'Canes settle for Carlos Huerta's 28-yard field goal and an early 3–0 lead.

With Samuels still dazed, Texas puts in Willie Mack Garza to return the kick. Huerta drills the ball, and Garza, who hasn't fielded a kickoff all season, slips and falls at the Texas 3. The Hurricanes storm off the field in celebration. Three plays later, Waits punts again.

Miami takes over at the Longhorn 48. After fullback Steve McGuire rambles for 11, Erickson again looks for Carroll, his favorite receiver. The soft-spoken Carroll is the product of a broken home in a Cleveland ghetto. His father moved out when he was an infant, and his mother fell into cocaine and alcohol addiction. She rehabilitated in a halfway house, but a former addict moved in and, in a rage over his need for a fix, fatally stabbed Carroll's mother with a steak knife.

Wesley Carroll wears a tattoo on his chest that reads "In Memory of Mother."

Richard's thinking Erickson may return to Carroll, and guesses correctly. Carroll runs a simple out route, and Richard times his move perfectly. He steps in front of Carroll at the Texas 35 and, with nothing but green ahead, he . . . drops the ball.

"That could have changed the whole game," Richard says.

Well, maybe.

Two plays later, Huerta nails a 50-yard field goal, tying a Cotton Bowl record, and Miami leads 6–0.

Down by 6 to Miami, it's starting to look like another emergency for the Longhorns. Texas has fallen behind in 8 of its 11 games and won 7, but those teams weren't Miami.

Consecutive sacks of quarterback Peter Gardere by linebacker Darrin Smith and Maryland doom the Longhorns' third possession. But for once, the Texas defense is able to push Miami out of Huerta's range and gets the ball back for its offense.

On the second play from the Texas 21, Gardere, who's been getting no time to throw, drops back and is smothered by Maryland. Smith recovers the fumble, and two plays later, Erickson finds Carroll for a 12-yard touchdown and a 12–0 lead.

"It just looked like we were dead," an offensive starter says. "It was probably from practicing and partying for the last month or so."

Not until 11 minutes remain in the first half does Texas manage a first down. Another Miami personal foul moves the ball to the 'Canes' 33. Hadnot rumbles for 14, but Robert Bailey almost picks off a Gardere pass. Texas settles for a 29-yard field goal from Pollak.

The next time Texas gets the ball, Gardere tries to hit Adrian

Walker over the middle. He tips the ball with his left hand, and Bailey is there to send another message. Interception.

Texas's Brian Jones gets to Erickson for a sack, but the cool Miami quarterback isn't fazed. Leon Fuller sends Jones and Anthony Curl on a blitz, but Carroll slips behind Grady Cavness on a flag route for a 24-yard score. Miami 19, Texas 3.

Texas has to do something. A facemask penalty and another personal foul help Texas along, but the Longhorns are going to have to get into the end zone on their own. They reach the Miami 3, where they face a second-and-goal. Samuels tries off guard, but Shane Curry meets him head-on for no gain. Gardere rolls to his right, sees 6-foot-4 tight end Kerry Cash in the end zone, but can't get him the ball.

With fourth-and-goal, Bailey knows what's coming. He and the other Hurricane defensive backs had put in overtime all week to prepare for the fade route to Cash. Get inside position, the coaches had told him. He was ready, but as he says later, "I didn't know he was *that* tall."

Cash didn't know Gardere would throw the ball that wide. He leaps for the ball along the right sideline of the end zone, but his momentum takes him out of bounds with a little help from Bailey's right arm. No flag, no catch, no points.

The Longhorns trudge into the locker room at halftime, down 19-3. Thomas waits until everyone else has left to make his way up the tunnel.

By halftime Miami already owns the Cotton Bowl record for penalties for an entire game. Ten penalties, an embarrassing 132 yards.

Sam Jankovich, wearing dark green suspenders, is livid. The Miami athletic director, who only a week earlier had announced he was taking a new job as general manager of the New England Patriots, catches up with a few of the Hurricanes' assistants in the press box.

"You all are in trouble," bellows a furious Jankovich. "You all had better figure this game out."

To everyone else, the 'Canes already had. Texas has managed only 52 yards in 33 plays. On the sixth-floor press box, Royal and Campbell sip coffee and visit in the hallway. Royal frets that the second half could even be worse.

"We've been down before and come back," Royal says. "We did it against Baylor, but this ain't Baylor."

In the locker room, McWilliams talks a good game even though he is second-guessing his decision not to have Pollak kick a field goal and come away with something, anything.

"Coach Mac was real calm, like he had been all year," Thomas says. "Everybody was pretty quiet. I was so mad I kind of kept to myself."

Most of the team knows what's coming.

"When we went in down nineteen to three, I really didn't believe we were going to win the game," Pollak says. "I think a lot of people were down, disappointed. When you're down to a team like Baylor, Baylor's a great team, but we just knew we were going to win. When you're down nineteen to three against Miami, it's tough to come back. When I kicked off, they returned it to the fifty-yard line. I knew it was over."

Seven plays later, he's right. Miami's Darrin Smith steps in front of a lazy sideline pass intended for Keith Cash, latches onto the ball, and zips 34 yards up the sideline for a crushing touchdown and a 26–3 lead.

Many Longhorn fans, beaten and tired of the weather, head for the exits. As the fourth quarter starts, there's a traffic jam outside the Cotton Bowl as frustrated fans clog Pennsylvania and Washington avenues.

Texas's one last gasp comes immediately after Smith's interception. Hadnot gains 26 on an option play. Texas reaches the Miami 28, but Mark Caesar comes to bury Gardere. He goes down for one of nine Hurricane sacks on the day.

Pushed back to the 37, McWilliams sends out the field goal team. Pollak's 54-yard try—McWilliams refers to it later as "that nine-hundred-yard field goal"—falls far short.

Three plays later, Erickson finds split end Randal Hill behind Garza on a fly route up the left sideline. He leads Hill perfectly, and the Miami senior with the 4.3 speed in the 40-yard dash catches the ball in stride for a 48-yard touchdown. Hill drops the ball in the end zone but keeps running all the way up the tunnel and toward the dressing rooms.

Miami scores twice more in the fourth quarter. The game is so far out of hand that the Miami assistant coaches leave their stations in the press box and run across the field in celebration during a time-out. The final score of 46–3 is the most lopsided of the fifty-five Cotton Bowls. Texas's Shock-the-Nation tour continues, but it's because of a stunning loss.

Darrell Royal likes to say a team has to win six or seven of the eleven individual battles being waged each snap.

"Your extra hustle will cover up for the mistakes," Royal says. "It comes down to each individual. You can fool your coaches and the guy next to you, but not yourself."

No one's sure just whom Stan Thomas is fooling. He's wearing a turned-around black baseball cap after the game. In his mind, he's the only Longhorn who came out ahead.

"I won my battles," he says. "Look at the film. I must have gone against Maryland twelve times and I won eleven of them. The other time, Peter held the ball too long. But I can't do it all."

The Hurricanes say Thomas must be grading on the curve. Shane Curry, for one, isn't all that impressed. He accuses Thomas of spitting in the faces of the Miami players during the game.

"He's an infantile, young kid," Curry says, walking off the field. "He needs to grow up. Texas came in here very, very cocky. Or they were trying to build themselves up with a bunch of false chatter. The way they were talking, I thought they were going to be some kind of monster, and they weren't."

Two Miami teammates hoist Curry to their shoulders and begin parading him around the field.

Craig Erickson tries to toss the Longhorns a compliment inside the locker room. It is one of his few incompletions.

"They're the best secondary we've faced all year long," he says.

"Ah, Craig," butts in Lamar Thomas, one of his receivers, incredulously, "what are you doing standing over there lying for? Their secondary reminded me of Boston College."

On the field the celebration continues. Even the team chaplain is swept away with the emotion. To no one in particular, the Reverend Leo Armbrust, a Roman Catholic priest, shouts, "How's that for a Texas barbecue?"

In Austin, William Graham sat through the bloody game. The former Longhorn defensive back had invited friends over to his house in Northeast Austin. He'd set out all his UT paraphernalia and was prepared to gloat.

"I physically got sick by the end of the day," Graham says. "I kept hoping something good would happen. Those guys are going to live with it the rest of their lives. They don't know it, but that will haunt 'em the rest of their lives. Ask Craig Curry."

Curry is the unfortunate former Texas player who dropped a punt in the 1983 Cotton Bowl against Georgia. It cost the Longhorns a national championship, which was won by Miami.

More than 1,500 miles away in Pasadena, former Texas quarterback Shannon Kelley is staring at his television set in his room at the Hyatt

Regency in disbelief, while wife Mary Lou Retton rides in a float in the Rose Bowl parade.

"I felt sorry for the guys," Kelley says. "They had worked so hard to get there. Once they got there, they just got smoked. But I think Coach Mac's got 'em on the right track. I think we can use that as a recruiting tool.

"People believe in Coach Mac. He stepped up to the line and took the shots. He did exactly what nobody thought he'd do. Nobody in the world picked him to go to the Cotton Bowl."

Nobody expected a 46–3 disaster in Dallas, either. Texas has had a glorious 1990 season, its best in seven years. It's painfully clear, however, that the Longhorns will have to kick it up a couple of notches to win the national championship that's eluded them for two frustrating decades.

24

Never Again

Almost a month has passed since the debacle against Miami, but 275-pound Chuck Johnson is still pissed about that Rice Krispies line.

"I couldn't believe they told this joke—they let this guy tell the joke—on the radio," he says outside of the Neuhaus-Royal weight complex as the sun is just starting to lighten the winter sky. "You know, what's the difference between Texas and Rice Krispies? Rice Krispies know what to do in a bowl.

"I mean, that made me mad. I grabbed my car phone and called the station right then. After all the money we'd made for the merchants, the hotels, and the restaurants. After all we'd done for this school and this city . . ."

At Texas, the only option is to do more. Practice harder. Recruit better. Aim higher. Get up earlier for workouts. Stay up later to call blue chips.

Be number one, or no one. Kick butt, or be the butt of drive-time jokes.

Even the sun isn't bleeding orange when Johnson and his teammates trudge to their predawn workouts at Memorial Stadium. In the darkness, when the grackles are still asleep in the trees, the Longhorns are going through the same conditioning drills they resurrected before the 1990 season. They sweat in the same old weight room. They hear strength coach Dana LeDuc once again exhorting them to higher levels. Their jump ropes make eerie arcs in the artificial light as they run down the field, skipping rope.

There are, however, a couple of distinct differences. The players are now running in every direction in agility drills instead of just straight ahead. They're trying to develop the kind of lateral speed they just couldn't match with Miami.

The players are also leaner. "Last year we had to shed about three hundred pounds from the offensive linemen," says trainer Spanky Stephens, who is in charge of the drills.

"Hell, the guys we recruited used to come in at three hundred pounds," Johnson says. "Last year we were just trying to make it through the practices. Now we're encouraging one another. If someone is having trouble, we run over to help him. Last year we were all just worried about whether we could make it through the workouts ourselves."

"Texas, National Champions!" a player bundled in sweats screams in the predawn light of Memorial Stadium. It's an echo of a gut feeling that began just moments after the loss to Miami.

The seniors were asked to leave the locker room. One of them, offensive tackle Stan Thomas, had gone to the press tent and claimed that he'd beaten Russell Maryland on eleven of the twelve plays they'd gone head-to-head on, while safety Stanley Richard groused to friends at the top of the tunnel that Texas should have gone to its nickel defense much earlier.

In the locker room sophomore Shane Dronett jumped up yelling, "This is our team now!" He and defensive tackle James Patton made an impassioned plea not to forget this game. Together, the underclassmen all vowed to come back to the Cotton Bowl next year. And win.

"Everyone hold together," Johnson urged in the sweat-soaked sting of the 46–3 defeat just before coach David McWilliams went out to try to accept the blame for defeat.

He shouldn't have tried that long field goal, McWilliams said. He should have taken the field goal before halftime, instead of going for the touchdown. He should have prepared the team better. Should have, should have, should have.

But Texas was never really a coach's team. It was a players' team. They took it upon themselves to win. They did that ten times while losing only two.

As senior defensive end Oscar Giles said before Dallas, "This year will be a blueprint. This is where it started. We started from scratch. Maybe this is the new legacy for Texas football. This is the new foundation. This team will be talked about till the twenty-first century.

"I don't think anybody knew what it'd take to win. But they do now, and they'll work even harder."

Then, they took the Cotton Bowl as a reward for three—and sometimes four—years of football hell at a place they thought was heaven when they visited as recruits.

In Dallas before the game, they partied hard, but not together. They separated and went to black bars, country-and-western bars, yuppie bars, and piano bars. Some players—and not just the walk-ons and special teamers—stayed out past 3 A.M., drifted into the swanky Loews Anatole, and then went through the motions in practice some four hours later.

On New Year's Day, they ran into the Hurricanes, who just wanted to kick some ass on the football field and get out of Dallas.

"I'm not saying that if we played ten times, we'd win five," Spanky Stephens says, "but it was one of those days."

"Texas knew Miami was two touchdowns better going in," Cotton Bowl head honcho Hoss Brock shrugged the day after he watched his potential showcase turn into a near shutout.

"I don't know if you build on games like that. You try to forget them, like the Baylor game last year," Johnson says. He can't forget the game, can't let it go, and can't believe that Miami was really 43 points better than Texas. "I must have watched that game twenty times on the VCR. We had plays that would have worked if we'd just given Peter some time. If I knew then what I know now—we just didn't adjust to their stunts. Stan, I don't know what game he was watching when he said he beat Russell Maryland. You just don't talk like that, or say things about your teammates, say they were intimidated. That was uncalled for."

There is, however, one thing Johnson has learned from Thomas, and that is that being big helps, especially in the pro draft. He's trying to add fifteen pounds of muscle. He has a T-shirt that's specially made for squeezing out one more rep in the weight room. From the front, it looks as though the letters on it are written backward. But when Johnson looks in the mirror and is trying to max out his pump, he can read the Miami-inspired message in the mirror.

"Never again," it says.

Johnson should be the anchor of a solid offensive line that will be opening holes for potential superstars in Butch Hadnot and Phil Brown. Maybe even Heisman candidate Butch Hadnot. The defense, with Shane Dronett crashing through the lines from his spot at left end and safety Lance Gunn rattling the bones of opposing receivers, should be even better than last year's. At quarterback—although you never know at Texas—Gardere returns with almost two full seasons of experience.

All that's missing are a few pieces, a big tight end, and a stronger-armed quarterback that offensive coordinator Lynn Amedee loves better than Bud Light or golf. That, and a burner of a wide receiver like little Mike Miller at Sugar Land Willowridge, who just might be the flat-out fastest football player in the country. Texas, after all, lost all three senior receivers, Johnny Walker and Keith and Kerry Cash, from a senior-laden team that didn't quite get Texas all the way back to the top.

At Texas, if you can't beat them, you have to outrecruit them so you can beat them in three or four years. Not long after the Cotton Bowl loss, the Texas staff scattered across the state and tried to make inroads into the rest of the nation. They're going to emphasize nationwide recruiting.

"They need to go out of state," says Californian Stan Thomas, who nonetheless predicts Texas will contend for a national championship again next year. "They found me out in the middle of nowhere. They keep thinking Texas football players are the best ones in the country. That's not true. You've got 'em all over. You need to go to Miami. Go down south. Alabama, Louisiana, Miami, Michigan, everywhere. They also need to recruit more junior college players. These guys have more experience. No out-of-state recruiting, that's what's killing 'em. If they want a national championship team, they got to go out of state and recruit."

The recruiting results start coming in. Texas jumps out to a big lead in the SWC, grabbing just the kind of big, small-town linemen that Texas always finds it easiest to recruit. Center Toby Pevoto of Texas City. Tim Barron of McKinney. Tim Crain of Lufkin. Joe Phillips of Midland. Two potential Outland Trophy–type studs in 6-foot-5, 260-pound Blake Brockermeyer of Arlington Heights and 6-foot-1, 260 pound John Elmore of Sherman, maybe the best offensive guard in the nation. Of course, Brockermeyer's dad just happened to be a former roommate of consensus All-America Longhorn running back James Saxton, whose son, Jimmy, will push Gardere for the quarterback spot or maybe be moved, perhaps to running back. Seems like old times.

Robert Heard of *Inside Texas* gushes that it could be the best haul for Texas since the famous "Worster Bunch," which included bruising fullback Steve Worster, defensive tackle Bill Atessis, and split end

Charles "Cotton" Speyrer and was the backbone of the Darrell Royal teams that won 30 straight games from 1968 to 1970.

In the latter part of January, Texas recruiting hits a dead calm. Seventeen days pass without a single recruit publicly announcing for Texas. Miller, who could step right in and put some zip into Texas's passing attack with his 4.3 speed, starts talking about going to Notre Dame and becoming the next Raghib "Rocket" Ismail.

The second-best player in Texas is still a big enough deal to write his own recruiting diary for the *Houston Chronicle*. Sam Adams's dad played pro ball for twelve seasons with the Los Angeles Rams, New England Patriots, and New Orleans Saints, and his 6-foot-4, 260-pound son had a whopping 23 sacks as a defensive end at Cypress Creek. Fans are calling recruiting expert Max Emfinger's 900 number just to find out which way Adams is leaning. It's down to Texas, Oklahoma, or Texas A&M. The Longhorns may have an in because Sam Adams, Sr., is tight with former Houston Oilers guard Conway Hayman, who just happens to be one of Earl Campbell's best buddies. One of Sam Jr.'s cousins is Butch Hadnot. Sam Jr. is praying over the matter of which school to select.

Word comes out that he had a great trip to Oklahoma. He even writes in his diary that he couldn't believe there were that many beautiful women in Norman. Suddenly, unexpectedly, he crosses Oklahoma off his list.

"I think you could see how confused he was by reading his diary," Texas Angels president Madelon Highsmith says. "He'd say he really liked some place, then he'd cross it off his list."

It's down to Texas and A&M, which is coming on fast.

Finally, Adams makes his choice. He picks the Aggies and talks about how together they are as a team. "He said the Aggies were like brothers and we were like first cousins, whatever that means," Highsmith says. "Maybe some good will come out of that. As someone who's not with the program, he had a different perspective. Maybe we can learn from that."

A&M gets Sam Adams. Texas settles for Bo Adams, a 5-foot-7 quarterback from tiny Schulenburg, who had been headed down the road to Division I-AA Southwest Texas in San Marcos before Texas offered. A story circulates throughout the state that Dronett insulted Sam Adams with a racial slur during his visit to campus. Dronett denies it and Adams refuses to talk about it.

With Kerry Cash and backup Stephen Clark both graduating, Texas is in dire need of a big tight end who can play immediately. Tight end Jeremy Kennedy of Oklahoma City fell in love with the Texas campus but was also considering Southern Cal and Florida. "It was so quiet, so peaceful; it was like walking through the Garden of Eden," he says of the Austin campus. He chooses Florida.

The Longhorns grab Jason Reeves. He's a talented tight end from Anderson High School in Austin, but he weighs only 210 and, some say, perhaps less than that. Texas coach David McWilliams even makes one last-ditch offer to tight end Scott Waterbury of Arlington Lamar, even though Waterbury has been ripping Texas in the papers for being arrogant. "He gave me that attitude," Waterbury says before signing with Oklahoma State. "I could only take so much." Waterbury said he needed an hour to think about it. Texas said forget it. He did.

In College Station, Texas A&M coach R. C. Slocum is crowing over a class that Max Emfinger ranks eighth in the nation. "There seems to have been an assumption—because Texas won games this year—that Texas had come back. Not everyone wants to go to Texas. If we work hard at A&M, we will get our share."

One Southwest Conference coach adds, "Texas is arrogant. They walk around, figuring everybody will fall over dead for them. It doesn't work that way anymore. They can't accept that."

McWilliams isn't quitting.

"I've probably been on the phone till midnight for the last ten days," he says from his office on the February 6 national signing day. "I've either been talking to recruits or I've been on hold."

The late-night effort helps land speedy Irving linebacker Norman Watkins to top off a solid, almost spectacular, class. Illinois-based recruiting expert Tom Lemming puts Texas in his top ten, behind leaders Michigan, Florida State, and Penn State. Houston's Max Emfinger isn't so kind. He ranks Texas thirteenth, right behind Baylor. Notre Dame, in a down year, has gone south to Texas and snatched two of the Top 10 players in the state, Miller and Dallas White linebacker Huntley Bakich.

Close to home, the news is even worse. Mario Freeman of Austin LBJ, one of the top linebackers in the state, snubs Texas and picks Oklahoma. Wide receiver Chris Sanders of the same school actually commits to the Longhorns in December, then has a change of heart and signs with A&M. Two more LBJ products—linebacker Kenneth Alexander and defensive back Greg Lane—also went elsewhere the previous signing day. To Florida State and Notre Dame. Four big-time players from Texas's own backyard.

"I'd give us about an A-minus," McWilliams says of his latest recruiting class.

An A-minus. Kind of like the 1990 season. It's a good grade. An acceptable grade. Somewhere. Almost anywhere. But not at Texas, never at Texas. The orangebloods won't accept it, won't tolerate it, won't stand for it.

They will, however, have trouble escaping it. Texas can never quite be Texas again.

"It never will," says former Texas A&M coach Jackie Sherrill, who in 1991 opens his first season at Mississippi State against Texas. "No program in the country will be back like it was. It's because of the twenty-five scholarships. Take Colorado and Georgia Tech. Why did they win the national championship? Because of the twenty-five-scholarship limit.

"An independent's schedule is much easier. Miami's got excellent players, but a team gets better when you don't have to line up week after week after week and get the shit kicked out of you. Notre Dame's got things going for 'em. Also, they recruit the best players."

For now, Texas is trying to hang on to its players.

In late February, a walk-on Texas football player is arrested and charged with obtaining drugs by fraud. Police say he used a fake prescription to buy the male hormone testosterone at an Austin pharmacy. Longhorn starter James Patton is with the player when the walk-on is arrested in the stakeout. More arrests may follow, the authorities say. DeLoss Dodds tests thirty-eight players for steroid use the following Monday. The results are not made public.

But how long till the Tower is lit up for another national championship in football? How long?

Spring practice ends on an upbeat note. The normally boring orange-white game turns into a spirited contest. Running back Phil Brown breaks one long touchdown, flashing the promise he showed at Penn State. Butch Hadnot is showing all the signs of a legitimate Heisman candidate. *The Sporting News* plans to tout Texas's defensive line as the best in America. The 1991 schedule isn't soft, but it's not as tough as 1990's was.

"If we can just find some guys who can catch the ball . . ." says coach David McWilliams as spring practice closes in April. "I feel better than I did at this point last year."

The players are no longer thinking about just making the Cotton Bowl. They're talking national championship.

Maybe, just maybe, 1991 is that year. And the bleeding will stop.